D0867366

352

kiss the kids for dad.

Don't forget to write.

Kiss the kids for dad.

THE WARTIME LETTERS *of* GEORGE TIMMINS, 1916-18

Don't forget to write.

EDITED BY Y.A. BENNETT

UBCPress

Dedicated to the memory of George Timmins,
late of "D" Company, the 116th Ontario County Battalion, CEF,
and one-time lance corporal,
18th Battalion, 4th Brigade, 2nd Division, CEF,
and to that of his wife, May,
and their children, Winnie, Jim, and Molly.

Also to his faithful grandson, Joseph (Joe) George Houlden.

20 19 18 17 16 15 14 13 12 11 10 09   5 4 3 2 1

Printed in Canada with vegetable-based inks on FSC-certified ancient-forest-free
paper (100% post-consumer recycled) that is processed chlorine- and acid-free.

LIBRARY AND ARCHIVES CANADA CATALOGUING IN PUBLICATION

Timmins, George
Kiss the kids for dad, don't forget to write : the wartime letters of George
Timmins, 1916-18 / edited by Y.A. Bennett.

Includes bibliographical references and index.
ISBN 978-0-7748-1608-3 (bound); 978-0-7748-1609-0 (pbk);
978-0-7748-1610-6 (e-book)

1. Timmins, George – Correspondence. 2. Soldiers – Canada – Correspondence.
3. World War, 1914-1918 – Personal narratives, Canadian. I. Bennett, Yvonne
Aleksandra, 1953- II. Title.

D640.T54 2009   940.4'8171   C2009-900920-X

Canadä

UBC Press gratefully acknowledges the financial support for our publishing
program of the Government of Canada through the Book Publishing Industry
Development Program (BPIDP), and of the Canada Council for the Arts, and
the British Columbia Arts Council.

UBC Press
The University of British Columbia
2029 West Mall
Vancouver, BC V6T 1Z2
604-822-5959 / Fax: 604-822-6083
www.ubcpress.ca

CONTENTS

FOREWORD

On one of my family's regular visits to Oshawa when I was a child, my grandmother asked me to run upstairs and fetch a sweater from her dresser drawer. In doing so, I came across a bundle of letters tied together with a ribbon. Even now, I remember feeling somewhat guilty for peeking and seeing the word "Sweetheart." They turned out to be Grandpa's letters home during the First World War, carefully preserved by Grandma. Grandpa did not speak of the war very much: he would just say that it was "all a long time ago." A few years after Grandma died, my grandfather decided to move into a retirement home in Oshawa to be with friends. Grandpa was quite whole-sale in discarding possessions in preparing for the move and would likely have destroyed the letters. Fortunately, they were saved once again, by my mother, his eldest daughter, Winnie. Many years later, when the time came for my mother to move into a nursing home, I asked her to pass the letters on to me, which she did. By then I had read beyond "Sweetheart" and had resolved that Grandpa Timmins' letters would have further adventures. I wish them well.

Joseph George Houlden
Ottawa, May 2008

ACKNOWLEDGMENTS

In researching the material that supports the George Timmins letters, I have used the records, materials, and resources of Library and Archives Canada and the Canadian War Museum in Ottawa, and the Oshawa Community Museum and Archives, the Oshawa Public Library, and the Oshawa Military Museum in Oshawa, Ontario. In the United Kingdom, I have used the records deposited in the Dudley Archives and Local History Centre, Coseley, West Midlands. I have also used the resources of my home library at Carleton University and the services of its Inter-Library Loans Department. The staff and the volunteers in all of these places have given generously and engagingly of their time and of their expertise: to all of them I owe my sincerest thanks. My family have accompanied me on my visits to the battlefields, memorials, and cemeteries in France. To them, to Emily Andrew and her colleagues at UBC Press, and to Kerry Abel, and especially to Robert Goheen, Frances Montgomery, and Joe Houlden, I owe an inexpressible debt of thanks.

A NOTE ON THE TEXT

George Timmins' letters posed few issues of transcription, although the passage of time and use occasionally compromised legibility. Save for those written before Timmins' departure overseas, the wartime letters are written in pencil and on poor-quality paper, which is showing signs of deterioration, notably along the folds. Where the original text fails to provide the date and year of entry, they appear here within square brackets. The editor has arrived at these dates by correlating internal evidence with other sources. The original punctuation, spelling, and paragraphing of this edition are George Timmins' own. The interventions of the military censors are indicated by the use of [*censored*] inserted into the text. If words have been censored but are still legible, these have been identified by an endnote. Timmins frequently added a postscript, either at the head of a letter or more usually at the end, depending on space. Sometimes, however, he did not use the conventional "p.s." to signal a postscript. In transcribing his letters, the postscripts have been left where he placed them and set in slightly smaller type.

Kiss the kids for dad.

Don't forget to write.

INTRODUCTION

I see in the papers that we are still pushing ahead and & Canucks are doing fine work Such is the peculiar make-up of a man that often as I have wished myself out of it & knowing as I do, none better, the horrors of it, I almost find myself wishing I was into it again. Its so good to feel you are in & <u>winning</u>. Advancing all the time. Its so different to fighting on the defensive like we were in March & April. That's what gets your goat. Anyway, kiddie, I suppose I should be thankful to be lying here in a good warm bed with lots to eat, instead of being suffering what I know the boys are suffering out there. Its adding to my chances of eventually getting home again & seeing you all. I often imagine what it will be like to have you all round me again. Sometimes squabbling eh? I'll guarantee to be good natured and every other old thing that goes to make a model husband.[1]

Writing from the safety of an English hospital, this is how George Timmins confided to his wife, May, the conflicting emotions he was experiencing in August 1918 at the end of his effective military service. At the outset, in March 1916, when he enlisted in the 116th Battalion of the Canadian Expeditionary Force, he was a thirty-three-year-old devoted husband and father of three children living at 460 Albert Street in Oshawa, Ontario. By October, he had been transferred to the 18th, and it was with this battalion that he served at

Vimy, Lens, Passchendaele, and Amiens, where he was wounded on 8 August 1918 in the advance that he describes in the quotation above.[2] After a brief period of training at Niagara Camp, George left Halifax bound for England, on 23 July 1916.[3] Nine days later, he arrived in Liverpool.[4] Letters became the only means of communication between the couple, and between the children and their father, for over two years.[5]

The George Timmins letters are an important collection because they draw us into the everyday life and relationships, at home and abroad, of a married Canadian infantryman.[6] Unfortunately, not much is known about the lives of soldiers' wives since so little of their correspondence survives. Little, too, is known of the perspective of children. This is true of the Timmins family as well. None of the letters from May and the children have survived, but such is the strength of George's devotion that they do not remain as shadows. It is one side of a conversation, but the portrait of a marriage and family still emerges with clarity. A man of limited formal education, George chooses simple words, but he employs them well, with a sense of humour and a keen sense of observation.[7]

The simple words introduce us to a world of multiple issues. Four intersecting communities – the family, Oshawa, the Front, and civilian society behind the lines – significantly sustained, and shaped, George Timmins' experiences of the war. The endnotes initiate a dialogue between the themes in the war letters – and those subsequent to the war included in the Epilogue – and their discussion in current historical writing: soldiers' censorship and self-censorship; civilians' knowledge of the conflict; everyday life as a refracting medium of that knowledge; and the tides of enthusiasm and disillusionment for the war.[8]

May and George were both twenty-two years old when they married in Holy Trinity Anglican Church, Old Hill (near Birmingham), on 1 March 1905.[9] George described his birthplace of Old Hill as "a village in the fields on the outskirts of industrial harshness and poverty."[10] May Dunn came from Cradley Heath, about a mile's distance, and "the heart of the iron trade."[11] Her father was a chainmaker, in an industry described by Robert Sherard, one of England's social investigators, in 1896, as one of "the worst paid and most murderous trades of England."[12] To escape poverty and the class system, the couple sailed for Canada a week after their marriage. In a letter written to his grandson, Joseph Houlden, and his wife, Nicole, in 1965,

George commented: "The old empire is through, I guess, and about time. There was always too great a division between the different grades, the classes and the masses. That's the reason I came over here. I didn't like the touching of hats to the minister etc."[13] George had taken his first trip to Canada in 1902, travelling westward with two friends to Kamloops, where he worked for an unknown period in the Iron Mask Mine.[14] The decision to settle with his wife in Oshawa was likely connected with the chainmaking industry.[15] Before General Motors came to dwarf every industry in the town, the Ontario Malleable Iron Works – the Malle – had the largest payroll. One of the Malle's products was chain-links, used extensively in Great Lakes shipping.[16] On his wedding certificate, George gave his profession as "striker." He worked at the Malle, and at the Steel Range Company. The couple appear to have prospered. Their first child, Winnifred Mary (Winnie), was born in 1906, Walter James (Jim) in 1907, and Margaret Ann (Mollie) in 1914.[17] By 1916, George was no longer engaged in physical work but employed as a clerk.[18] May, it seems, did not work outside the home for any sustained period. Indeed, from at least one comment made by George, it seems clear that he believed that his duty was to support his wife and children, and that his wife's role was to stay at home and look after the family.[19]

We know that the couple discussed enlistment at length and what that commitment might entail.[20] By the time the decision was taken in March 1916, both British and Canadian troops had been bloodied in battle. The Whitby *Gazette and Chronicle* and the few surviving copies of two Oshawa newspapers, the *Ontario Reformer* and the *Oshawa Vindicator,* make clear that the domestic populations of those two small Ontario communities knew a great deal about the war and its dangers.[21] Family information tells us that George's timing was primarily dictated by his desire to ensure that, before he left, his youngest child could walk well enough to be less of a burden to his wife.[22] His motive for enlisting would seem to have been a sense of obligation: "You can tell anybody that asks you, that your husband is doing his bit as best he can."[23] It would also appear that George was caught up in the community regiment strategy developed by the Department of Militia and Defence to combat declining voluntary enlistments.[24] Tapping into local civic pride and identity and seeking to generate a strong sense of esprit de corps, individual citizens and local communities were to be the genesis of community-based regiments: in Ontario, the county battalions, such as the 116th, were the very successful products of this approach. By May 1916, the battalion was 1,145 strong. "D" Company was made up of men from Oshawa, the company commander being Cptn. (later Maj.) Alfred Hind, the town's former chief of police.[25]

On Saturday, 27 May 1916, George and the other members of the 116th Battalion paraded through the crowded streets of Oshawa, the last leg of their two-week trek through Ontario County. It was a multipurpose occasion designed to raise awareness of the battalion and of the conflict, in order to increase recruitment and garner funds for equipment.[26] The *Gazette and Chronicle* newspaper, rather like a contemporary gift registry, listed desired items and their prices.[27] In Oshawa, various local groups presented cheques to Colonel Sharpe, the battalion's commanding officer, while Mr. George W. McLaughlin, the vice-president of the McLaughlin Motor Car Company, presented a car.[28] The parading men became proxies for a community and a nation at war.[29]

The mails were the primary medium for the expression of support for the troops, which was widely recognized as crucial to morale.[30] This was certainly true for George. He hungered for this contact with his wife and children. Correspondence enabled George and May to convert the pain of separation into an experience of absence that might be better endured.[31] "Don't you forget your two a week as they are about all that I care about now," he wrote. "Of course its very nice to have a letter from anybody but its your letters that count."[32] However, a long-standing habit of totally open communication was now constrained. Of the surviving letters, several refer to the censor and to George's inhibitions about writing in intimate terms to his wife. In one of his first letters from France, he confessed, "I have tried to write letters since I have been in France but somehow they have always seemed so unsatisfactory to me on account of the thoughts of the censor having to read them."[33] Letters often went astray or would arrive all of a heap.[34] The irregularity of the mails compounded George's longing for his wife and his children, and his anxiety over their health and welfare. Just two months after his arrival in England, George expressed concern and puzzlement over the Canadian army's pay arrangements: "I hope you are getting your pay all right. They have cut us down. It seems they stop 5 dollars a month for 4 months so as to always have a balance in hand of 20 dollars, after that they just pay us up in 1 pound & 10 shilling notes, so that if your pay is 19 shillings you draw only 10 and the balance is kept by somewhere. God knows where. It certainly seems very unsatisfactory."[35]

George's primary community was his family – his wife and children. They were the focal point of his life. For the couple and for the children, communication was vital, offering to each companionship, comfort, and security. George tried to give his family the encouragement they needed to meet the challenges caused by his absence, while May in particular gave George the opportunity to discuss the difficulties he faced. The hardship experienced by his family only increased as the war progressed and his absence lengthened: "Look out dear you don't do too much. Never fear about me having to worry, financially or otherwise. Beleive me nothing is worth worrying about any more except you and our kiddies."[36] George was most concerned about his wife's working: "Say! I don't want you to be working this summer like you did last and making yourself sick with the heat & hard work. You are too much to me to do that and take chances of a serious illness especially as the kiddies need you so much. If you do a bit around our own garden you are doing enough for anybody."[37] But it is clear from George's letter of late April 1918 that May had been hinting at the necessity of work: "So all the soldiers wives are working eh? Hope you don't have to sweetheart. I can understand it must be hard on you all the way prices are & the way your pay has remained stationary. Never mind, hon, we'll soon be talking it over together."[38] The opportunity did not materialize. By the end of June 1918, May was working on Saturday nights and holidays, and the issue of volunteering for land work had also been raised. This time, speaking in a rare voice of insistent direction, George wrote: "You have enough to do at home. I dont want you doing anything like that. You can do your share by staying home & looking after the home & kids."[39] The urgency in George's voice might be accounted for by the perilous nature of his own employment. In the same period, he told her: "We were standing in a row in the bay when a shell hit the parapet ... [I] escaped with a mouth & nose all full of dust & powder smoke. I was sent flying on my back but scrambled up in about 5 seconds and made my way to the heap of dirt & dead as best I could."[40]

His exchanges with May regularly employ phrases that imply involvement in a community of effort: "you are doing enough for anybody"; "you can do your share."[41] They also reflect George's conviction that his contribution to the war effort should make her feel easy in the amount that might fairly be asked of her. The details of this contribution were shared openly with May, who became familiar with the daily realities of life in the trenches. George frequently refers to the extremes of heat and cold, the rain, and the mud underfoot. In the period from October 1916 to April 1917, he freely comments on both the paucity and the inferiority of the rations.[42] In one letter, George explains how the complete absence of vegetables in the diet was playing havoc with his digestion.[43] For many periods during the war, parcels were not a luxury but an important means of supplementing and varying the diet. George did not think it right that "you have to spend your income on food to keep alive & well so you wont be a casualty & a burden to your country."[44] His letters underscore the importance of food for morale and the part families played in maintaining that morale, often at considerable cost. They also make clear his profound sense of fair play, which he felt on occasion to be violated by the inadequacy of state provisions both for his family at home and the men at the front.[45]

In early January 1917, George had to reassure his wife about his postwar employment prospects. May's anxieties on this score grew in direct proportion to the prosperity of the men who stayed behind in Oshawa. George tried to comfort his wife and to minimize her concerns: "Say hon. don't you let the fact that so and so is doing so well worry you that don't amount to a row of pins. You bet we'll be all right. If good jobs are scarce I guess I'll be able to hunt one. You just look after yourself and the children, that's all that really matters you know. You must'nt get sick."[46] However, it is clear that May continued to be very worried. One of George's fellow soldiers, in exchanging news of home, expanded on the same theme, which George then relayed to May: "Frank Powell ... making 10 dollars a day in an aeroplane factory and being exempted from military service is pretty soft, what? Hicks is looking pretty good though but like myself he rather envies Frank Powell. I'm thinking that I am as good a man as he is to be making 10 bucks per diem and he has no kiddies, and I have three to be raised yet. It is a little unfair all things considered, I think."[47] Throughout his letters it is clear that when George Timmins is critical, it is almost without exception on the basis of fairness and equality of effort. The standard of equity applied to his children, too: "I'm inclined to socialism. If the war workers get so much why should my boy have to pick fruit at the same old price. You mustnt show him this but just think it over. I'd rather have him loafing down by the creek than working for some measly fruit grower. [48]

Almost every letter mentions his children. Like May, they were central to his being. He wrote to them frequently, sending letters, postcards, birthday greetings, and Christmas presents. He was very aware of the price they paid for being inescapably drawn into the war effort. At the end of January 1917, he wrote: "Received your <u>very</u> welcome parcel last night containing candy, nuts, apples oranges etc. So good of you dear. Also the kids to send some of their Christmas things to dad."[49] Jim, nine years old, was expected to assume the role of the man of the house: "Tell him he's to get up the coal etc & not to let his mother do it all." In the same letter, George commented on the boys at the front who were doing the job of full-grown men: "There's boys here under 18 doing men's work ... Never missing a turn & doing exactly the same, & in some cases more, than full grown men."[50] To Jim fell the role of relieving his mother of heavy work and toiling in the garden that was being cultivated to augment the family's food supply. In May 1917, George told May to tell their son, still shy of his tenth birthday, that "I won't forget him for that."[51] Winnie, almost two years older than her brother, was also encouraged to help her mother with chores, and especially with looking after her little sister.

George understood that May's proximity to the children meant that she must be the primary decision maker. He acknowledged that the physical distance between them meant that he could not properly assess the circumstances of any given moment as well as she could, yet he sought to participate in their lives as much as possible. To do so, though, George generally took care not to employ "the old bullying spirit you used to resent so much" and the advice that he tendered was couched as an observation, a gentle nudge.[52] After George sent Jim a German dagger as a souvenir ("I can imagine Jim being the authority on the war amongst his mates now, especially when he gets his dagger"[53]), he observed to May: "Rather dangerous, hon, to let him carry it around."[54] His eldest daughter edged toward puberty in his absence. It seems that her maturity and good looks began to dawn on George when his fellow soldiers admired her photograph, saying, "'Gee thats a fine girl you have there.'"[55] Several months later, he wrote to May, "Winnie must be getting quite a big girl now so just keep an extra look out over her. Sweetheart! I know this advice is needless but I feel much better for giving it."[56] Of their youngest daughter he often wrote with longing and pathos: "I can always imagine her without much effort of mind."[57] George was certainly very conscious of the burden May had to bear because of his absence and of the debt that he owed her. Although there clearly was a sense of a division of labour between them, the letters leave one with the sense that George thought that May bore the greater part, and with less emotional support than he enjoyed. "That's the worst thing of all for me to contemplate," he wrote. "You there without anybody to help you a little."[58] To support her, George frequently reminded May of her importance, of how much he missed her, and of how much in love he continued to be.

Reciprocally, May played a critical role in sustaining George's morale. Her letters were "like a ray of sunshine."[59] They helped him face the moment of entering the trenches: "I always go in feeling better for a cheery letter from my girl. I'm never worrying much when I do get in, its the going in that makes a fellow feel a little blue."[60] George in fact recognized that there was a direct correlation between the tone of his letters and whether he was going into the line, was in the line, or was coming out and into rest: "A letter is generally in the same vein as your feelings at the time of writing."[61] The flow of May's letters was as important as their content, since the arrival of mail had a rallying effect: "I was the happiest man in my platoon last night. What with having no mail, cold, misery, & short rations I was rapidly developing into a morbid, uninteresting, bad tempered piece of humanity. Even my letters of the last few days must have reflected it. My own special section, (I'm section commander you know) got to saying 'What the H--- is wrong with old Tim'? But its all over again now. Last night at 9.30, mail came up & I got 5 letters. 4 from you."[62]

In order that May might better understand his experience, George often evoked images familiar to her: "I tell you, hon, you in Canada, (except for the lonliness of wives who really miss their husbands) don't know what war is. In our last billet we had table, chairs, a writing desk, old beds etc. belonging to the former tenants. Just imagine, kiddo, if it was Oshawa. Our tables and chairs and stoves in use by troops. I say it is a shame. And its so common one never notices it."[63]

Second only to his relationship with his family was the relationship George had with Oshawa. Thanks to the method of recruitment, George was able to maintain this community contact abroad. His strong peacetime ties and interests endured in the 116th Battalion and the 18th Battalion to which he was transferred along with numerous fellow Oshawans in October 1916. They significantly shaped his military experience.[64] The Oshawa community also featured more broadly in easing the sense of isolation felt by the couple. News or the prospect of news was the passport for contact with others. May fed George's need for local news, and he responded with reports of the Oshawa men serving overseas with him that May could share with their families.[65] Forty-nine local men (three officers and forty-six other ranks) are mentioned in George's letters. Eight came from Albert Street, where the Timmins family lived, and the vast majority of the remainder from its vicinity. One was Jack Burr, who lived a short distance from George. In a letter written on 31 October, just nine days after his transfer from the 116th to the 18th Battalion, George reported that he and Jack Burr were the closest of friends.[66] In the 18th Battalion, George and Jack were in the company bombers together, but they were separated when George was sent to the battalion bombers. In early December 1916, George confided to May, "I sure miss him. although I'm with a first class bunch; but Jack & I could compare notes and speculate on what you people were doing at home. He is certainly a cheerful kind of a guy. Just after my own heart."[67] Their friendship was lifelong: both men and their wives are buried side by side in Whitby's Mount Lawn Cemetery. In November 1916, George reported to May that he was chumming with an Oshawa man who knew his half-brother: "If you see his wife any time you can tell her he's a fine chap which will be no flattery at all."[68] Sometimes George makes the front line sound like a walk through his neighbourhood back home: "Oh, Say I forgot to mention in my recent letters. The last time in the line I met Tom Milgate from Jackson St. He was pleased to see me & we had a great talk about home."[69] Clearly responding to an inquiry from May, he wrote: "Yes! I see Fred Cooper most days.[70] He is looking FINE." When George's old battalion, the 116th, crossed to France and he was able to visit the men, he told May: "Say Mr Jacobi & Henry and Hinds & last but not least Fred Palmer were tickled to death to see us fellows. Shook hands about 10 minutes. Talking about the good times we will have when we all meet in Oshawa ... I got a pair of socks down there from the Oshawa knitting society. S.M. Palmer took us to his tent & dished them out."[71] Jacobi, Henry, and Hind were all officers. On this occasion, the community of "Oshawa" trumped rank.[72]

There were also those who would not meet again. "Oshawa is sure getting hit hard eh? Young Gibbie gone now has he," George wrote.[73] The memories were indelible: "Well I've come through all right so far so I don't mind past experiences, though they've been heart breaking sometimes. That J. Mc-Mullen who was killed on April 9 reported in the Vindicator was a chum of mine in our bombing section. He was killed by my side. A first class man too. One of the 116th too."[74] In recounting the fighting for Hill 70, overlooking Lens, George shared with May still more local losses, reporting on 29 August 1917: "We are sure giving the Boche something to remember us by.[75] Though its not without a price of course. Three more of our old fellows were killed this last trip in. All of Oshawa. One used to work in the Steel Range. Harry West was his name. Also one badly wounded. Gee! they are getting scarce all right now."[76] In early September, he commented in the same vein, "By God! we lost some good boys too, but I'm still here. There's only a few of the old boys left now. C. & J. Gibbs are here yet with me."[77]

These Oshawans, alive and dead, were part of a much larger Canadian fellowship of the trenches. In a letter to May written after several weeks of arduous fighting to turn back the German spring offensive, which had begun in March 1918, it is the regard of the men of the battalion that is important: "Its sure great though to have the good-will of so many good boys."[78] For George rank did not define worth, nor were medals always a measure of a man "I beleive in giving honor where its due," he commented. "Its the same all the world over. I know justice is seldom done. In the army the man with a little influence gets decorated if he never sees anything and the man that does the work is ignored. You hear <u>men</u> in our bunch saying 'I don't want no medals, they're getting too cheap.' Its so too. At Passchendael we had some decorations handed out and the one that got the highest did the least to deserve it. The men that stayed with it to the last got nothing not even rations or rum, nothing but mud & misery."[79] Again, what determined value for George was doing the job and doing it well. Frequently in his letters he tells his wife of the courageous effort and toil of the men, as when he recounted that "we marched all night. I say marched but I think after the first three hours it was more like a stagger. We 'carried on' though, grouching, swearing, and staggering. I don't think a single man dropped out."[80] In August 1917, George lost an officer whom he much admired. The man George describes was Lt. Thomas Dougall, MC, MM, who in the early hours of 17

August 1917 received shrapnel wounds to the scalp, spine, arm, and back from an enemy 5.9 shell. Dougall had enlisted as a private with the 18th Battalion in October 1914. It is apparent from the entries in the 18th Battalion's war diary and the 18th Battalion historical records that Dougall became an exceptional non-commissioned officer and subaltern, active and daring in patrol and reconnaissance work.[81] Recording his death, the battalion diarist wrote: "His courage and energy had been a source of pride in the Battalion and his work had been of the greatest value, not only to the Battalion, but also to the Brigade and Division."[82] George's assessment of Lieutenant Dougall was similar: "A good man he was too. Rose from the ranks. Many a night I crawled in the mud behind him in No Man's Land seeing what was doing. Just looking for adventure à la Don Quixote and at the same time finding out valuable information. He would go anywhere if he had a man or two for cover. He'd say 'You stay here and watch those houses, if you see anybody shoot him so that I get a chance to get out of here.'"[83] Lieutenant Dougall was awarded the Military Cross for the action that took his life. He was nineteen.[84] Lieutenant Dougall "and the men that stayed with it to the last [who] got nothing not even rations or rum, nothing but mud & misery" passed George Timmins' test: their contribution to the common effort.

George's commitment to the common effort steadied him in the face of temptation. "Beleive me hon," he wrote, "sometimes I feel I'd do any thing to get out of this and come home to you and the kids ... but I have'nt got the nerve to swing it. Never went on sick parade yet ... I'm here now and its up to me to do my best I guess. Anyway my self pride would'nt let me do any less."[85] And if good service in the line earned his respect, and helped him to keep his own, the failure to do so earned his undying opprobrium. On 1 November 1917, days before George was to enter the fighting around Passchendaele, he wrote to May about some of the men who were no longer in the fight and who were likely to be among those returning to Oshawa: "Say there must be a bunch of men coming back to Oshawa all right, but by what I know of them that's judging by their names, they are all men who have done no service in the line."[86] Generals, too, could place themselves outside the community. In scathing terms, George reported: "We were inspected by Gen Horne on Saturday last. It took about 3 months to persuade the men to clean up sufficiently to satisfy the officers that they would pass on this eventful day, and it took the General just about 3 minutes to inspect each battn, 12 minutes to inspect the brigade. We had to walk about six miles to the place of inspection. The common soldier had to carry a load that is almost a disgrace to humanity, on purpose to be looked at. The general, who has a motor car supplied by the Gov. could'nt condescend to visit us and save us the walk. oh! no. Its sure a great life alright. Talk about militarism. We are supposed to be here to suppress it, and it seems we are getting in the toils of the same infamous machine ourselves. We need to win the war I know, but it seems we will have a fight on afterwards to rid ourselves of the obnoxious habit made infamous by the Germans."[87]

George's comments are telling ones. Although he was being bitingly critical of the army administration's common practices, and the pointless burdens being imposed on men who had already borne so much, he was still acknowledging to May the validity of the war as he saw it. He also believed that it was the common soldier, the "good men" of whom he so often speaks, who would be the determining factor in the winning of the war. In January 1918, he wrote: "The Canadian Army is the rottenest affair in the world in its administration. If it was'nt for the <u>men</u> they have in the ranks it would'nt be as good as Cox's army of Yankee fame as a fighting unit."[88] And in the same letter, George once again returned to his concerns about militarism, expressing in his analysis of the problem the crux of the wartime liberal dilemma: "I beleive in conscription myself for the duration of this war, voted for it in fact, but if we build up a military party we are just building what we are supposed to be fighting to break down, 'Militarism.' Its the predominating power in England to-day. They are calling for more & more men, & women to fill men's places. Realizing that they must have a stronger 'militarism' than Germany has to be able to beat her. Where will it all end. No one knows, but I'd hate to be at the mercy of a 'military' power, German or otherwise."[89]

The criticism and even sometimes the bitterness that creep into George's letters after Vimy vary in their depth, quality, and consistency, though they become quite distinct by the time of Passchendaele. His account of his journey back to France after ten days' leave in late November 1917 includes powerful images of soldiers rounded up like cattle and herded on to trains. He conjectures that there would not have been enough rope to hang all of the men, including himself, who were guilty of seditious talk.[90] But while

George often used the expressions "fed up" and "war weary," he was not ready to give up on the war.

Along with his family, the Oshawa connection, and the brotherhood of the trenches, George drew strength from the communities behind the lines. The precarious existence shared by civilians not far from the front, family life violated by war, reaffirmed in George the values for which he believed he was fighting. A number of George's letters mention the children whom he met while soldiering. George was profoundly conscious of the war's toll on them. In July 1917, resting by the side of a road, he encountered a displaced mother with two daughters. "Say! one was like Mollie must be," he wrote May. "Fair, with blue eyes and long fair hair, and healthy fat old cheeks. I spoke to her in my <u>best</u> French and asked her for a kiss. Say! her mother told her to kiss the 'Bon Soldat' and she came right over & kissed me. Hon! I made a kid of myself right there I just had to hug that kid for as long as she'd stand for it. Her mother informed me that they were refugees from La Bassee, and that the Germans had come right through the place where they were living & they had had to beat it without a thing and had to go hungry and nowhere to sleep. I felt I could kill a German any old time for the sake of that kid, and the way she must have suffered."[91] George's civilian encounters behind the lines were not always as fleeting. In February 1918, George recounted to May "a Sunday dinner in a French village."[92] The friendship with his hostess, which had begun in the summer of 1917, led first to an exchange of letters and, several months later, to a meal, George's description of which forms one of the wittiest and longest letters in the collection. The letter concludes, however, on a darker note. The husband of his generous French hostess was a prisoner of war in starving Germany; "She had to send him food or else as she expressed it, namely, 'Him dead.'"[93] George's family in England also offered him the domestic space and comfort he craved: "I spent my first night in Blighty at Mary's at Small Heath being treated like a prince."[94] He recounted to his children with evident delight the antics of his nephew: "I have seen Aunt Mary's baby boy twice. He is a beauty. He thinks his Uncle George is all right I guess, as he just laughs all the time I'm there and climbs all over me."[95] But his family in England, like his French hosts, faced serious difficulties. The long shadows of war produced food shortages and inflationary conditions. "Things look bad here," George wrote to May from England in late November 1917. "You should see the women lined up about a block to buy ½ pound of margarine or tea."[96] There was also a serious illness in the family. George's father, Felix, apparently suffering from mental illness, died sometime between August and early September 1917, when George speaks of him in the past tense.[97] These troubles notwithstanding, George received a steady supply of letters and parcels from his family in England, who were also in close touch with May and the children. One is struck by the closeness and evident warmth of George's family ties and the degree to which the family was able to maintain them across such distances and in such trying times.

From his sixty-three surviving wartime letters, George Timmins emerges as a man of principle with a strong sense of the value of family, of duty and fairness, friendship and community. George reveals himself as a man who measured himself against himself. He was a man of ethical substance, whose ability to maintain his perspective, equilibrium, and "genial love of little ordinary human things"[98] owed much to the strength that he derived from intersecting communities of effort, civilian and military, at home and abroad. Foremost among these was his family, who went to war in March of 1916 as surely as he did.

CHAPTER 1

about 35 yds from Fritz.

MAY–DECEMBER 1916

LETTER 1   *Notes appear on pages 138-39*

Niagara Camp[1]
Monday Night [24 May 1916]

Dear May[2]

Just arrived here after a very pleasant trip. The lake was lovly to day. There were quite a number of soldiers on board & quite a few who had drunk not wisely but too well. The latest camp news is that we get a medical exam. to morrow. Report says that the 98th had theirs & about 50 per cent were turned down.[3] If we get it as strict as that, there's quite a few unnecessary tears been spilt in Oshawa to-day.[4] I'd hate to be turned down now after people have cried over me. You, girl, are a heroine. When poor little Winnie & "Jim" started it nearly got my goat. Never mind honey; if I get through (and there's only one thing will stop me) you can tell anybody that asks you, that your husband is doing his bit as best he can. What got into May Timmins to day?[5] See her crying. I am wondering if it was over me or maybe it was just the influence of the crowd. Good luck and lots of love from yours as always

George.

Kiss the kids for dad. Poor old Jim I never thought he could cry!

Buy some choc. for them from daddie[6]

can tell anybody that asks you, that your husband is doing his bit as best he can. What got into May Simmins to day? See here crying. I am wondering if it was over me or maybe it was just the influence of the crowd. Good luck and lots of love from yours as always

George.

Kiss the kids for dad. Poor old Jim, I never thought he could cry!

Letter 1, Niagara Camp, 24 May 1916

LETTER 2   *Notes appear on pages 139-40*
[*On letterhead bearing the words "Brotherhood
of St. Andrew Reading Room."*][7]

"D" Company 116th Battalion
Niagara Military Camp
[June or July 1916]

Dear May

Thought you would'nt mind if I wrote you an extra letter, not that the supply is written on schedule though I'm always willing to write but infinitely more willing to receive letters as you know. Well I have just finished my job as chaperon. I have just seen Lillie on the "Corona," Toronto bound. It was too bad. Yesterday, after expecting to be dismissed after 11.30 as orders called for we were kept at the ranges until 4 never reaching camp till 4.30, and all the Oshawa people waiting to see their friends.[8] Well, I was with Lillie to the boat. Having previously engaged a room for her & her friends in case they could'nt get a boat in time for the train home. When they got inside the gate I came away satisfied they were all right, & went to bed. What was my surprise to be wakened up by a friend of the other girl to tell me they had not gone after all as the boat was too full, and they had gone to their room. He having telephoned Oshawa in the meantime. So I looked them up after church parade & so ended another episode of my experience.[9] Lillie seems to have had a good time though. I guess she'll be home on the 10 to night. There is still all kinds of rumors going around about our departure, but nothing definite. I don't pay any attention to them any more. Plenty of time to think of going when our packs are on our backs. By the look of the paper last night I guess we won't be needed after all.[10] Is'nt that good news though. Not that I don't want to go. Far from it, but for the good of the whole bunch. It certainly won't last much longer I dont think. We are doing all our shooting in a hurry so we will be ready I suppose when the time comes. I see a big bunch of Oshawa people round here to day. There's going to be a big storm here in a few minutes by the way the wind is blowing so I must get over to camp and see things are all right as all the other occupants of our tent are away at the Falls.[11] I'm going to keep all my money if I can until we go over or until I get another trip to Oshawa. We were paid the other day I got 7´25.[12] But I had a misfortune I either lost or had swiped my big knife. So I have to swipe or buy another Love to all & don't forget to write soon to yours as always George.

Love to the kiddies from dad. There's lots of little kids round here to day about like Mollie. I feel I'd like to steal one for a little while

LETTER 3 · *Notes appear on pages 140-41*
*[On the letterhead of the 116th Overseas
Battalion, CEF Ontario County.]*

Aug. 1ˢᵗ [1916]

Dear May

Arrived in camp last night at 2 o'clock after a long trip by train. We had quite a time on the boat.[13] We had lots of good food, but the boat was so crowded we could hardly move. We slept in hammocks slung over the tables and any old place. Then we had to wear lifebelts all the time.[14] Could'nt move any place without them on. They are very inconvenient too. You have to wear them to meals & to the wash house & every place you go. When you go to wash you lay it down & maybe there's some fellow there who has forgotten his & has been lucky enough to escape being held up by the M.P's, but does'nt want to run the gauntlet again so he swipes yours. What can you do then with perhaps 100 men in there. Its no use hunting for your own, the best thing you can do is to swipe somebody else's. That is if you are slick enough I used to average about 6 Lifebelts a day. Every time I took mine off, it seemed that somebody took it further. So the first one I could see had to be mine. We also had practise alarms every day: When the whistle blew we had to drop whatever we were doing, and run up on top deck at our best speed. We were supposed to be up there in about two minutes. The last alarm that sounded I was snatching a little siesta when somebody yelled in my ear "General Alarm, beat it. Well believe me I beat a few records in getting through crowds on the stairways (Crowds is right as there were about 6500 troops on board). I had just got on deck in my place & was rubbing a little slumber from my eyes when up came two fellows who had evidently been caught in the swimming pool (there was a dandy on board) to judge by their costume, which consisted of a short (very short) shirt and the inevitable lifebelt. Cold on deck too. I think modesty would win with me in a battle with fear of death by drowning. I'd take a chance on catching the last boat and put on a pair of socks anyway. We came right through England in the train. It looks good too at this season. We passed through the Black Country.[15] Wolverhampton Bilston Smetwich West Bromwich, Handsworth, Birmingham. The Black Country is rightly named. It does'nt compare with the rest of the country very favorably. That's from the train of course. But it was like a glimpse of home to me and I was stuck half way out of the window all the way. Well there's one thing about it, the people of the Black Country gave us the best reception passing through of any. Women & children lined the back fences & railroad banks & pit banks. Women with Union Jacks & the inevitable grimy baby. But the hundreds of school kids on the fences warmed my heart. Nice white "pinners"

on the little girls & collars on the little boys.[16] There must have been
"thousands" My God talk about kids I said hundreds before but on
considering I'm sure there was thousands. I mention this so that you
won't say "exaggerating as usual." No race suicide for Staffordshire.[17] I am
going up as soon as I get a pass. I am going to have a pint with your old
man if he is still drinking (Save the mark).[18] There's lots of camps &
soldiers in England as far as I can see.[19] We are in huts, as they are called
here, but in Canada they would be termed houses all right. They are fine.
But I think we wont be here long as this seems to be just a clearing house
sort of a place. They examine the men here & pass them on to other
places for their training. They say the medical exam is terribly severe. So
I don't know where I'll get off at. Well I'll do the best I can any way. I hope
you are getting your money all right. They say we don't get much money
here as there's so much [*words illegible*] back as deferred pay. Remember
me to all & say I'll write as soon as I get a chance, but it seems every chance
I get I want to write to you, hon. Love to the kiddies. Kiss them for dad.
Love from your loving husband
George.

Address   Pte G Timmins
746180 D Coy
116 Batt C.E.F.
c/o Army Post Office
London England

FRAGMENT 1   *Notes appear on pages 141-42*
*[On the letterhead of the 116th Overseas
Battalion, CEF Ontario County.]*

[Monday, 25 September 1916]
[Part of this letter is missing.]
looking forward to it too. Its a grand summer here as far as we have seen
yet. Its never rained so far since we came. We are in Hampshire.[20] About
7 hours from the trenches. So we can quickly get there eh?. Its so nice to
have a walk through the lanes at night and call at a wayside inn & get a
pint of beer. But the hours are awfully restricted. 12 till 2.30 & 6 till 9 P.M.[21]

This is an awfully out of the way place. Nothing but a small town & lots of soldiers. And the prices![22] Ye Gods its ridiculous. And after us telling the Canucks how cheaply they could get a good time in England.[23] They certainly rub it in to us. We can all sing "O. Canada," with feeling, believe me.[24] The grub is cut down fine too. No waste, as you think you might need it to sustain you. The first time I went for a walk through the lanes, I was pleased to see the hedges full of honeysuckles, so I got a few to send to you as I remember you used to think so much of them. I mention this so you wont think I got the idea from the snaps. you sent to me, for which many thanks. They say the Medical Exam is very severe here, so I am a little anxious as to how I will fare, as they don't send you back if you are rejected, they just keep you here for fatigues & guards etc. In a god forsaken hole like this. Just imagine. There's quite a lot of the 84th here waiting their discharge, for several minor reasons, for which you would think there would be no kick at all.[25] I was sorry to hear that the report was circulated in Oshawa that we had been submarined 2 days out. I can almost imagine your feelings. Just the same it might easily have been. It was no fault of the subs. It was skill on the part of the captain of the boat. We were all ready to land in England for Sunday morning, even to sandwiches for the train, when suddenly the ship was put about, & we struck for sea again. Of course we could only surmise, but you can bet they dont go 24 hours out of their course just to give the soldiers an extra ride on the ocean.[26] We heard since that the Germans tried their best to get us, also that the betting in New York was 10 to 1 that they did. Any way they did'nt, so we should worry Glad to hear the garden is doing so well. Also that the kids are so good. Poor little Jim. Got knocked down did he at the station that night. Well there's going to be a settlement with those damn Polacks one of these days.[27] In the meantime stand clear. Look after yourself & the kids & wait. We are supposed to be reviewed by Sam Hughes this afternoon.[28] Sunday at that. Bless his heart, you know what I mean. I will now close with the best of wishes for you all, and lots of love from your loving husband George. Kiss the little fellows for "dad."

P.S. The same address you put on before is all right. Geo

LETTER 4   *Notes appear on pages 142-44*

Bramshott Camp[29]
Tuesday Sept 26th [1916]

Dear old sweetheart

Just a little scribble in answer to the dandy long letter you sent to me.
The news is still about the same here That is as far as we are concerned.
I got a week end pass last Saturday and went to London with a bunch of
the boys. We only got from Saturday noon until 10.30 Sunday Night, so
you can bet we did'nt have much time to spare. But it was enough time
in which to dispose of all the money we had. Gee! they soak it to you,
especially when they see you are up there for the first time.[30] You would
admire the masterly way in which the bus conductresses handle their
passengers.[31] Some of them are good looking too, in their uniforms and
puttees. Everything seems to be run by women or girls even the milk
routes. You can't move for girls and soldiers, at least you could'nt on
Sunday evening. We had to leave there about 9 o'clock. We saw all the
sights though, and lived high. Dinner (you know late dinner or supper if
you like) at the "Monico" both nights.[32] Some class for Tommies, eh?[33] We
thought we might as well have a good time while the chance was good.
We were inspected by Sir Sam Hughes yesterday (Monday) morning & he
said he was very pleased with our appearance and we were the best Batt
on parade out of the whole Brigade.[34] Rumor has it now that we shall go
over as a Batt and not be broken up It may be shortly too, according to
what an instructor told us yesterday afternoon.[35] Oh. I forgot the main
news. While in London on Saturday we saw a Zepp raid. I suppose you
will have read about it before you get this. Anyway we heard the guns &
the people cheering but we were too far away to see the downfall. It was
on the outskirts of London & we were in the West End at Marble Arch.
They got two but not before they had done an awful lot of damage,
according to one of our chaps who was on leave right in the place that
was hit. I was on guard last night (after a pass oh Lor!) and behold another
one was over. They say she raided over the Midlands. Though we did'nt
get any particulars yet.[36] Well, dear, I suppose you will be getting fed up
with this stuff. I hope everything is first-class with you all, as yours truly

is at present though sadly in need of a little sleep. Say kid I never got a
parcel at all yet, and I had your letter 2 weeks ago to-day saying that first
parcel was posted the same day. Don't waste any more money on parcels
until you hear from me about having received the others. I don't like
other people to get whats sent for me and its plain somebody else must
be. I suppose some of the mail handlers like cigarettes & candies, though
believe me it would come handy now as its a week until pay day. I hope
you are getting your pay all right. They have cut us down. It seems they
stop 5 dollars a month for 4 months so as to always have a balance in
hand of 20 dollars, after that they just pay us up in 1 pound & 10 shilling
notes, so that if your pay is 19 shillings you draw only 10 and the balance
is kept by somewhere. God knows where. It certainly seems very
unsatisfactory[37] Well, honey, I will now say good bye with all kinds of love
to you & the little fellows from yours as always George.

Did the kiddies like the post cards I sent for them?

LETTER 5   *Notes appear on pages 144-48*

Say do you remember last Hallow'een. J. Burr was laughing about the
kids only last night
Don't forget to write.

27th Letter[38]

France
Oct 31st [1916][39]

Dear May
    Got two letters from you yesterday, when we came [*censored*].
I assure you I was delighted to get them, especially to hear that you had
got two from me, as I can understand kid, how you must feel when the
others get mail & you don't. Its about the same here I guess. When other
men get a letter and my name is not called out I immediately begin to
wonder whats gone wrong at home. Glad to hear the kiddies got their
cards alright. But I am still wondering what became of Mollies birthday
present I sent from your home through Mary.[40] You never said anything
about it yet. Don't you worry dear, about the money. Get what ever you &
the kids want. If the money you get from the Gov. & mine is'nt enough,

you know where there's some more. We don't get any scarcely, so I can't help that way, but don't go short of any old thing at all. I'll have a good job again some day, old girl. It seems Mrs Burr is asking for a photo of Jack the same as you want one of mine. Well Jack & I are the closest friends now and we are going to have a try to get them.[41] Of course it may be difficult here in France to get them & to send them away. Your second letter was a dandy. Say Hon, it just seemed you were talking to me. Sorry to hear you had been a bit sick though also Jim. Don't take any chances, you know you have nobody to bully you into self protection like you used to have when I was home. Oh! you asked if the cake, etc, was eatable. Say when we get back I'll bring a dozen witnesses to prove it was equal if not superior to manna from heaven. Also I got the hankies & papers. That rumor you heard was correct. We were in France on the [*censored*]. Its funny is'nt it? I think Capt. Hinds cabled. He was sure cut up about it too. I was surprised at the amount of feeling he showed. Shook hands with every man of us & wished us luck.[42] Don't worry about the parcels dear if it gives you any trouble or too much expense. Any way don't put in any plugs as they get damp & we can't smoke them. Send Senator if any.[43] I did'nt get Maimie's yet altho she said she sent it the same time as the letter. If you hear anybody talking about the beauties of France tell them from me they handle the truth carelessly. Round here is the muddiest, dirtiest place you ever saw. Of course its badly knocked about too. Say you knew Jack Cash (that's the man who married the widow Batton) well he got the Military Medal last Sunday from the General for gallantry under fire.[44] Just imagine eh? I saw Bert Norris & Albert Wallace on Sunday & they were telling us about it. Bert Norris says he's (J. Cash) the best man in the army. I saw Billie Bircham on Sunday too but I never saw Charlie yet but he's round here so I will see him to night likely.[45] Its a good thing for the widows that they have raised the pensions.[46] I guess the Gov. can stand it all right. They can find any amount of money to pay to have the men killed so they should be able to keep those who are left dependant. Don't worry though, that won't affect you. Me & old Jack have a decent time as far as resources go of course. A little beer each night this week now we [*censored*] when we are in [the line].[47] Well we should worry. I guess that's all I can write this time The censor is pretty strict now. One man got a letter saying all that was left of his last three letters was "<u>Dear</u> <u>Mother</u>" the other was all censored.[48] So good bye & lots of love to you all from yrs as always Geo.

The Timmins children – Winnifred Mary (Winnie), Margaret Ann (Mollie), and James (Jim) – probably in Oshawa, summer of 1915. Photo courtesy of J.G. Houlden.

LETTER 6　*Notes appear on pages 146*

France. Nov 6th [1916][49]

Dear girl

Just a little letter to reassure you. We are back for another turn of six days, and then six days in reserve, then six days in billets and so on <u>ad. infinitum</u>.[50] A kind of endless chain, which we hope will find an end some day in the near future, at least I think that's the sentiments of the majority. Its getting to be nasty weather here now. rain about half the time which makes things unpleasant.[51] I got a letter from Florrie yesterday[52] They were awfully disappointed that I had'nt been to see them again before I left. Beleive me it was no fault of mine, as I would have gone with the greatest pleasure in life. Jack & I have got parted now. After working together in what we thought would be a permanent job. We were in the company bombers, but I was sent to the battalion bombers on Saturday last.[53] I have'nt seen Jack since, but will see him anyway on Friday or Saturday next. Maybe he'll come with us then. Well, hon, it will soon be Christmas. I don't know how I am going to send anything for the little fellows from here, but I'll have a try. Good luck to them. I guess its up to Jim this year to get the Xmas tree eh? Say you would have laughed if you could have seen us last Thursday. It was pay day. All our fellows from 116th drew the magnificent sum of 5 Franc, thats just one dollar as a franc is 10 pence. Well the other fellows of course drew more, so we organized a concert & impromptu dance in our billet (which by the way was an old dry goods store I should imagine) Jack & I slept together on the counter. Well we got the dixies (that's the pots the cook makes tea, soup, boiled rice, or anything there happens to be, in) and also borrowed a pail from some people at the back somewhere & got them full of beer, which by the way was also French beer, like water, you know like Sid complimented Rose on, "Well its wet"! Well we had a very successful evening. Which is to be repeated when we again come out, if its possible to raise the price. Well sweetheart it just seems I can't write an interesting letter any more, but will be able to <u>tell</u> you the news soon. Remember me to Maimie & Annie. Tell them I'll write again soon. Love to yourself and our kiddies from yours as always <u>George</u>.

Tell Jack Long I'll write to him too.[54]

LETTER 7   *Notes appear on pages 146-48*
*[On letterhead bearing the YMCA logo
and the words "And Canadian War Contingent
Association With The Canadian Forces."][55]*

Somewhere in France
Nov 17th 1916 [56]

Dear old girl

Just got your letter dated Oct 29th . That's pretty quick work eh?
The quickest I have yet received. Nevertheless it was extremely welcome
beleive me. Rather glad to hear that Rose & Gid are interested a little in
as much as to send me a nice parcel. I am going to write and thank them
very much. You must be rather a busy little woman now a days. Two
babies to look after besides the extra fussing with meals. Look out dear
you don't do too much. Never fear about me having to worry, financially
or otherwise. Beleive me nothing is worth worrying about any more
except you and our kiddies I'll be content all right just to have them
climbing over me. Even for Jim to be throwing lumps of baked clay at me
while I am working in the garden. Do you remember the young villain,
how he used to throw and sometimes make a hit and then laugh? Poor
little old Mollie, having her toes bruised like that. I suppose Jim got his
for that. She'll be able to tell her dad about it soon I hope. Say I'm in luck
all right. Got a letter from Sarah Dunn yesterday saying she had some
money from Harry, and asked to send me something.[57] I sent word not to
buy cigs or tobac. in England as its so dear there but to send some good
eats, especially raisin pie. I taught her how to make them while I was on
pass. Sure hope they come soon too. We just look forward to a good feed
like that. Looks bad for England when they are starting to issue food
tickets & to stop any more white bread being sold.[58] It will be a good thing
I think when the war is ended favorably, for everybody concerned. Miss
McLeod will think I'm a poor correspondent wont she. Well I'll write as
soon as I can think up some news to tell her. Don't you forget your two a
week as they are about all I care about now Of course its very nice to have
a letter from anybody but its your letters that count. I got a lovly pair of
socks from the 116th Oshawa Knitting Society.[59] Just what I needed too.

Though I had 3 prs already Its so cold at night now.[60] So I've got a big pair
of boots & wear 3 prs of socks with them. Appearances don't count here.
It would break the hearts of all the military officers of Canada to see us
now. They used to be so strict as to have us all alike even to rolled or
unrolled shirt sleeves. Now some wear overcoats some have'nt any, so
don't wear them. Some wear woollen caps, some ordinary caps, some steel
helmets. Its sure a funny sight to see them coming out of the trenches or
going in. If we could be suddenly transported, just as we were to Canada,
I'll bet the country would go wild. Mud caked on shoes, clothes, even to
the hat. Rifles looking in some cases like a stick of mud.[61] Fully loaded
with ammunition and perhaps a sand bag full of bread in case the rations
turn up short. Say it looks like a caravan starting on a journey over the
desert only instead of camels they use men as beasts of burden. Believe
me I would just like to see "Winnie & Mollie in bed looking like angels." I
sure just love those two kids. Roll on! Tell Jim I think just as much of him
too. Glad to hear you go to church if its passing a pleasant evening away
for you. You can tell De Penuir from me that his theory of the soldiers
must be right. I certainly don't see what else is coming to a soldier if he
does go under. That should certainly square accounts. If it don't I would'nt
give much for the chance most of them stand Its certainly educative to
hear their descriptive language when referring to mud, rain, cold or bum
rations. It must be old Bob Gibbie that's sick although I've never heard
about it. He was left in Bramshott you know.[62] Oh say I'd be glad of a little
Zam buk.[63] Mrs Burr makes it for Jack. I saw him to day just going in as I
was coming out at 5.30 AM. Also a few apples & cheap candies. You the
15 ¢ a pound variety of mixtures from 5. 10, 15. Pack in a little wooden box.
Jack Long will find one for you any time I guess. Address 18th Batt'n
Canucks, "Grenade Section" France.[64] This seems rather a tall order, but
your offer was pretty wide. Well sweetheart I can't think of anything else I
want, only you & the kids so I will say goodbye with all sorts of love from
yours as ever George

P.S. Saw Jack Darley & Harry Winship yesterday[65]

LETTER 8   *Notes appear on pages 148-50*

Somewhere in France
[23] Nov. [1916]

Dearest May

I've sure been in luck this week I got 5 letters on Wednesday night and one last night. The five included 2 from you, one from Miss McLeod addressed by you, one from May Timmins, and one from Gid.[66] Last night I got one from you dated Sept 25 It had been all over the country I guess trying to find me, judging from the erased addresses on it. It was the one I had been expecting so long, containing the news that you had received Mollie's birthday present. She was a lucky little girl eh? Is'nt everybody good to her? Well she's worth it & more I always think. I can always imagine her without much effort of mind, I can assure you. I have tried to write letters since I have been in France but somehow they have always seemed so unsatisfactory to me on account of the thoughts of the censor having to read them. Well they have begun to issue the green envelope again, (it was stopped last spring) which is inscripted with an oath to the effect that the writer is disclosing no military secrets, (as though a man has nothing else to write to his own wife about) and then it <u>may</u> escape censorship.[67] Well anyway I'm going to take a chance & call you all the nicest things I can think of just for once, expecting you to understand when I don't (as I am awfully shy about anybody else reading my love letters) that I am just as much in love with my wife as ever I was, whether I can write about it or not. Never forget sweetheart when my letters are as unemotional as a schoolboys essay on horticulture, that its not the lack of love on my part, but fear of the eye of the ----- censor. We came out yesterday for 6 days in the reserve.[68] We are in a district formerly a colliery district. All little model villages, you know "company houses." But they must have been great at one time. all smashed now.[69] Trenches in their streets, billets in their schools etc. I tell you, hon, you in Canada, (except for the lonliness of wives who really miss their husbands) don't know what war is. In our last billet we had table, chairs, a writing desk, old beds etc. belonging to the former tenants. Just imagine, kiddo, if it was Oshawa. Our tables & chairs & stoves in use by troops. I say it is a shame. And its so common one never notices it. I'm just quit laughing at two of our men who wanted something to use to write their letters on & went to the little school house and got a desk, you know the kind, two kiddies seats with holes for inkwells and every accessory. Say it was almost a tradegy. Poor little devils. Believe me it brought ours to mind after I had had a laugh at the ludicrous appearance of the men with it over their shoulders on a stick. We have to do lots of foraging in that way. We have to get fuel too, as best we can, probably we are in luck and get some old wood or go to the mine dump & get some slack & screen it, only at the latter job Fritz is likely to see us and drop over a shell or two as he has the mine under his guns all the time[70] The other day three of us went to get coal & were just coming back when a shell dropped just behind us. Believe me we hastened our footsteps considerable. Then again if he sees much smoke coming out of the chimneys he slings a shell as near the house as he can Hits it if he can of course. Thats only when we are on reserve. When we are "in" of course he gives us as many as he can. All kinds too Snipers, machine guns, trench mortars, big shells etc, to keep us busy.[71] Its been wet this last week and the mud is over our knees, in fact up to our thighs in places. I used to think the mud tales were exaggerated, but now I see its as true as the scripture.[72] Us gang only go out nights to hold the advanced posts and believe me its some job getting there in the dark.[73] It sounds impossible for men to travel with sticky mud to their thighs with rubber boots right to the top of their legs & strapped on, but we do it everytime we go out on duty.[74] The other morning coming in, the front line had fell in & we had to come over the top. Pitch dark. Got mixed in our own wire.[75] You should have heard the muttered curses. Could'nt express ourselves out loud as Fritz is only a very little distant from us at this one point and if he hears you he is liable to help to swell the population of the nether regions, if you have'nt lived a good life that is of course.[76] Well I always seem to drop into a good bunch of fellows. The bunch here, ("The bombers") are a fine bunch. Don't give a hang for anything. That's what the job calls for. I hope I can show up as good as they have when the occasion comes There's two or three D.C.M.s among us now.[77] Some record eh? Of course there's quite a few left in the Somme region. Left for good poor chaps.[78] Well I'll do all I can. There's a fellow here from College Hill that I am chumming with now. He's old Tom Parker's son in law. He's named Stan Harrison He moulded in the Malle. He knows Gid all right. He came over with the 37th.[79] If you see his wife any time you can tell her he's a fine chap which will be no flattery at all. Well kiddie Gibson seems to be making money yet eh? I hope it does him good, nix. I got Jim's letter in Miss McLeod's. Tell him he's to get up the coal etc & not to let his mother do it all. You are right when you say <u>we</u> are blessed with fine children. I showed the snapshot of you all eating plums to the fellows here & the first thing they did was to say "Gee thats a fine girl you have there," meaning Winnie. She's sure to get spoilt that kid is. Just keep her to you, girl. Make her as much like her mother in ways as she is in looks & she'll be all "Jake" as they say out here.[80] Some time at Norman's party eh? I suppose he was in his glory. Also Winnie & Mollie & Jim. Tom Knott never wrote at all. He's some gas meter all right. So they are not giving the slackers much peace eh?[81] If they had the wishes of the men out here come true they'd sure have a fancy time I tell you. Say this is hard in streaks & seldom exactly comfortable, (as we would call it in civilization) but I would'nt have missed it on any kind of chance I don't think. We curse it at times too. There's boys here under 18 doing men's work & bluffing they are 20 & so on. Never missing a turn & doing exactly the same, & in some cases more, than full grown men. And men in Canada keeping out of it. Hell, it dont matter any way. Probably the war can be ended without them. Well sweetheart it dont seem to be much of a love letter does it. I'll be glad of a parcel as soon as you can send one. What about a good big cake. Send to Mary if you like as it gets smashed up so in transit. Not that the quality is deteriorated at all. Its fine, but the postage for a parcel to stand the trip is so exorbitant. Its eats of the "delicacy" variety we seem to need most. Our rations by no stretch of the imagination can scarcely be called delicate.[82] You say you are always thinking & talking about me. Well [*remainder missing*]

LETTER 9   *Notes appear on pages 150-51*
[*On letterhead bearing the YMCA logo
and the words "And Canadian War Contingent
Association With The Canadian Forces."*]

Somewhere in France[83]
Dec 7th [1916]

Dear Girl

Just received your letter, also a parcel of candy from Mamie and Annie. Yours contained a note from Mrs Foster & a card with a hymn or a prayer on it.[84] I don't know which. Their's contained snapshots of Winnie & Jim, by far the most acceptable. Don't they look fine? Winnie gets to be quite a young lady. Jim is still the old Jim just the same as always. He sure looks good to me though. The girls had wrapped them in a grand way. I thought I had about a dozen pictures instead of two. Quite a delicious sensation of suspense while unwrapping it, wondering when the end was coming. Sorry dear to hear you had been sick. Take more care of yourself, whatever else goes wrong it must'nt be you, you know. You speak of repeating the same sentence in all your letters. Please don't forget to repeat it each time. I like to read it. I wrote to Mamie & Annie this week acknowledging receipt of S R. Co parcel. I guess you will get this as soon as they get their's. To night I got a type-written letter from Michie & Co Toronto, with addressed envelope to let them know if I had got a parcel sent through a London firm through them which was the steel range parcel. I am returning their letter the next mail with "received" written on it, which is all they want. So Jim bought me a pipe eh? Tell the girls I'm still using the one presented by them last May 21st. Just as good as new only a little tasty. Give Billy Clarke the address if he wants it. It will do no harm to him nor me. Let him send all he likes. Say, hon, I don't need that underwear. You see the system which is worked out here, is this. When we come out we get a bath & change of underwear & socks, not before we need them I assure you, but its some joke I tell you. They don't measure the men for the suits but just issue them as they come a whole outfit complete. Well maybe you have just taken off a good new suit, probably two sizes too large and get in exchange an old suit worn pretty thin & two sizes too small you have to stretch them to make the buttons come anywhere near the button holes, and they will probably be English make with short sleeves, some exchange. Its where exchange is as near robbery as its possible to get. But the bath is fine. A shower bath with hot water, lasting <u>4 whole minutes</u>.[85] I can use a good pair of gloves or mitts though. Its pretty cold here at night. I still have the leather mitts issued to us in Canada but they are somewhat clumsy to use. The pair I had at home would be fine if you will please stick them in the next parcel. Say its a good thought of yours that pack of cards. I was intending to ask for some in this letter. We pass away the time with a pack very pleasantly. Miss McLeod seems very kind to you does'nt she? I certainly appreciate her thoughtfulness. I wrote to Gid last week. I think you did right telling Tom Knott to wait a while, as if things come in a rush they are wasted & not appreciated half as much, & we have to use them up as we have enough to carry when we are moving. I wish Enoch all kinds of luck. I have'nt seen J Burr for a week again. I sure miss him. although I'm with a first class bunch; but Jack & I could compare notes and speculate on what you people were doing at home. He is certainly a cheerful kind of a guy. Just after my own heart. I hear from Bramshott that P Williams has his discharge & is home with his wife's people at Hull.[86] That's all right for him eh? You'll get this about Christmas I guess. Say did you get those pictures of J Burr & I you never mentioned them yet. Let me know if you get them also the money I sent you as I will send some more this pay. They give us an extra big pay for Xmas and its no use me carrying it round with me. We get 50 francs extra for Christmas pay. A franc is 10 <u>d</u>. So you see its quite a little sum for an extra. We ordinarily get 30 francs a month, small enough you will admit, but as we only get a short time each month to spend it in it suffices, as we generally get nearly enough tobacco & cigarettes issued to do us, also matches. We have to buy candles though. Again wishing you and the kids a very, very Merry Christmas and a Happy New Year I remain as always your loving husband George.

P.S. Write as often as you can

LETTER 10   *Notes appear on pages 151-52*

Somewhere in France[87]
Dec 10th [1916]

Dear May

What Ho! another green envelope. Hope you got the last intact. Its the only chance we get to write to our wives without the knowledge that some other guys are going to read our innermost thoughts. That's a fact though. when I went to the orderly room to register that £1 note, which by the way I hope you have received safely, the fellow in there calmly pulls out the little epistle I had written to you, reads every word with as little emotion as a judge trying a drunk, examined the money to see if he was registering something worth while, then sticks down the envelope & seals it as though its all in the day's work which of course it is, but believe me it does gall to stand by while they do it. I bought a lace collar last night off a fellow who had bought it for his wife & afterwards went broke in a poker game. It is Flemish handmade lace made by the Sisters of some Convent round here. I hope you'll like it. I just missed the chance to buy another thing in the shape of a hand worked silk apron, another man beat me to it. But trust me you'll have one yet. They are beautiful, in my estimation anyway. Its certainly too bad that the Steel Range got burned out.[88] Hope it is'nt too bad. I suppose Mr Gibson <u>would</u> be prominent in the excitement. He's in his element at a fire anyway. I just wish some of the cold footed ----- could hear what the boys out here say about them. I wonder it does'nt reach over there sometimes anyway. Its so vehement. What they'll do when they get back too if any of them speak to them. You remember the notorious 33 Batt that J Canuck was always giving it to.[89] Well there's a few of them with us I tell you they are fine fellows. There's one just now writing to Sarah thanking her for the pie she sent me which of course he shared. He is a Scotchman from Toronto. A particular chum of mine already. He is going to hint for some more pie. Say but that pie was good. Five of us had just come off listening post, pretty near frozen to death 12.30 P.M. Just imagine kiddo 6 hours laying down in mud & water about 35 yds from Fritz. You dare not move around to get warmed up as that would attract to much attention, we creep in in a manner that would be the envy of the noble redskin at his best. You see the bombers have to hold the most advanced post. For this extra hazardous work they are allowed to be off extra work when out in billets. We go armed to the teeth. Each man carries 6 or more bombs besides rifle & ammunition. Gee when I first carried those bombs (& we had to get 'em in the dark) the first time I handled them like eggs at 75 c a dozen believe me, but familiarity breeds contempt you know. Of course they are not to be monkeyed with, with impunity, those some of them juggle with them like you see the guys on the stage. But to return to my narrative of how to hold an outpost. Just try sitting on the arm chair with a paper & a bottle of beer & everything that spells comfort. try it for 6 hours, don't move only slowly so that the darkness will swallow each move & see how you like it. Then imagine doing the same in oozy mud with a nice steady, cold rain falling on you. Its hard to be optimistic in those circumstances, but as soon as its over & your through for probably 24 hours, (if things are quiet) you are in the best of spirits especially if the rum's up, though that damn rum has the hardest time getting up the communication trench, its worse than the Pilgrims had in getting to the Glory Land in John Bunyan's immortal work.[90] Sometimes its "spilled" & the guy that spins the yarn smells badly of it & wobbles as he walks, next night it is fortunate & makes the haven, the next night the jar gets broken the next night its only half issue & the non-com's breath is highly perfumed and the rum weak.[91] Say its good though on the whole. I mean both the life itself and the rum. There's all kinds of good times when we're out you know. The best time of the day is when the rations come up with the mail included. There's a great rush outside then you can bet. We are in a place now in what is called reserve We are billeted in a house, 6 of us in one room We have fixed it up like a home. Little stove in, a table, & two beds of course there's no room to waltz nor anything like that but we just eat & sleep as in this billet there can be no inspections & drills like there is further from the front line as "Heinie" is likely to drop a few shells into us as the drill is in progress. There was a man killed getting his morning wash here the other day & another lost his arm.[92] We have to find our own fuel & it takes quite a lot these days. Wood has to be carried & also cut up so its obvious that coal is more easy to use. But the mine is in full view of HIS front line & his snipers are always busy, but coal we must have. We go sneaking round the corner of the mine buildings, (this afternoon is in my mind now) with a sandbag each, intent on stealing coal, (stealing is right as the French Gov. is going to presecute anyone found getting coal.) we just get around a railroad car & get busy when a sniper opens up. It just comes over my bean & cuts a hole in the shed by which I am working. I just stoop a little lower & go on digging for coal with my hands as my only tools. Its precious coal by the time you chance your arm on the Gov & snipers as well beleive me. By the time we got out we had 50 lbs about of coal & 4 shots from Fritz's rifle.[93] But oh! the glorious fire we had all afternoon. I lay on the floor & smoked the pipe of well earned peace. Say last night I dreamt I was home & you were so pleased to see me Mollie was in bed you said so I went upstairs and woke her & she jumped up with both arms out & shouts "Daddy." Say I did'nt want to wake up I tell you. You'd laugh, if you were here <u>sometimes</u>. We get stuck for something to fill in the time. Somebody suggests Let's have a peace conference. So we straightway sit down draw up terms & settle the war off hand to our own satisfaction. Of course Germany always pays a huge indemnity & rebuilds Belgium, reinstates Poland, Gives Alsace Lorraine back to France & reimburses Canada's sons for their trouble. We are going to win of course, but us fellows so seldom see a paper we can't form an opinion as to how its going except in our own immediate neighborhood. Its quiet now anyway as its bad weather etc, but still there are lots [*remainder missing*]

LETTER 11   *Notes appear on page 152*

> Somewhere in France
> Dec 15th [1916]

Dear

I got two letters from you last night after having had none for 10 days. Gee! It seemed a long time too, as its about the most pleasurable thing that happens when we are in the line. The parcels are coming thick and fast now but, alas, not to me. I have'nt had one except the S.R. Co's yet. The other fellows are getting them every night so I am getting lots of candy cake nuts & raisins etc, as everybody throws his parcel open as soon as he gets it. Of course socks etc are not to be divided just eats. We came out the other night at 1 AM. and there was a parcel for one in our relief, so we were all right. We had our rum (most wonderful too there was 1½ issue) and a good feed of cake & biscuits, candy and we had'nt a hardship

nor a grouch in the world, where a ½ hour before we had been ready to
fight at the drop of the hat. It was the worst night we had had this trip in.
Rain all the time & mud clean to the ears. beleive me we needed that food
& drink. To make it worse Heinie had been raising H---- all night with
high explosive. We never had a casualty either Providence sure is looking
after the soldiers I should think. Its quiet now though as far as fighting is
concerned. You see its winter & the roads are so bad that I should say
either side could'nt advance without getting into trouble.[94] I sure am glad
you got my pictures. Jim & Win think I'm thin, why they must be bad
judges. I am a whole lot fatter. My cheeks are like Jim's now round & red,
that is of course when I get a wash which is only occasionally You would
laugh to see us sometimes, 6 or 7 days whiskers and unwashed as well. You
don't recognise your own partner when he has had a wash & shave. Talk
about your sporty guys; there's a kid here from Toronto, one of those
good looking kids who the girls all spoil you understand takes pride in
a mop of curly hair etc you can plainly see what he was all right. well he
takes delight in being the dirtiest and most unkempt of the whole lot &
always cheery. He's a wonder. I take off my hat to a "nut" this time all
right. He volunteers if there's anything doing so that he can see the fun.
I often think of Jack L. jr when I look at him he a lot like him except the
cheeriness you know. But you will be getting sick of this. Tell May and
Lillie I'm pleased to hear they think so much of me as to decorate my
photo, but please tell them to place 18th in place of 116th or to put it 18
late of 116. You see I belong to a fighting batt'n now & don't want to get
classed with the other again.[95] And Mollie knew her daddy again eh? Don't
let her forget as I'm jealous now I think of having to miss her growing up.
We never enjoyed the others to the full like we ought to have done. We had
enough to do through did'nt we kiddo? So J.L. sr is enjoying her company
instead of me, well I'm glad she is so companionable. You must have had
some time at Campbell's with her. And Jim plucked up courage to ask an
officer to let him see his cap eh? Jim will be a salesman yet. I'll be glad to
get their photo's I got the snaps from Mamie and they were good. I was
thinking of getting taken again myself and as they are in demand probably
I'd better. You see I'm still vain enough to want to be fussed. Say isn't that
too bad about Mabel Farrow. She must have been crazy. So Joe Wilson is
wounded now. Mr. Pooke seems to be a humorist all right.[96] I guess its

A cap badge of the 18th Battalion

easy to be funny when you are in Blighty & on the high road to recovery with your wife along. It must be a cinch. I know what the hospital suits are like. of course I've seen hundreds. Bramshott was full of them, also London but you can hear the fellows wishing they could wear one. What do you think of our latest war news, and peace proposals. I guess there was great speculation on Albert St Dec 12th eh?[97] I know we were all a little excited here about it, but I see the Allies have refused to listen, but it's the thin end of the wedge & I don't think it will be very much longer before some definite proposal comes forward. We don't want to quit until we get what we go after, no chance. It would only mean a draw after all this expense in blood & money. I got a letter from mother this week & she is sending me a parcel, after me writing and telling her to be sure not to. You ask me if I get tired of hearing the exploits of the kids. Say thats the only news of Oshawa I care to hear anyway [*remainder missing*]

LETTER 12   *Notes appear on pages 152-53*

Somewhere in France
Dec. 20th [1916][98]
& cold as : ------

Dear sweetheart

Just stealing a few minutes to write to you as I may not be able to write
again for maybe a couple of weeks. We are putting in our supposed rest
period at a bombing school.[99] It is an old French chateau. The kind you
read about in Dumas and its easy to beleive this one existed in those
days.[100] Its a great big place built of blocks of stone, Park, & driveway
leading under a stone arch to the stables & cowsheds at the back. Then a
huge kitchen garden. There's some of the family living here yet as I saw a
fancy dressed madmeslle yesterday, & a young man dressed as a French
staff officer, her brother, & an old man, evidently her father. The officers
who take a course here of course stay in the house, the men of which I am
one, stay in the barn, and beleive me she's some barn. But the course is all
right. You learn all about bombs and all explosives. How to handle & not
to handle etc. Well, dearie I guess you are not interested in bombing at all
now. You will be more interested in Xmas. Its sure dreary here for Xmas
beleive me. We have to leave our billets to sit down & get warm I am
writing this in an estaminet where we come to get a meal of eggs & chips,
and to get warm. The meal is very welcome I can assure you.[101] I got a
parcel from the Sons of England day before yesterday, thru the Junior
Army & Navy Stores, & a good one it was too.[102] Well I've just had a good
feed of 2 eggs & a plate of chips & two glasses of beer & two cups of French
coffee & feel much better in my innards. Got to have one meal a day you
know We never get vegetables at all now you know. Its a little hard on the
digestion though. Its a terror when you have to spend your income on
food to keep alive & well so you wont be a casualty & a burden to your
country. Well the kids are all ready for Christmas now I guess. Did Jim
have a good tree ready? I suppose he would all right. Well I just about
know where I'll be Christmas Eve. Just imagine us singing "Peace on earth
goodwill towards men" to Fritz over the parapet. Well we were to have
our pictures taken this week when we got out, but my chum got into an
argument with a flare pistol. The flare hit him on the nose & cut it all up

so of course he could'nt show his mother how he looked all plastered up, so he had to postpone it, but its due to occur the very next chance we get. A very funny thing thing happened yesterday You know the Germans have what they call tear gas, besides the other deadly gas.[103] This stuff just makes your eyes burn & water, its excrutiating. Of course at these courses we get all this to prepare us for possibilities. It is exploded out of a shell. The sergeant got our bunch to carry the empty shells down to the dump as we clean up the grounds every day. A couple of fellows got this gas, (which smells exactly like pineapple) on their clothes. We got to the pub at night & the warmth got it going. Say it cleaned out the house. You talk about the companionship of a skunk. I was sorry for the lady who runs it & she is a lady too Her eyes were red & streaming with tears. She was too polite to ask them to go, though she knew what was the trouble and they were too hungry to go as they were waiting for their chips & eggs. Its sure a fierce invention of Fritz's. Well hon, I guess you will think I'm uninteresting, but really there's nothing to tell you except the old, old story. Lots of love to the kids & the same for yourself from yrs as always George.

FRAGMENT 2[104]   *Notes appear on page 153*

rotten things to get though. So all the casuals from England have to work or fight. Its about time they did something except form fours & eat rations anyway. I hear Arthur Day is coming home. He soon got away did'nt he?[105] Never spread any talk about on the remarks I make as its only hearsay with me, of course, then spoken of with my usual sudden impulses. You remember me I'll bet along those lines eh? You will be finding it hard work by now with winter on you with all its rottenness. Well! Jim must dig in and help, which I've no doubt he will anyway. Winnie is getting to be a big girl by this time I suppose. Say it seems a long time to me. What's the matter with the Malle? No Polacks left or what is it?. They'll get back at their employees just as soon as the opportunity offers, which will be as soon as the country is flooded with discharged men. Well sweetheart I'll have to repeat myself again. Always remember I'm thinking of you & the children all the time, and all the time loving you all. It's the best I can do now to write about it, but It won't last like this for ever I guess. Heaps of love & best wishes from your always George

LETTER 13   *Notes appear on pages 153-54*

Somewhere in France
Dec 24th [1916][106]

Dear girl

Just got back from the course after six days and got a parcel from you
and a letter, a letter from Edith & one from Sarah, also the promise of
2 parcels one from Edith & one from Mary.[107] I guess you wont be very
proud of the last letter I wrote about 3 days ago. Well I suppose I should'nt
have written then feeling as I did, you know what I mean don't you? A
letter is generally in the same vein as your feelings at the time of writing.
Well I was hungry, tired, and uncomfortable almost frozen etc. Well
sweetheart you must have been feeling cheerful when you wrote yours. It
was like a ray of sunshine to me. Your parcels will sure be welcome as the
rations are fierce. I guess this will be crossed out, but its the truth all right.
We never get vegetables at all, sometimes a handful of dirty currants or
raisins. Mind you kiddo I'm not grouching, but like you I feel bitter &
resentful sometimes, especially when the grub is a little worse than usual
& then I get a Vindicator, containing a letter from some guy in the steenth
Batt saying how well they live & giving in detail the menu which looks
like a hotel menu.[108] We know its true too as we took the same when we
were there. But the difference is so vast.[109] Say hon, I told you I was in the
bombers when I first was placed with them. Jack Burr & I were put in the
company bombers together. Then there were some men wanted for the
Batt bombing section and I, fortunately, or otherwise was chosen. It is
generally referred to as the "Suicide Club."[110] I suppose its the same
wherever you are, if one comes your way your chances of stopping it and
getting away with it are about equal, bombers or not. I have'nt seen Jack
again for 3 weeks. You see the Batt bombers are on their own. We only
have a chance to see our friends in the companies when we get out, & this
time our "out" was used up in a course at the school. Well kiddo I guess
you wont want to hear any more of this. Your parcels are very satisfactory
indeed. Cakes, cocoa, etc. You can cut out tobac altogether as I always have
tobacco to burn, also less choc. ever since I've been up the line anyway.
Candles I would'nt send, as we are always buying them: We have to have
lots of them as we use them all the time except when actually on duty. So

Mrs Knott seems to be in trouble again Let them carry on. Dont you get mixed up with it all. Be on good terms with them all as far as possible & let it go at that I know you have a lot of good judgment of your own any way. So the Malle is having difficulty in keeping men eh? That sounds funny for them don't it? Well I guess they will soon have lots of men. Get the war over and they will have more than they want I guess. Well I suppose you are talking about dad now as its so near Christmas. I can easily imagine you now. Its about supper time with you and one day before Christmas. Never mind sweetheart just wait a while longer. We will be fixed all right for another Christmas anyway, with a little good luck. Remember me to Maimie & Annie also Miss McLeod. Oh, shall be very pleased to get the kids photo. Good luck to them. Hope they enjoy themselves to the highest to-morrow even if dad is away. Give them a kiss from me for luck and with all kinds of love for yourself I remain yours as always. George.

P.S. Hope this is a little more cheerful Please write as often as possible

LETTER 14   *Notes appear on pages 154-55*

Somewhere in France[111]
Dec 29th 1916

Dear old girl

I suppose you will be wondering how I put in the festive season. Well on Dec 23rd I got a parcel from you and one from mother, so naturally I expected great things the next night, Christmas Eve, but it was a calamity. The mail comes up with the rations and on this particular night you can [*one line illegible*] though usually we like the "other fellow" to go as carrying rations is work, and of course work is objectionable to a fighting unit.[112] But to continue, we were all there. The transports were piled high we could see this much in the darkness. (They only come up in the dark you see for fear they may be shelled.) They began to unload, our anxiety increasing as the grub & mail was shot off. Every body being mentioned in turn. "A" Co, "B," "C," "D." Machine Gunners Scouts, Signallers etc. We began to get anxious No welcome call of "Bombers" except for rations. Then somebody broke the spell & asked the transport sergeant "– ain't there no ---- mail for us." The answer was "no." We have 44 men & not one letter even. We got the grub home & first there was no bacon. There was plum pudding.[113] One 8 lb tin, marked on was the legend [*one line illegible*]. You will probably see pictures of happy soldiers eating plum duff subscribed by a generous public, but don't examine them to see if there's anybody belonging to you, it will be useless. We were a pretty gloomy bunch on that rotten Christmas Eve I will tell you until somebody says "Oh ------ lets have a little melody." So we started singing everything we could think of. You will recollect I had'nt opened my two parcels yet except to glance through them to see contents, so I came forward and saved the situation. We had Christmas cake Christmas pudding cookies, chocolates, and those cherries.[114] I hope you know where they grow those kind of cherries as I want to get a tree like that when I get home. Well we sung & ate until 12.30 and imagined we could hear Xmas bells ringing "Peace on earth goodwill towards men" between the explosions of the shells etc. [*one line illegible*] up about 7.30 to breakfast. We got a slice of bread & jam & some cold tea. Dinner we got a minute slice of beef, a portion of the 16 rations of plum duff, divided into 44 parts, some raisins & prunes, as an extra. We enjoyed it very much and then we were booked for "up the line" at 2.30 P.M. for 72 hours on an old mine slack dump. About like the one in Lomey Town only more isolated and much larger & I should say wetter.[115] Its a new departure for us. Its a post about 20 yards from "Heinie's." We do 6 hours on and 6 hours off all the time we are there. There's nowhere to sleep except what looks like an enlarged rat hole a narrow tunnel which runs about 20 feet into the side of the hill only about the six feet furthest from the entrance being any way at all inhabitable, & that only for two men side by side. The rest is [*one line illegible*] that six feet is not exactly a bed of roses, more like waterlilies if we are to use a horticultural term.[116] Well I went on at 4.30 P.M. until 10.30 P.M. for my first relief. About 9.30 I witnessed the most inspiring sight possible to see I should think. A Battle in progress on the frontage right next to us probably ½ a mile away.[117] Some other battalion giving Heinie his Christmas box. We were away up in the air and could see it all. Just think. A pitch dark night then suddenly H---- let loose. Shells bursting with a red flame and a terrible roar. Flares going up a dozen at a time and all colors. The Germans send up rockets for their artillery to open up you know. Well it lasted about a couple of hours I should think, and not a shell near us which was the best of it from a personal point of view. Well the next [*one line illegible*] exciting <u>for us</u> anyway. The shells came all over us in our beautifully isolated position, but luck was with us. It seemed to be a period of thrills for next morning Dec 27th I had just come down to my rat hole (which by the way we shared with the original owners who seemed inclined to be resentful and keep us awake all they could by running over us while we endeavour to sleep & by eating our grub) when I saw signs of a little excitement.[118] A bunch of aeroplanes up in the air over the German lines and German guns firing all they could at them. Suddenly one of them begins to circle down, and gracefully it settled until about 50 feet from the ground then flop. Broke in two. I saw them carry the men away but of course it was too far away for me to reach them but they fell in our own lines so they did well beleive me. Well by golly the same [*words illegible*] did'nt blow up a mine right in front of our post.[119] It sure shook us up where we were but it was an awe inspiring sight to see in the dark. Some Christmas week I tell you. More exciting than being at Knotts or some other house & listening to the strains of the "Norseman" or something like that, and drinking beer and eating things until you feel on the verge of an explosion. Also its not hardly as comfortable. I'd used to get a wet shirt dancing sometimes, but now its wet probably the first half the night with rain, then the miserable weather of this mis-named Sunny France changes and the rest of the night it freezes. A beautiful experience. [*words illegible*] trying while it lasts but not so bad to recollect while sitting by a little fire in billets when we are "<u>out</u>." Well sweetheart this seems to be an [*words illegible*] has a green envelope and can call [*word missing*] nice things with impunity. Its bad to waste it with recounting my own experiences but its also the only chance I shall ever get of sending news at all, as ordinary letters are more apt to be censored than one with a green envelope. That's not saying that this one is certain of going unmolested. Let me know if a green "special" envelope ever comes to you which has had portions erased. They are not supposed to be but they are subject to censorship. Well sweetheart I hope you and the children had a good time Christmas. Also lots of presents. I could imagine the scene perfectly on Christmas morning. Say don't Mollie look good with Jack on the snapshot. She is a nice little girl now and I'm [*one line illegible*] on, hon, the time when I'll see you all again. Tell Winnie & Jim [*letter torn*] was delighted with their letters [*letter torn*] where Winnie says I'm a better dad than lots of men, you see I like a

little flattery even yet. Tell Rose next door that I received her lovly card &
letter and appreciate the thoughtfulness that prompted the deed & will
write as soon as I can. Love to you & our kiddies sweetheart from yours
as always George.

my grammar is going the way of my table manners it seems.

LETTER 15   *Note appears on page 155*

On Active Service
Dec 30th [1916][120]

Dear Winnie

Just received your letter in with your mothers. So glad to hear that
you got you cards and handkerchiefs safely, and that you liked them. Also
pleased to hear that mother got the registered letter I sent her. You tell
her I say, she is to use it for a present for herself. Say it's too bad about
poor little Mollie having whooping cough. Hope she soon gets better I
remember when you & Jim had it. It sure was fierce to hear you coughing.
Did May, Lillie & Annie get their cards? I saw your name in the paper on
the honor roll of your class at school. Glad you are doing so well. I'm
quite proud of you. Write again honey to your loving "<u>Dad</u>"

CHAPTER 2

He was killed by my side.

JANUARY–JUNE 1917

LETTER 16   *Notes appear on pages 155-56*

Somewhere in France
Jan 2nd [1917]

Dear May

Just a few lines wishing you and the children the very best of
everything for the coming year. I hope you had a good time New Year's
Eve. I could well imagine what it would have been had I been home. This
year it was a little different for me as I was <u>working</u>. "Business as usual" is
the motto out here, what ever time of the day or day of the year its always,
business still doing and booming.[1] When you have once heard the shells
coming over you realize how the business of war does rush & boom.[2] Well
roll on the time when they shut up shop. I received you letter of Dec 12th
saying you had the handkerchiefs etc. Glad to hear you thought them
pretty. About the other, you just use it if you need to. We'll buy that
present as soon as I get back. It'll be fine eh? Winnie's and Jim's letters
were all right. I answered them both immediately.[3] I have been busy
writing this week all right. I've been writing every chance I have had to
catch up on Christmas "thank you s" and "Compliments of the Season,"
and such like stuff. It makes a touch of the holiday spirit where's there's
no holiday. Say hon. don't you let the fact that so and so is doing so well

worry you that don't amount to a row of pins. You bet we'll be all right. If good jobs are scarce I guess I'll be able to hunt one.[4] You just look after yourself and the children, that's all that really matters you know. You must'nt get sick. Hope Mollie is improving. Poor little girl. You look after her and Jim will do your heavy work for you. He's quite big enough now. Well, dear, I guess I'll have to close as we want to get the mail away as soon as we can. Will write a longer letter next time. Best of wishes & lots of love from yrs as always George

LETTER 17   *Notes appear on pages 156-57*

P.S. Please pack my small razor strop in next parcel. Have lost mine. Ge

> Somewhere in France
> Jan 27th [1917][5]

Dear girl

Received your <u>very</u> welcome parcel last night containing candy, nuts, apples oranges etc. So good of you dear. Also the kids to send some of their Christmas things to dad. We are sure having a cold spell of it here now. Cold as Canada I should say. Certainly feel it as much or more anyway & the conditions are so much more inclined towards the cold side too.[6] I am going to write to J Burr as I have an address which I think will reach him.[7] According to it, he is still in France didn't make "Blighty."[8] Too bad if he did'nt. Hope the kids are all right by this and that your worst troubles are over as far as they are concerned. It must certainly have kept you busy all right. I hope you get Jim to do his share. He ought to. Some news about my successor eh? I just expected as much any way. I've seen it before with him. Well he's sure got a good taste according to the class he comes in contact with in that business, especially when in partnership with his old friend. Apropos! I never got the parcel nor letter from said friend.[9] Just as well eh? Glad to hear Gid is doing so well though I'd like to know <u>what</u> he's doing at that price. Must have a specialty, or else they have jumped the prices enormously. Good luck to him anyway. Hope I get as good a chance soon. We're still <u>resting</u>.[10] Ye Gods! resting is right.[11] Well I was going to write a good long letter hon, but it seems there's nothing to write about. I must write to Jack & as its too cold to write much I'll have to divide the time it takes to freeze in into two letters instead of devoting it all to one. The best of everything for you & the kiddies is the only thought of yours as always George

LETTER 18   *Notes appear on pages 157-59*

Somewhere in France
Feb 4th [1917][12]

Dearest girl

Received another letter from you to-day dated Jan 14 also one from Mamie of Jan 16, & last but not least, (especially as it came in particular times of famine) a parcel from you through Sarah. A dandy parcel too. It contained about a dozen mince pies (made by herself) and believe me she's some cook nearly as good as yourself.) 2 tins OXO cubes, 1 cake, 1 Pork Pie, 8 apples All eats you see & me half starved. Gee! was'nt it all right. It seems a fellow is always hungry here, its so cold, and we are always in the fresh air, too much we think sometimes.[13] Glad to hear that Mollie is feeling fine again. I'd sure have liked to have seen her when she was stealing the sausages. Some trick for her to do. Pretty rotten deal you are getting from the coal men eh?[14] They should be shot as it surely is'nt necessary to pile on the price like that. Just taking advantage of the times I guess. Please don't bother sending me canned vegetables, hon. The weight in the parcels is so limited anyway. I guess I'll manage with what we get with an occasional parcel & a cake. I wrote asking for my razor strop. If you have'nt sent it when you get this please put in some Colgate's Soap (Shaving) & a couple of plugs of chewing.[15] Say! it seems to me that I mentioned the cherries I got at Christmas. If I did'nt I will say now they were grand Also the deck of cards. I guess we wore the cards out pretty soon though, as we have to play in some queer places. Not quite like playing on a table that is smooth & shiny. Oh! about the magazine I would'nt send any over here I think. Say I have'nt read more than 2 hours since I've been in the army. I like to be in comfort when I'm reading, you know that. Lots of warmth & light And that's one thing which seems to be entirely absent, at least in soldiers quarters out here. If we are in billets its generally old houses or barns with boards for windows & of course in the line its underground, dugouts as they are termed.[16] We were inspected yesterday by the C.O.[17] Expect to be inspected by General Byng to morrow.[18] Some thing doing again pretty soon I guess. We are all getting fully equiped again.[19] I was charged 15 Francs or 3 dollars (again or) ½ months pay in France for a ---- ---- gas helmet which I got spoiled in our last trip up the line by pieces of stuff thrown up by a shell.[20] I suppose its all right, as I was supposed to hand in my old one to get another, but I did'nt want to lug a dirty old bag of stinking rag around, suspended from my neck.[21] Could'nt get away with it though. Must be studying economy in the army. Its as bad out here to get anything as it was in Canada. Well enough of this. This is the best town I've seen in France yet. Its got a full civilian population. Mostly miners as is usual all over this part of the country. Its all coal mines. And such mines too. Must employ 1000 or 1500 men anyway. You see them coming home you would'nt think they were colliers. All cleaned up. They have big shower baths & drying rooms in the mine buildings all white tile. Its where we got our last bath & change.[22] There's a beer & wine house every second house on the street. All doing a good business now you can bet. The regular miners hobbies too, pigeons, birds, rabbits etc. Say you would never think the war was on at all to judge from here, except the occasional French soldier you see at home on leave from the trenches. You see they get a leave from the line every 3 months.[23] They say its for reasons of State.[24] Some cinch eh? Of course they are in their own country & right [*remainder missing*]

LETTER 19   *Notes appear on pages 159-60*
[*On letterhead bearing the YMCA logo and the words "On Active Service With The British Expeditionary Force."*]

Somewhere in France
Feb 17th [1917][25]

Dear sweetheart

Was in luck to day again Got two letters from you. One 19th & one 21st of Jan. Our mail is sure erratic. I got one from you dated Jan 26 a week ago. I sent Mollie a note the other night so I anticipated her request for a letter from dad. Glad indeed to hear you are all well again. I don't blame her for not wanting to be dumped into the snow out of her sleigh. I guess Jim does it on purpose. I think I understand him well enough. Winnie was right about us being likely to loose our table manners Say we live like pigs. Eat, sleep, and every thing else in mud. Though they seem to be cutting down our chance of preserving our table manners by cutting down our chance to practise. Gee its the limit to be hungry all the time. Stone must be lucky. I think from what I can gather, that he writes to all the people he ever knew in the old country to see if by any chance they will send him a parcel. I think he gets one oftener than not. Some scheme eh?[26] Mrs C's social efforts seem to be as successful as ever don't they? Glad Miss McLeod liked her letter. Hope to hear from her again soon. I saw a lot of the old bunch up hear the other day. The second draft that came over They have a cinch. They are attached to a work battalion.[27] Have'nt seen the line yet. They are just back of where we are billeted now. We expect to go in the line [*censored*]. [We are on a new front.][28] Just where we don't know & don't care much as its all the same wherever you are out here. The Germans raided the place the other morning in aeroplanes at 4.30. [*censored*] but dropped 3 bombs in the village. Killed 3 civilians & destroyed two houses. It shook us considerably in our "beds." We all thought for a minute that we were going up too. Funny you never mentioned Jack's being wounded. The weather has changed again here. Its almost like spring, But you should see the mud.[29] Well I guess I'll have to quit. Tell Mollie I got & appreciated her post card very much. Tell her that dad <u>does</u> love her & thinks of her every day and hopes to see her soon. I guess that photo will have to wait some more favorable opportunity. I get it as soon as I can though hon. Love to you all from yours as always Geo.

LETTER 20   *Notes appear on page 160*

Somewhere in France
March 1ˢᵗ [1917]

Dearest girl

Congratulations. May we have many happy returns of this day.[30] Its about 8 o'clock here so about 3 o'clock in Canada. Seems to me you must be thinking along the same lines as myself about now. Never mind, sweetheart, we had a few years of it did'nt we? Hope to have a lot more yet. I'm just longing for a letter from you as I have not had one for 2 weeks or a little more. It seems a long time all right. I will write as often as I can, you can bet on that, when I can't do any better I'll send along a field post card to let you know, even in such an unsatisfactory manner, that I am alright or otherwise.[31] Hope to keep alright anyway. We are on a pretty rough front now [*censored*]. [Losing a few each day you know.][32] Just luck or the otherway I guess. I never got that parcel yet. Is'nt it the limit. Just when I need it too. The weather seems to be improving here now. To-day was quite shiny & warm. Consequently the mud is getting a little less & a little less hard work to move around. It was sure the limit a week ago Say! it took a man all his time to pull his feet out of it at all. It just seemed that your feet would pull off. I never heard any more from Mary. Hope she is getting along all right. She was doing fine when Sarah wrote to tell me of the happy event.[33] I hope the kiddies are all fine. Remember me to Jack Long & Rose, also Gid & his wife. I cant write any more letters until I get out where I can get some paper & envelopes as I had to beg this, but will write to you all again at the first opportunity. Good luck, the best of health & lots of love until I get home is the best I can wish you all Yours as always George.

LETTER 21   *Note appears on page 160*

France
March 7 [1917][34]

Dear Winnie

Just a line or two to show that dad thinks about you, which I do all the time. Glad to hear you got over your accident all right. Don't do the same again whatever you do. You seem unfortunate or else your bones must break easily eh! honey? Hope you are helping "Mom" all you can, dear, as she needs all the help you can give her. You will understand all about it later on. Hope you are still doing your best at school too. How's Mollie getting on eh? You must do you're best to look after her & help mother until dad gets home. Lots of love from your affectionate "dad"

LETTER 22   *Notes appear on page 161*

Somewhere in France
March 26 [1917]³⁵

Sweetheart

Got your letter last night, dated Feb 26th. You are quite right, hon, the mails <u>are</u> irregular. It was the first time I'd had from you for nearly a month but I have been writing at every opportunity just the same thinking you would be getting mine anyway and <u>knowing</u> you would be writing to me as usual, so I'd get them sooner or later. We must not get impatient, dear. I guess we will just have to wait until it does come trusting each other as usual. Poor girl, no wonder you thought I was indifferent to Winnie's accident and your Xmas presents, when I was most concerned indeed. Say honey, I was pleased indeed to hear that Miss MacLeod invited you for a day's outing. Also that your objections were overruled. It would have been a shame for you not to have had that day's pleasure I'm sure, and as for the money, kid, just make that a secondary consideration, which it really is. This is the place to make you realize that all right. Self preservation seems the paramount idea with us fellows, and that even, seems to be an off chance sometimes. This is sure a hot place, not climatically though. We pulled off a bombing raid the morning before yesterday. About 60 men go over to Heinie's trenches and another 40 or so act as covering party about half way over to cover their retreat. I was with the latter party which of course has to be the last to retire just when the Heinie's guns are busiest.³⁶ Well it seems there had been a series of raids pulled off all along the line so our friend the enemy in this particular instance was waiting for us & the only thing that brings success in a venture of this kind [*remainder missing*]

LETTER 23   *Notes appear on pages 161-62*

Somewhere in France
Mar 30th [1917]³⁷

Dear girl

I received your letter dated Mar 6th to-day. Was pleased indeed to get it and to hear you were all well. Also got a letter from May, containing a

couple of snaps of her and Lillie. They are pretty good pictures too. So
the plating room closed down eh? What's Gid doing now? Say its too bad
about Rose being sick so long, but you will just have to quit working at
both places. You must just remember the responsibility you have now
with our children, and you must keep healthy for their sake if you can,
not go looking for a spell of sickness. I can't see how you would manage
if it should happen that you were sick for some time. I wonder who'd
look after you? It sure worries me when I think of it I can assure you. We
considered all sides of the question before my enlistment you remember,
and you understood the chances did'nt you. Poor girl you must be having
it hard these days. I can quite understand how you feel about it. I sent
thirty francs to mother to-day. It will be 25 shillings if they get full value
for it. Its all I had. Wish it had been twice as much. Guess they can stand
it all right. Say hon, when you have sent those little things I asked for don't
send me any more parcels from Canada or England. We are doing pretty
well now in the way of rations so the parcels are in the shape of a luxury
anyway and easily to be dispensed with. You just have as good a time as
you can on what money you get and keep well until I get home. That's all
I desire, hon. I should sure like to releive Mollie's feelings by coming home
too, beleive me. Poor kid, wants her dad eh? Well you can rest assured that
the feeling is reciprocated. The weather is getting a little better here now,
though it still rains quite a lot, consequently lots of mud. I don't know
whether you got my letter saying I had received your parcel containing
cookies and all kinds of eats also Jack Long's. The mail seems so uncertain
these days I thought I had better tell you again as I know you always like
to hear when I get them. What's Jack and the girls going to do if the place
closes down totally? Don't forget to write and tell me all about it. I don't
seem to have any news to write about, but you are probably more
enlightened about the war news than we are as I suppose you read the
papers every day and so keep posted.[38] Say some laugh on Mrs. K. what?
Would sure have liked to have seen her when she had been marooned
with the bunch of kids for a couple of hours. I'll bet she enjoyed herself
exceedingly. Remember me to her. I often think of the good times we used
to have at their house also at ours I also often look forward to lots more
you bet your life, kiddo. I got Winnie's exam. paper. She's getting along
fine is'nt she? So glad to know it. Hope you had a good time in Toronto.

Enough to make the sick spell after, worth while, eh? Never mind dear we'll go together after a while. Surely we can beat Wilhelm pretty soon. We have lots of faith anyway that we can do it. Hope its justified. Guess I'll close now with lots & lots of love to you & our kiddies from yours as always George.

LETTER 24   *Notes appear on pages 162-63*

Somewhere in France
April 24th [1917]³⁹

Dear old sweetheart

So sorry I could'nt write a letter before, but circumstances made it necessary to compromise with Field cards or whizz bangs as they are usually called here.[40] Glad to say I'm still alive and well in spite of hostile attempts to exterminate the whole outfit.[41] We seem to be doing very well these days according to all reports. Hope it continues that way, so as to get it over as quickly as possible.[42] The weather seems to have changed to favourable these last few days, so its not so bad. Gee! Easter week was something fierce, snow hail, rain, and everything that was rotten, and we were in the open nearly all the time.[43] That was when the Canadians made their advance. We seem to be able to win now at any point. The Germans must be getting discouraged I should think. They must have had a good time all winter though by the appearance of their dugouts. They were fine compared to ours. Beds for all the men, good stoves, electric lights etc. They must have thought they were there for good I guess. Beleive me when our artillery opened up, they soon vacated their nice homes. We could'nt occupy them though as he had too fine a line on them and could make it pretty hot for us. So we had to do the same as the rabbit, dig a hole in the ground and lie low. [*censored*] It was some experience to see the Germans coming up to us with their hands up and crying "Camarade." They were made to carry out our wounded and they seemed to be tickled to death with the chance as it took them away back from the shell fire, though I did'nt envy one poor fellow I saw. Four Germans had him shoulder high on a stretcher and every time they heard the screech of a shell coming their way they would all duck into a shell hole and the poor guy on the stretcher would probably roll off. They would immediately load him up again & proceed on their journey to safety. I hear Gower & a bunch of ours made "Blighty." Lucky too. Gower was only slightly hurt as he walked out 4 or 5 miles.⁴⁴ [*censored*], hon. I guess this don't seem much news to you but the censor is so strict these days. I got a letter from Esther last night. She says father got the money I sent also 25 Sh. from Gid.⁴⁵ He is in receipt of the pension now so it all helps although he is still sick. How are you all getting on? Hope you are fine Just anxious to hear from you More anxious to see you though Roll on the time sweetheart. Beleive me it will be a great time for me. Remember me to all Love to Win, Jim & Mollie. Heaps of love to yourself sweetheart from yours as always George

LETTER 25   *Notes appear on pages 163-65*

France
April 28ᵗʰ [1917]⁴⁶

Dear old girl

Just got a longed for letter from you. We came out last night again & of course I was most anxious to hear from you. Went down to see the old Batt. to night. Say Mr Jacobi & Henry & Hinds & last but not least Fred Palmer were tickled to death to see us fellows.⁴⁷ Shook hands about 10 minutes. Talking about the good times we will have when we all meet in Oshawa. It did me good to see "Gobi" laugh again. He is sure a cheery cuss. He says his only regret is that he has'nt got his own old platoon. Says they can't be beat especially now they are getting to be veterans. I got a pair of socks down there from the Oshawa knitting society. S.M. Palmer took us to his tent & dished them out. Oshawa is sure getting hit hard eh? Young Gibbie gone now has he.⁴⁸ Say every bunch of artillery I come across I've hunted for some of the boys I used to know but have never seen any yet. Well if the old town is getting casualties, she's also getting laurels. Jack Cash was recommended again for gallantry in the advance. He already holds the Military Medal.⁴⁹ Jack Darby was also mentioned on the same day for distinguished conduct in action. They say he captured a machine gun & its crew.⁵⁰ Good work eh? Guess it takes the cockneys to shov'em yet. Well, hon, glad to hear you are still doing all right. The weather is still uncertain here though its improved quite a bit. Say sorry to hear about old Jack getting his at last though he must have expected it for some time.

A German soldier, probably L/Cp. Siegfried Schulze

Does he have any plans for the future? Pretty hard for him I guess. So all the soldiers wives are working eh? Hope you don't have to sweetheart. I can understand it must be hard on you all the way prices are & the way your pay has remained stationary. Never mind, hon, we'll soon be talking it over together. So Mollie went to school with Miss McLeod. Guess she felt quite grown up. Still longing to see you all again. I sent some little souvenirs home in my last two letters. Please let me know if you get them as they were in official green envelopes. German coins, a button, small comb etc.[51] Let me know as soon as you get them. Lots & lots of love from yours as always. <u>George</u> Love to Winnie, Jim, & Mollie <u>from dad</u>.

> P.S. Yes! I got all the parcels you have mentioned, also Rose's. Say just you let that garden go to the deuce. It is'nt necessary at all to work in <u>that</u>. The whole works is'nt worth working yourself to death for. That Burley you saw marked wounded was a little fellow who used to drive Ross's hardware delivery waggon.[52] Lived down towards Harmony,
> <u>Geo</u>

LETTER 26   *Notes appear on pages 165-66*

Somewhere in France
May 12th [1917][53]

Dear sweetheart

I got two letters from you this morning dated April 14th and 23rd. It was sure a great pleasure to get them especially as we had just come through an ordeal which was to say the very least trying in the extreme and its reassuring to get a pleasant letter from ones wife on coming out saying she still beleives in him and holds the same old regard eh? We have been holding the line for 4 days and now are back about a mile for 4 more. Say those days in the line if often repeated will put us all in the mad house. Its the place we drove the Germans back and we had to dig ourselves in, in a big plain like a huge meadow. You see the French farmer never fences his land. Well you can understand that our defences were almost nothing. We had to crouch in little "Funk" holes dug in the side of the trench and take all his shell fire without a kick except of course from our own artillery.[54] We were there in case he came over to recapture what we held. He had guns all round us and he pounded away pretty nearly all the time. A big 5´9 would come over and bury somebody, sometimes as in one case it did, buried four. They came so near they would shake every bone in your body. We sure lost a lot of good men, but I'm here yet thank God. When we first moved in there was some mixup in places and we had to change. I was good & mad as I considered I had a good spot. Well the poor guy that got that particular spot, one of my own section too, was killed the last afternoon in. Poor fellow he was unlucky. Just joined the Batt on Jan 16th, wounded on Jan 17th, the same day as Jack Burr, came out of hospital and rejoined two days before we came in & killed on his first trip. We are now living in little holes dug in a bank on the side of a sunken road, each man has his own little home, just room to lay down in case of shell fire covering the road.[55] You'd laugh if you could see us. All winter we lived with the rats & now we are sharing with the fishworms & beetles of which there are thousands. But I guess we are giving the Germans all they want. Their shell fire was awful to stand, but ours must be 10 times worse for them. Say when our barrage opens up the air is so full of shells, you'd wonder how they get past each other without colliding, and the miracle of it is when there's a little lull you will hear a skylark singing up there amongst it. You'd wonder how he ever got through. I sure admire a skylark from now on.[56] We do fatigues at midnight now while we are here, such as carrying stuff up to the front line, and carrying poor fellows out. Well sweetheart I guess you will be tired of this stuff, but this is the inside of what you see in the papers when you read about a "Great British & Canadian advance." This is what it entails. Good men gone to "Blighty" & worse. But its necessary if we are to ever end this war. I want you to always think that I'm doing my little bit for you and our kiddies, hon. The weather fortunately has been ideal for two weeks now only its too cold to sleep at night and too hot in the day as we have no cover from the weather except an oil cloth sheet. Tell May I got her letter too. Will write to her as soon as I can. So Tom Knott has an auto now eh? Gee! that's fine. Glad to hear he's fairly generous with it too. Jim sure must be a little man now eh? Doing his work in the garden as you say he does. Tell him I won't forget him for that. By what you say the prices of things are fierce, but in England I believe its worse if anything. Hope you got my watch safely before this. Please let me know. I am enclosing a German coin I got from our first batch of prisoners on Easter Monday. I sent two before. Hope you got them all right. You can give one to Tom Knott for a "pocket piece" if you like from me. I can't send it to him as green envelopes are scarce. I've a belt for Gid if I can ever get it through. Its so hard to do you know.   A few hours later.

Dear

I think I'll wait before I send the souvenir for Tom to see if you got the others all [*word illegible*].[57] I should get an answer in a week or so as I sent them on the Sunday after Easter. Please excuse this poor disjointed letter as the circumstances are not conducive of a very good effort at letter writing. Tell Mollie & Winnie dad just wants to see them ever so much & hopes it wont be <u>too</u> long. This includes you sweetheart just as much as ever. Remember me to Miss McLeod & Rose Mitchell, Gid & his bunch also Mr & Mrs Knott. Lots & lots of love hon from yours as ever George.

P.S. Don't send parcels to me, hon, at the price of things you must be hard pressed enough. G.

LETTER 27   *Notes appear on pages 166-67*

Somewhere in France

May 18th [1917]

Dear sweetheart

Just a year since I left home eh? Seems a great deal longer I assure you. Hope I'll be home again before another has passed. Well I wrote to you the day before we came out of the line the last time. This is the day before we go in again presumably.[58] It was a great relief to be out that time, though getting out was bad enough. Its quite a long trip, especially when you are tired out and pretty well loaded, and then the Heinie drops a few shells as close to you as he can immediately he gets wise that a movement of troops is going on. Changing releifs is always a very nerve trying job, especially in a place like we are in now. First you have to wait until dark. The road is full of shell holes into which you often fall, or as in the case of our coming out dead horses & men line the road and you are as likely to fall over, or into them as you are shell holes unless the dreadful smell warns you to look out. And the smell is awful beleive me this warm weather. Well you get into range of the enemy's flares or star shells, and he maybe sees you then its watch out if you want to get away whole. It sure is a nerve trying job as I said before. I'm always glad when its over either going in or out. The last time we came out I had a nice little lift on my way. We had come possibly 2½ or 3 miles & were having a rest on the side of the road this was about 1 A.M. & dark as possible, when an artillery ammunition limber passed us.[59] We asked them if we were on the right road for – He (the sergeant in charge) says "Yes, are you just out of the line, if so jump up I'll give as many a ride as I can." I was first there beleive me, but found out afterwards I was in too big a hurry as I had left my bread in a sandbag where I had been sitting on the roadside. Bread is not always so plentiful that you can afford to leave it lying around.[60] Well anyway I got on the limber, which is an iron box affair very heavily studded with sharp pointed rivetheads. We were going over a new road what is called a corduroy road made of logs laid side by side across the road.[61] Well I almost wished I'd walked, although that's a terrible hardship when you are tired out. I was certainly sore when I got off that jaunting car. I don't think I want to be a gunner after that. Gee my teeth were almost rattled out. Well we have had a nice time this time out. Nice weather pretty good grub & not too many parades, that's to settle our nerves after the awful trip we had in last time. Honest, kid I never expected that any of us would ever get out alive. We are being inspected by Gen Byng to-morrow and we expect to hear the usual line of bull. Beginning "Men, I am proud of you" etc. etc. etc. etc.[62] It makes me sick. Well, hon, it seems I'm getting to be a poor letter writer these days. I got a letter from Mary a few days ago Everything was lovly. She had received your present for her baby.[63] Also Walt must be getting married right away as he is looking for a house in Barrow I presume. I got a parcel from Rose & Gid this last week. A good one too. Say hon did you ever get some French & German coins & other little things I have sent for the kids from time to time. You have never mentioned them and as I have just placed them loose in the envelopes I have wondered if the censor–. Please let me know as I would like you to get them after me getting them. I sent my watch & some small stuff in a parcel some time ago & some German souvenirs this week so let me know as soon as you get them. Give my love to Win Jim & Mollie. Accept same for yourself sweetheart from yours as ever <u>George</u>.

Don't forget to write.

releifs is always a very nerve trying job, especially in a place like we are in now. First you have to wait until dark. The road is full of shell holes into which you often fall, or as in the case of our coming out dead horses & men line the road and you are as likely to fall over, or into them as you are shell holes unless the dreadful smell warns you to look out. And the smell is awful beleive me this warm weather. Well you get into range of the enemy's flare or star shells, and he maybe sees you then its watch out if you want to get away whole It sure is a nerve trying job as I said before. I'm always glad when its over either going in or out. The last

Letter 27, 18 May 1917

me know as I would like you to get them after me getting them. I sent my watch to some small stuff in a parcel some time ago & some German souvenirs this week so let me know as soon as you get them. Give my love to him Jim & Mollie. Accept same for yourself sweetheart from yours as ever George.
Don't forget to write.

Letter 27, 18 May 1917

LETTER 28   *Notes appear on page 167*

Somewhere in France
June 5th [1917][64]

Dear sweetheart

This is my first chance to write to you for a week or more, though I sure did good in the week preceding that as we were "out." I got your two letters one dated May 10th with Harry's letter enclosed & one May 12th with Jim's. Its just does seem good to hear from you when we get out after a hard trip, and beleive me every trip is pretty tough these days.[65] Its funny too that I should generally get yours & Miss McLeod's the night we are going in. The last 3 or 4 trips it has been my luck to get one at the last minute. I tell you it seems good when you are looking forward to the next

Letter 28, 5 June 1917

few days with anything but pleasure, in spite of the pictures you see in the "Toronto World" of soldiers going into the line feeling like spring lambs on a sunny morning. Its much better now though as the weather is beautiful & an occasional thunderstorm don't bother very much as you soon get dried out again. Its sure a beautiful country. I take back all I ever called it during the winter. Its a crying shame that it should be blown to pieces by artillery. Around our battle field of Vimy Ridge, (I don't think there's any harm in mentioning it now) there nestles a little village about every 1 or ½ mile.[66] Right on the bottom of the ridge where the plain starts. Say they are the prettiest sight you ever saw. Houses mostly built of chalk blocks, though some are a bright red brick. Well! You will maybe be admiring the pretty scenery when you hear a rushing sound with which you are too familiar, and you see a cloud of red & white dust mixed with smoke, and there's a vacant lot in the village, to mark the spot where somebody's little home was struck by a German 9´2. Its hell all right. We are out now for a rest & change. Back a few miles so we can't hear the roar of guns. We are billeted in barns etc in a town that just reminds one of home. Its a working man's town you know and you see the men after the

The gravestone of Pte. John McMullen (see Letter 28, 5 June 1917)

days work having their drink of beer and working round in their gardens And the little gardens are just the same and about the size they used to be in England. We are out for 3 weeks some say so I suppose its just the calm before the storm. We will be due for something violent by the time you get this probably. Well we did our share on Vimy Ridge all right. We helped to take it & did our turn holding it ever since April 9 against all efforts Fritz made it get it back. So glad you are all so proud of us. Beleive me it makes a fellow feel much better when he knows somebody cares. Even Jim & Win are tickled to death eh? I can imagine Jim being the authority on the war amongst his mates now, especially when he gets his dagger. Say he does write a good letter. It surprises me the way he has got on. He seems to have his mothers welfare at heart too. I just would like to show him how I appreciate him & his efforts. He's come out great. So Harry is going to Vancouver to join. He wont be able to come to see you from there I guess. Too bad. I thought possibly he would make for Toronto.[67] I got a letter from Stoney two days ago. He's in hospital in Boulogne. He was "gassed" about a month ago.[68] He was'nt with us at the time. He was sent with a party on an engineers fatigue for a few weeks. I hear the 182nd are at the base.[69] Time too I should think. They've had a cinch. Just imagine the bunch that joined out of the Malle the day before I joined. Just got to

France and I've got eight months in the line to my credit or otherwise. Well I've come through all right so far so I don't mind past experiences, though they've been heart breaking sometimes. That J. McMullen who was killed on April 9 reported in the Vindicator was a chum of mine in our bombing section. He was killed by my side.[70] A first class man too. One of the 116th too. You ought to see the way the boys fix up the last resting places of their chums. That's when its possible of course. There's a cross erected with the name etc of the man [*remainder missing*][71]

CHAPTER 3

I'm still fine.

JULY–NOVEMBER 1917

LETTER 29   *Notes appear on pages 167-68*

France
July 2nd [1917][1]

Sweetheart

Feel I <u>must</u> write to night to thank you for two letters I received to night dated June 9 & 10 containing a short essay from our "big" girl. God bless her. Just as I thought. I'd get letters from you the day we were leaving for the line. Well its a little early this time as we are not going until to morrow. We are going, as usual, to a hot place on a new piece of front where there's some dirty work to be done by all account.[2] We seem to get in for all these beauty spots somehow. Well maybe I'll have luck this time in the shape of a decent little "Blighty" as its the only way out of it for a while. Hope to God, hon, for your sake that its no worse than a "Blighty." The monotony of life out here in a French town when we are supposed to be out for a change and a rest is so great that the line will be an almost welcome change. <u>So</u> glad dear you received and appreciated my souvenirs. Sorry now I cut the helmet. Will get you another on our next advance. Didnt think I'd be able to send it you see so I cut the piece out to carry it around the easier. Winnie says Mr Carswell saw & deciphered the inscription. That's dead easy. Some have the words "Gott mitt uns" which is "God with us." Well beleive me he needs to be You'd think so if you could hear our guns to night or any night. Say its fierce. You know how an extra severe clap of thunder sounds in Canada. Well its like that only it lasts all the time. Just imagine we are several miles behind the line now You can fancy what its like in the line So glad Jim likes <u>his</u> souvenir. Rather dangerous, hon, to let him carry it around. Am expecting to hear from Miss McLeod any time now. Rather disappointed not to hear the same time as from you. Generally do when going into the line. Glad to hear you got some chickens out of your venture, but its strange the way Rose acted eh? God! some people are generous. Remember me to Tom Knott. Say I got a bit of bad luck I got a chunk of metal from a German 'plane we brought down & gave it to a fellow to make some little souvenirs for Tom Knott Miss McLeod & yourself, now I've not seen him for a month.[3] Too bad eh? Never mind I'll send something the first chance I get. Say I know the reason we did'nt get our pictures taken on Vimy. It was 3 days after the advance April 12 to be exact. We had just gone over again to releive some Imperials the West Kent's I think.[4] Our platoon was first as usual. The next platoon was taken. We saw it in the Sunday World inscribed "<u>Waiting</u>" to be releived.[5] So Jimmy Richards has got an auto eh? Well I'll be Well sweetheart "doing your bit" may be very gratifying to your conscience but I'm hanged if it gathers much substance Never mind kiddo if I ever get home again it will take more than an auto to tempt me off that verandah and beleive me I'll only fight for that little bit of property after this & then the enemy has to be on the steps. I am going to repeat my little lesson again to you, listen, Jim is to be disillusionised. No soldiering for him, never at any price. Tell him dad says so. I'll explain when I get home. Do you ever hear from Mamie? I got a letter from your home yesterday, but sweetheart, I feel better to night than I have for some time as I've been sure down hearted at not hearing from you. Say, hon, I miss you more every day. My God I wonder how much longer this is going on. Not long I hope. See little kids about 3 years old & imagine how my little 3 year-old looks. Bless her little heart. Love to her & <u>you</u> hon & Win & Jim & remember I'm <u>always</u> thinking of you all. More love from yours as always George.

LETTER 30   *Notes appear on pages 168-69*

Let me have Harry's address or better still tell him to write me. Please.

France

Aug. 2nd [1917][6]

Sweetheart

Got a letter from you to night. Glad to hear from you, you bet. I have written to Enoch to-night too. I've often thought about him too & wished I had his address. Well I hope to hear from him shortly. Yes! I got all your parcels I guess. Jack Long writes a pretty good letter when he does write. Say I've often wondered what became of Frank Powell. He sure lost a good job down the Can. Malle. You ask how the cakes keep. Well say the only fault I've ever found with them that they were'nt like the loaves & fishes that Christ had to use when he was on that big, famous ration party.[7] I generally cut them up immediately I get them Generally reserving the smallest piece for myself. You know how its done. They all do the same so it works all round. So glad you liked the photo. I was rather scared to send it. It looked so fierce to me. I have another one yet so will send it with this. I have enclosed one in Enoch's letter too.[8] I sent Sarah one & she said I looked "tired out." Yes! I got those snapshots of you & the kiddies which May took & they sure made me homesick. Glad my photo reminded you of those good old times which seem about a decade ago to me. Never mind, hon, it can't be that this war will last for ever. Then we'll have that trip to Lake Forest which we have promised ourselves for so long. How's Sid & Soaf getting along?[9] Ever hear from them at all. You speak of the wet weather over there. Well you should just be here now. Its rained for two days straight now Just imagine the boys in the trenches. Gee! its fierce. So Glad the little fellow liked the cards I sent her. Kiss her for dad. Also the others. Tell them I think of them every day, and just long to see them. Lots of love to you & our kiddies from yours as always

George

For Mollie, Jim & Winnie xxx & Ma X

LETTER 31   *Notes appear on pages 169-70*

France
August 29th [1917][10]

Dear May

Just a line or two to let you know I'm still fine. I am disappointed this week in not having received a letter from you since the one dated July 24th. I'm sure longing for one you can bet. Say! I got a card from young Will Ford to day. He's in Bramshott Camp, England.[11] Expects to be here soon he says. Guess he will too. Looks as though they will be able to use all they can get. We are sure giving the Boche something to remember us by.[12] Though its not without a price of course. Three more of our old fellows were killed this last trip in. All of Oshawa. One used to work in the Steel Range. Harry West was his name.[13] Also one badly wounded. Gee! they are getting scarce all right now. Well I did'nt get that newspaper report yet written by McCleese.[14] Am rather curious to see what part of my correspondence he used, and what is described How's all my family coming along. Hope you are all fine. Also hope your efforts as a gardener are successful. I sent you a couple of registered letters just lately. One containing money and the other some little things for the children. Let me know if they arrive safely. I got a letter from home the other day. Father is very sick again. The same old thing. I think he's worried until he is about all in. Its affected his head it seems. They are rather afraid he will have to go away. Mother hopes you will excuse her not writing to you as its rather difficult under the circumstances.[15] Hoping to hear from you soon I remain yours as always George

Love from dad to all the kiddies

LETTER 32   *Notes appear on pages 170-71*
[*On letterhead bearing the YMCA logo
and the words "And Canadian War Contingent
Association With The Canadian Forces."*]

France
Sept 10th 1917[16]

Dear sweetheart

I feel I <u>must</u> write to you to-night in spite of the fact that I'm still
waiting for a letter from you. I was almost saying I wouldn't write again
until I did hear, but I reflected that it could'nt be your fault, as I knew you
must be writing as often as usual. The last I got was dated Aug 1st so I've
surely missed 5 or 6 letters. We are at present resting as a reward for
services rendered in the work round a town which I suppose I must leave
unnamed, but which is now coupled with the name of "Canadians" in all
the newspapers.[17] Possibly you will know where I mean. It was pretty
costly work too for us, as the Huns counter attacked 11 times, so you can
imagine it meant some names for the Canadian Casualty lists. By God! we
lost some good boys too, but I'm still here. There's only a few of the old
boys left now. C. & J. Gibbs are here yet with me.[18] We are all filled up
again or nearly so now, with new men from Canadian Battns in England
and fine fellows too, bigger than the average drafts I've seen before I guess
the biggest & best men must have waited until last to enlist. Well I hope
they can soon finish it, as I'm just homesick for a look at you and our
family, especially as I've not even heard from you for so long. Well, I've
just a very few days before going in again, in which to hope for a letter.
I always go in feeling better for a cheery letter from my girl. I'm never
worrying much when I do get in, its the going in that makes a fellow feel
a little blue. I hear we have to go on with the strenuous stuff again this
time. Old Heinie must be getting a skinful of it all right, as its attack after
attack these days & no hesitation about it. I could'nt get souvenirs out last
time Pretty lucky to get out myself I consider. Gee! it was fierce. We were
inspected and congratulated by Gen. Horne the commander of the
Canadian Division.[19] He said we had done fine, but we still had lots to do
as Heinie was still in front of us. Well beleive me if killing Germans will

end this affair the Canucks are not taking many more prisoners.[20] They are pretty foxy too. Imagine the last time in, our bunch had taken two or three trenches from him. We had men in the front line and men in the second as a kind of support for them. We held the place for two days and after that we found a big dugout <u>between</u> the two trenches <u>full</u> of live, unwounded Huns, just waiting for a chance to give us one, or to escape which ever was the most favorable. Just think they had been there two days sniping a good man once in a while, before they were even suspected. Our scout officer and some men found them and captured about 40 besides a few they had to make examples of. The officer was afterwards wounded severely and died in the Clearing station. A good man he was too. Rose from the ranks. Many a night I crawled in the mud behind him in No Man's Land seeing what was doing. Just looking for adventure à la Don Quixote and at the same time finding out valuable information. He would go anywhere if he had a man or two for cover. He'd say "You stay here & watch those houses, if you see anybody shoot him so that I get a chance to get out of here.[21] Of course I'm referring now to the street & house to house fighting round the place I mentioned before. It was not very genteel work either. Dead men buried in piles of bricks & mortar, and a hot summer sun. Unpleasant is a mild expression. Guess this is stuff and nonsense for you to read sweetheart so I will can it. How's things with all our little old family. I often think of them and feel I'd give anything to see them. The other Sunday when I was on that course a chum & I were sitting on a bank on the side of a road resting, when a French lady came by with two little girls Say! one was like Mollie must be. Fair, with blue eyes & long fair hair, and healthy fat old cheeks. I spoke to her in my <u>best</u> French and asked her for a kiss. Say! her mother told her to kiss the "Bon Soldat" and she came right over & kissed me. Hon! I made a kid of myself right there I just had to hug that kid for as long as she'd stand for it. Her mother informed me that they were refugees from La Bassee, and that the Germans had come right through the place where they were living & they had had to beat it without a thing and had to go hungry and nowhere to sleep.[22] I felt I could kill a German any old time for the sake of that kid, and the way she must have suffered. Well kiddo how's things going? The garden, the chickens, the loveliest old bunch of kids that any soldier has to dream about and last but not least by any means yourself sweetheart. Tell

The gravestone of Lt. Thomas Dougall (see letter 32, 10 September 1917)

me all the news, hon, I'm just hungry to hear from you. I wonder how poor mother is getting along now? Is'nt it too bad though I think I'd rather think of dad being dead than where he would inevitably have had to go if he had lived. Guess I'll quit now with lots of love to you & our kids from yours hopefully & always George.

P.S. I never got that Reformer yet that you wrote about or was it just a joke. I never knew McLease to be much of a "ministers son" as he discribed himself to you. Let me know if you got the two registered letters I wrote to you Geo.

LETTER 33   *Notes appear on pages 171-72*

France
Oct 22 [1917][23]

Dear May

Just a line or two to assure you that I am still fine, and still just as anxious to see you again. Roll on the time. We are still [*censored*].[24] Taking quite a long while. We have been in one place a <u>whole</u> week. We are so used to [*censored*] that a whole week makes a place as familiar to us as though we were born there. Its peculiar how soon a man gets used to leading the life of a Nomad. In fact we are more used to moving on than the average gipsy, and more easily prepared for the road. Always ready to move at 15 minutes notice. Like the snail too. Carry our abode on our back. We were inspected by Gen Horne on Saturday last. It took about 3 months to persuade the men to clean up sufficiently to satisfy the officers that they would pass on this eventful day, and it took the General just about 3 minutes to inspect each battn, 12 minutes to inspect the brigade. We had to walk about six miles to the place of inspection. The common soldier had to carry a load that is almost a disgrace to humanity, on purpose to be looked at.[25] The general, who has a motor car supplied by the Gov. could'nt condescend to visit us and save us the walk. oh! no. Its sure a great life alright. Talk about militarism. We are supposed to be here to suppress it, and it seems we are getting in the toils of the same infamous machine ourselves. We need to win the war I know, but it seems we will have a fight on afterwards to rid ourselves of the obnoxious habit made infamous by the Germans. I was glad to hear that the kiddies were all

right. All fine & healthy. Also yourself. Let me know if you got my letter
dated Oct 18th as I would like to know. Lots & lots of love from yours as
always George.

LETTER 34   *Notes appear on pages 172-74*

Remember me to Miss McLeod & R. Mitchell, Gid & family &
T. Knott and anybody else who's interested. Please write address
plainly. We have another Timmins in the battn somewhere.

Belgium[26]
Nov 1st [1917]

Sweetheart

Received your letter yesterday dated Oct 3rd. Was pleased to hear you
were feeling better, but I got a letter from Rose M. and she seemed to think
you were somewhat sick or rundown or something. Say there must be a
bunch of men coming back to Oshawa all right, but by what I know of
them that's judging by their names, they are all men who have done no
service in the line. Rorabic never came over, Pankhurst I suppose went
down sick as soon as he saw what he was up against, Northey the same.[27]
You see these weaklings or defectives come over here on a fluke knowing
they can get out by perpetually going sick so that the officers get sick of
them and shift them down the line. Charlie Danks worked every scheme
not to come over at all. But he over worked it and got sent over anyway.
Well he was in my platoon and beleive me he was only eating another
good man's rations. He had every <u>man</u> down on him in 10 days and the
sergeant in one day. Well he came through Vimy all right and when we
went in again as soon as he heard we were for the front line he went
violently ill and "swung the lead" and made the base.[28] Beleive me hon,
sometimes I feel I'd do any thing to get out of this and come home to you
and the kids. I'm sure homesick often enough, but I have'nt got the nerve
to swing it. Never went on sick parade yet. So I guess if I don't get disabled
by Heinie or disease I'll be here until the cessation of hostilities which by
all signs will be some time yet. Never mind hon. I'll be there some time,
never fear, but I want you to buck up and keep healthy for the poor kiddies
sake. I'm here now and its up to me to do my best I guess. Anyway my self

pride would'nt let me do any less. So hon, you know my opinion of you
So just live up to it, there's a kid. I just like to think when I'm getting too
badly fed up that you are at least thinking of me and would miss me if
anything happened or would be proud of me when I get home. Enough
of this though. You said Mrs Cooper told you I had a stripe. Well its so
but I was'nt going to mention it as its so insignificant. I should have had
more as I know I got a good report from the school, but you see in the
drafts that come over now are so many men who were sergeants in
England and know their drill & stuff so much better as they have been
in England a couple of years I tell you it makes our boys mad when they
have to be ordered about by what we call an "issue" serg. when we have
been bearing the brunt of it for all these months while these other guys
were having a good time in Blighty.[29] Its the way of the world I guess but
its sure a funny way. Anyway I seem to be having an easier time with just
one, than I had before. If there's a fatigue party and I'm on it I don't have
to work I just have to be kind of responsible, quite a bit easier than working
I can assure you. To day they sent a bunch including me to see the model
in clay of our next advance so as to get the NCO's familiar with the
general lay of the land, Its wonderful[30] Every little detail is shown and the
rise & fall of the land, the streams, swamps, railroads, concrete strong
points etc, etc, all modelled to scale from the maps and from photographs
taken by the airmen.[31] We went in London buses you know the old two
decker style. The distance was about 12 miles and a nice clear day. We went
through 3 or 4 small towns of course full of troops, but still with a good
percentage of their civilian population, and intact as far as shell fire is
concerned. Its a little different here to France. The first thing thats
noticable is the absence of the inevitable word on every second door
"Estaminet." Don't think for a moment though that we have now struck a
land for which the prohibitionist is so anxious. Oh no there's just as many
booze joints, but the word is altered. Here its Bierhuis, or maybe Drankhuis
though I can't explain the distinction between the two. Some places you
will see the fine delicate humor of Tommy Atkins. On some of the
Bierhuis's aforementioned you will probably notice a signboard with the
legend printed in really fine old English characters. We passed one with
Ye Olde Bulford Arms swinging gracefully from a bar of iron, a reminder
to some Tommy of the place he used to spend his leisure & incidentally

his money in that dim distant day "Before le Guerre."[32] Its some little excitement too riding on a bus through these narrow streets and the road just filled with moving troops & the paraphernalia of an army on the move. We passed 5 miles of limbers without a break on one piece of our journey. Well kiddie I just can't write any more. My shirt is so creepy I've just got to read it.[33] So Mollie wanted to know why I was'nt with that bunch of returned men eh? Poor little kiddie. Just tell her dad will sure come the very first chance. [*words illegible*] Lots of love to you & our kiddies from yours as always George.

LETTER 35   *Notes appear on pages 174-75*

Belgium
Nov 7th [1917][34]

Dear May

Just a line or two to let you know that I am still all right. I got all your letters safely of the latest dates. Hope you are feeling better in health than you were when you wrote to me last time. I got a letter from a chum of mine who is in England wounded and he says that Sisson and J Burr are still in Bramshott and not likely to be sent out here again for a while yet.[35] They are sure lucky as this is a fierce hole for mud and shells too.[36] I also heard from Esther. She had been home the previous week to see mother and mentioned the present you sent to her. Said she was very pleased with it, but wondered if you needed the money. Remember me to Miss McLeod & others who may be interested. Lots & Lots of love to you and our kiddies. You will have to excuse my short note this time. Will write you a real letter next time & will explain why this is so short yours as always George.

LETTER 36   *Notes appear on page 175*

France[37]
Nov 16th [1917]

Dear May

Just a couple of lines or so to let you know I am still all right. This is the first chance I've had of writing to you lately as they have not been collecting our mail this last little while Anyway I came out again alright, which I think I'm lucky to be able to say I told you some time ago that I had applied for a pass in France but it was cancelled so I waited for a Blighty pass and its a good thing for me now that I did as I expect it to night or to-morrow or anyway in a very few days.[38] I'll be glad to see mother again to see how things really are. I got a letter from her and I guess there's lots of room for improvement. Well I hope you and the kiddies are all right. You will understand as I have'nt been able to send any letters there's been none coming in either. Am sure longing to hear from you. This is all the paper I have just now and we only just hit camp but in Blighty or not I am going to buy a big writing pad and use it all up in a big long letter inside of two days Love from yrs as always George

LETTER 37   *Notes appear on pages 175-76*

Nov 24 [1917]

Dear sweetheart

Just a line to accompany my last literary effort.[39] I spent my first night in Blighty at Mary's at Small Heath being treated like a prince. I came on home the next day.[40] I am having an awful time After leaving Belgium my feet went bad and I intended to report sick as soon as we stayed some place but as soon as we reached our destination a whole lot of passes came thro as a reward for our hardships I imagine as they never came so fast before. Well I got mine & determined to say nothing about my feet or gas sores till I had had my leave as they might stop it.[41] I thought maybe that to sit by the fireside in the dry & warm would cure me right away. I think its the opposite. I'm here on a leave and am suffering agonies. Can just get my boots about ¼ time. I wear them till the pain is unbearable & then take them off. Immediately after my feet swell up so that I cant get them on again. Its either trench feet or chronic rheumatism. I'm going to try two more days & if they are no better Im going to report sick. Though I hate to do it as the men will think Im swinging the lead, but Its sure Im no good on active service in this condition. Will let you know anyway. Lots & lots of love to you & our children from yours as always Geo.

Everybody wishes to be remembered to you

LETTER 38   *Notes appear on page 176*

Nov 25 [1917]
Blighty

Dear old sweetheart

I'm still here and missing you more every second. My feet are still on the blink and the pain is something awful. Gee, how I miss your old sympathy although I know you would laugh at my antics afterwards. You should see me trying to walk. Say its a comedy to the onlookers probably but by heavens its a tradegy to me. I am thinking of reporting to a Military hospital to morrow. If they send me back to France in this condition I don't know what I'll do as immediately my feet get a little cool even they pain so much worse so you'll understand what that will mean in France. Say you ought to see Mary's baby. He is a great big boy & so good. Just sits where she puts him & laughs & laughs. Thinks Im all right evidently as he climbed all over me chuckling to himself.[42] I have'nt seen Edith or Florrie yet and Sarah & dad only once. You will understand I'm almost confined to the house completely as I can hardly wear my boots at all. Things look bad here You should see the women lined up about a block to buy ½ pound of margarine or tea.[43] The pubs only open once in a while as their supply is curtailed Then they'll only sell to their steadies. I tried six places in Cradley Heath 2 days ago before I could get a drink. Then I had an old chainmaker whose instinct was unerring to guide me. Lots & lots of love to you & our children from yours longingly Geo.

That stuff Im telling you about Belgium I don't think I'd give it to the papers yet. Wait til you get it all. Geo

LETTER 39   *Note appears on pages 176-77*

[Blighty, November 1917]

Sweetheart

Just a line to let you know I am pretty well but have still got that abominable pain in my feet. Its almost entirely spoiled my leave though I suppose I should be glad I was able to get away from France while they were so bad as I dont know how I'd have made out there with them. I'm

still longing, girl, for the time when I'll be home with you again. Hope
you have a good time this Christmas. Have the best thats possible. Lots of
love sweetheart from yours as always George

Keep these descriptive letters of Belgium to yourself for a while[44]

LETTER 40

Blighty [November 1917]

Dear Jim Winnie & Mollie

Guess it will be Christmas by the time you get this Hope you will have
a good time altogether Just wish, fellows, that I could be with you and
your mother for the festive season. I miss you more all the time. Beleive
me, kids, its lonesome even over in England without you. I have seen
Aunt Mary's baby boy twice. He is a beauty. He thinks his Uncle George is
all right I guess, as he just laughs all the time I'm there and climbs all over
me. I'm going to see if I can find some little thing to send each of you for
Xmas but things are pretty scarce here now. Lots & lots of love for you all
from Dad.

LETTER 41   *Notes appear on page 177*

Blighty
Nov 30th [1917]

Sweetheart

My birthday and in England. If I was at home I would hear you saying
the old, old stuff Many Happy Returns. And Winnie with all her old vigor
pounding (or at least having a good try, her success or otherwise depending
on the victim's temper at the moment) out 35, just imagine sweetheart its
sure worth writing in words (thirty five, there) won't I soon be old eh?
Funny though I'm as much a kid in spirits as I was 20 years ago it seems
to me. When I look at your girls & ours & think of their ages it seems so
funny. I always think of you as the young looking pretty mother you were
12 years ago. And also 2 years ago. I know you have'nt altered much in
spite of what you sometimes say in your letters. Great Scott. I always dream
of you just as you are, I know. Still longing sweetheart to have you again,
beleive me. I am sending a little parcel of presents for you for Christmas.

One of the two lockets with photos of himself that GT
sent home to his daughters from England (see Letter 41,
30 November 1917)

A Brooch for you. hope youll like it, a locket each for Mollie & Win. I have
put a photo of myself in each. If you want to remove them or change them,
the top removes by unscrewing.[45] It comes off right next locket. There's a
knife for Jim. The only one of the kind in town now as the man said he
could'nt get any more. There seems to be lots of things they can't get. See
a row of women waiting to get ¼ lb marg. no butter to be had, & often no
tea or sugar. Still they say we are winning.[46] Love from Geo.

CHAPTER 4

Its hell, kiddo, hell.

DECEMBER 1917–APRIL 1918

LETTER 42   *Notes appear on page 177*

[Blighty]
Dec 3ʳᵈ [1917]

Sweetheart

Just a line or two in a doleful note. I'm going back to France to-day. Not with so much enthusiasm as I went before I assure you. This thing looks like lasting for ever. You should see the women shopping over here. Standing in a line up for maybe two hours on the chance of getting ¼ lb margarine & finally getting there to be told its all sold.[1] The same with tea, sugar, bacon, eggs etc etc. Talk about starving Germany. She's sure doing it to England. But I never saw so much money here in my life. Thousands of girls working in every place. Some girls 16 make 4 Pounds a week & everything in proportion. I guess the manufacturers are satisfied to go on with the war they're making all kinds of money.[2] Well I drew all that was coming to me when I came on pass. Having the assigned pay allowance I did'nt have so much as some chaps, but I have had a pretty good time & have left some for mother so am sending you the remainder. Its only 3 £ but you will probably find it useful. May as well have it now as in the dim future which is referred to as after the war. Let me know if you receive it. Also the Xmas presents I sent for you. Everybody over here that belongs to us has used me fine. They are one & all doing well & are healthy. Good luck sweetheart & a Merry Xmas to you & our children. Lots & lots of love from yours as always George

LETTER 43 *Note appears on page 177*

> France
> Dec. 14/17[3]

Dear sweetheart

I think I told you about receiving the parcel but I wrote before I had sampled the peaches They were very good indeed. I have a chum here, a Scotchman who I divided it with in the trench one dark night, and cold, and he was in raptures. He said "Eh! mon, but that's guid"! I sure agreed with him as it was a bitter cold night. Its <u>Hell</u> being back here after being in England. I never told you about my pass although I wrote to you pretty often while in Blighty. Well you start from the Battn about 3 or 4 strong, by the time you reach the station there is quite a crowd, by the time you are embarked on the train you are packed like herrings. By the time you reach Bologne there is a parade that fills the street. Well there's all kinds of red tape to be gone through, but we stand it like angels. We are going to Blighty for 14 days. Finally we are on the boat, Canadians, N. Zealanders, Australians, Imperials & every [*The above passage accounts for pages 1 and 2 of Letter 43. Fragment 3, which follows, is almost certainly pages 9 to 12 of the same letter.*]

FRAGMENT 3

The munition worker £1 a day (& more) of 9 hrs & a good bed to sleep in & a pleasant place to spend his money in. Little girls making 3 or 4 quid a week & dressing like the proverbial actress. Ive seen hundreds of them. I'm feeling bitter about it yet so Id better get on with my story. Arrived in London we realize we are still in the army. Its, "Come on here you men hurry up, don't hang around there all day." Gee! its a rude awakening Peculiar too. Coming over there's a rush on to the train, boat, train again, growls at every stop. Going back there is a strange reluctance to be first to board the train or boat. Each man hangs back with a modesty which seems ill becoming when you look at the man. Nothing but curses about France & the war & the Big Bugs who sit at home and holler their heads off about fighting to a finish & the "honor" of their glorious country. Beleive me the most of us could have been hanged for our seditious talk on that journey, and our thoughts were even worse. Every man "fed up" completely & quite war weary. Its hell, kiddo, hell. Reach the accursed shores of France at last. Spend the night in a camp at Bologne. Next morning rounded up like cattle & herded on to different trains for the different fronts. Again no doors or windows. Can't coddle the soldier. Arrive at destination after 10 hrs freezing on the train at 6.30 PM. Just got off the train & land into a Heinie bombing raid. Nearly got it too. Spent the night in an old barn. Next morning on our way. No breakfast & 6 miles to go. Full pack. Arrive at battn transport at 12.30 AM. Report at orderly room. Battn in the line. Ordered to go at once to battn. Don't like the idea at all. No dinner only some bread. Sneak off until the party has gone & its too late. Buy some grub at the "Y" & sleep in an old hut. Join the battn next day. About 7 miles to walk. Get there just in time to "stand to" 15 hours until day light next morning. Stay at that 6 days. Just came out this morning & am easing my feelings by telling you, the only old girl on whom I can depend for sympathy. Some joyous existence. Only looking for the end of the war & rejoining you again. Hope you have a Merry Xmas sweetheart also our kids. Its obvious that this is not for publication. Show it to Miss McLeod if you like. I admire her every time.

LETTER 44   *Notes appear on page 178*

France
Dec 25th [1917]

Sweetheart
    Thought I would write to you and tell you how I am spending my Xmas, as I am still spending it, (along with some other material which I brought back from England, salvaged from the wreck as it were) this being just after dinner or to use the French, "apre midi," meaning afternoon. Well to commence right. This being the third Christmas the 18th has been in France, and only the first out of the line, the officers decided to make as good a time for the men, (of course with their usual self sacrifice they forgot themselves) as they could under the circumstances.[4] In the first place, the circumstances were very adverse to a merry time. We are billeted

in a small village where there are only about 10 houses & a school house & a blacksmith shop.[5] The 10 houses presumably are the property of the owner of the "chateau" which is situated about half a kilometre away. Much the same as the old feudal system. The "Lord of the Manor," as I've heard old men in England say in an awed voice, owns all the surrounding country & his vassals live on his land which is rented by them. Generation after generation live and work and die each in their turn on the same old place, in the same old house. I was in a place this morning drinking a glass of coffee, the floor of which, I am referring now to the house and <u>not</u> the coffee, was made with rough bricks, not quarrys like you see in England, and the laying of them must have been done by an amateur so rough and uneven were they. Guess you will see all the crossing out I'm doing.[6] I've just finished dinner as I told you in the first spasm of this emotional epistle. Well to get on with the story of this dinner. The difficulties were hard to overcome. First, suitable places for the men to eat in. We are billeted in barns, stables, lofts or any other old place where they can squeeze a platoon. Our own platoon is particularly unlucky. We are over a bunch of cows and pigs, and the smell is terrible Of course it does'nt matter all the other meals, but we could'nt eat a Christmas dinner under those conditions, oh. no! Well after great exertion it was arranged so that all the men were seated to a table to eat, quite a novelty too. The provisions were a source of great worry to the powers that be, but finally they got turkeys and pigs and puddings enough for each man to get a good meal. The stuff was cooked by our own cooks, who made a superhuman effort, quite different to their usual way of doing things. Usually if breakfast is supposed to be at 7 o'clock and the cooks are a little late in arising, we get breakfast on time all right because its an order but the bacon is raw and the tea is'nt boiled but we are generally hungry enough to eat it. We had two platoons at our place so one had to wait until second sitting, beleive me when it became known that ours was the unfortunate platoon and that we had to wait there was a terrible cry of disgust, but after a while disgust changed to the pangs of hunger, which in turn bred bad temper, which in turn gave place to exhaustion, the men being so hungry they were too weak even to swear. But every thing comes to an end. At last the word was passed to fall in, No 9 platoon having finished their meal. Joyously we fell in, not with the reluctance of a drill parade but with the joyous abandon displayed by a bunch of young pigs when they smell a pail of their favourite food. We marched down to the dining room engaged for us. I had judiciously placed myself at the head of the line so I could get served quicker. Again I was stung. "Fall out all N.C.O.'s" was the order. Fall out we did & had to dish out the grub which consisted of turkey, pork potatoes, peas, tea. I knew there was no more so I watched each piece of meat given out with ever increasing jealousy & anxiety as the sergeant, who was giving out the meat was feeling a little exhilarated and I thought that he would, try under the influence of Christmas spirit, to make up for meanness in dishing out every meal for the last 364 days, and give all the meat to the first 34 or so there being 41 of us, all ranks. However old habits told on him and he made the supply go round so that each man had a really generous helping. We were half way through when the captain comes along and says each man get a glass, then he passes along bottles of champagne to fill them. This time Dame Fortune sure smiled on me. I HAD A BEER GLASS. I drunk her down quickly beleiving in taking opportunity by the forelock as it were. He comes along & says "Did you have a drink, corporal." I says in my best military manner "Yes Sir." Says he "Well have another," again with military brusqueness I said Yes Sir. Then our machine gun corporal who for some reason or other is trying to be good to me, & he is a scion of a rich family in Canada, his uncle was our Major who was badly wounded in Passchendael.[7] He had bought about 6 bottles supposedly for his crew of 6 men, & they are quart bottles over here, and he insisted on including me in his crew Beleive me I was "well away" By the time we got to the plum duff I was feeling at peace with the whole world. It was quite a successful meal on the whole. But, kiddo believe me there was an under current of homesickness in all my enjoyment. When I got up out of my lousy blanket in the old loft this morning my first thought was of home and you & our kiddies. About 5 o'clock, (Canada) I could picture 'em, God bless 'em, running excitedly up and down the stairs finding new sources of delight & pleasure all the time, and a peculiar thing I could'nt picture Win or Jim any other way than wearing those "bunny" suits as they did 7 or 8 Christmas's ago. I wondered if they had a Christmas tree this year. I wondered lots of things beleive me, until I got to feeling mushy & foolish, which does'nt do at all, so I went hunting for a place to get a drink, there being no parade after about 10 o'clock. The best we could do,

I having by this time found some more fellows who were feeling much the same as myself, was coffee which we got at the house I mentioned as having the rough brick floor. Well I have still to put in the time this evening, its now 5 o'clock. The only thing to do is to go & drink Vin Blanc or Vin Rouge, meaning White or red wine as the case may be. Well sweetheart Christmas has come & gone (almost) again and I have no mail from you for some time again, I have not received your parcel yet but I got one from Gid some two or three days ago & one from the S.O.E. last night. Yours will possibly be along in a day or so. I fervently hope, dear, its the last Christmas parcel you'll have to send to me as I'm just feeling homesick pretty badly. Hope you had a good time, honey, also the kids and lots of nice presents. Remember me to Mr & Mrs Knott. Oh! say I saw Stoney the other day. He's got a dandy job. Working in the Y.M.C.A.[8] Sometimes as near the line as they can have one & sometimes way back. He's unfit for the line he says, but by the Gods he's healthier looking than myself. He was full of money too. The first thing he said to me was "Got any money" & I said "no." He says "I'll give you 10 francs," and pulls out his purse & hands over the ten. Lucky man him eh? Don't tell Mrs Stone about the money. She might wonder why he don't send it to her & of course that's his business. You said in one letter to me that you had a mind to send my letters to the Star. The next letter I got said, you had heard from the Star & they could use them. Did you send them samples or what was it. Now if you do send them there I want you to cross out, to thoroughly obliterate, everything even indirectly of a personal nature. Wherever I mention myself as doing, or being so & so, or mention you or the children I want that crossed out properly so that it can't be read as the boys out here don't think much of a man that "shoots the bull" as they call it, & there's a lot of them from Toronto. That last thing in the Reformer was fierce. I was scared lest somebody ask me if I was guilty of such an outrage on the public. Anyway I guess I'll have to confine myself to the usual soldier's letter while we are here as there's nothing to write about, & I don't want anything again as bad as Passchendael to describe Gee! Our fellows that were in it still speak in awestricken tones of the horrors of that trip. There's not many of us left that were through it but its still an occasion for us to remember and to converse on with regret for poor old so & so, or lucky old somebody else who got a "Blighty" up there. We are made up to strength again by a draft of new men & a draft of our own casualties from Vimy Ridge. Sisson & Arthur Judd among them.[9] Sisson says Jack Burr may be coming over with the next, but it is not likely we'll need any more until Spring. Just imagine Jack, been over there since last Jan. 17th he was hit. I think its about time I got a rest one way or [*remainder missing*]

LETTER 45   *Note appears on page 178*

> France
> Jan 2nd <u>1918</u>

Dear Winnie

Just a few lines to wish you many happy returns of your birthday, if this little note of mine has the good luck to reach you in time, but judging by the way the mail is coming in I guess it will keep it going.[10] I haven't received a letter dated later than Nov 16th yet. I don't understand what's coming but I had high hopes that of getting one for Christmas or New Year's. I hav'nt been able to get anything for your birthday as we are in a poor place to buy anything so you will have to be content with a greeting

An envelope addressed to Winnie by her father in 1918

this time, honey. Hope I'll be home for your next birthday. We'll make it
different, you bet. Hope you got the Christmas presents I sent you all
from England. Tell Jim I'll write to him too. Kiss Mollie for me, also
mother. Lots of love and best wishes from dad.

P.S Don't forget to write soon.

LETTER 46   *Notes appear on pages 178-80*

France
Jan 7th 1918[11]

Dear old sweetheart

I was the happiest man in my platoon last night. What with having no
mail, cold, misery, & short rations I was rapidly developing into a morbid,
uninteresting, bad tempered piece of humanity. Even my letters of the last
few days must have reflected it. My own special section, (I'm section
commander you know) got to saying "What the H---- is wrong with old
Tim"? But its all over again now. Last night at 9.30, mail came up & I got
5 letters. 4 from you, one of which contained Miss McLeod's and another
the letters of Win & Jim, and one from Tom Knott. I had written to Tom
only the night before, so will you please tell him I got his letter safely &
was very pleased to hear from him. Miss McLeod is the best letter writer
I know and her efforts are always <u>very</u> much appreciated by yours truly,
although of course I beleive I'd languish and die if you did'nt write for
two months. I beleive I think more of you the longer we are parted. I sure
long to see you more every day. Hon, don't get mixed up in those d----
society people and forget me in the slightest degree. You know how my
feelings always were in reference to ladies who had too many interests to
ever be able to stay at home. Guess you must have had a joyous time at
the election.[12] Should just like to have seen you in your post of honour,
not that its any too good for you. Mr Borden never knew the honour that
was his, at having a dear little woman like yourself at his meeting. You say
you only accepted a platform seat because you thought you had done as
much as any of them by giving up your husband, my humble self, to the
country's service. Dear! I assure you that in my estimation you were more
worthy than any of them for your own sweet sake besides the fact that
you have helped me through all kinds of despondency & misery by your

cheery letters, when I have been pitying myself and envying everybody else but myself, when I ought to know that you by rights ought to be the one to be cheered up. I've been feeling pretty bitter just lately about things in general, especially when I hear so & so's home again & see in the papers about his so called long term of service in the trenches, generally from 3 to 7 months. Tom Jeyes I suppose is spilling a story about what he's done. Well he was with us all told about 2 or 3 weeks and that when there was nothing doing. He "Swung the lead" so hard he got away with it.[13] If he wants to talk to you just cut him, as his reputation would disgrace a decent woman. Of course this is supposed to be on the quiet, but its the truth so I don't care. There were sure some rotters came out of Oshawa with us. I beleive in giving honor where its due. Its the same all the world over. I know justice is seldom done. In the army the man with a little influence gets decorated if he never sees anything and the man that does the work is ignored. You hear <u>men</u> in our bunch saying "I don't want no medals, they're getting too cheap." Its so too. At Passchendael we had some decorations handed out and the one that got the highest did the least to deserve it. The men that stayed with it to the last got nothing not even rations or rum, nothing but mud & misery. Beleive me, in spite of your efforts to institute conscription in Canada the Canadian Army is the rottenest affair in the world in its administration. If it was'nt for the <u>men</u> they have in the ranks it would'nt be as good as Cox's army of Yankee fame as a fighting unit.[14] I hope you have'nt made conscription a hard & fast law that can't be repealed as I'd hate to see my boy "called to the colors" to waste the best years of his life in a service that neither educates nor enriches its members. See what's happened already. The Conscription candidate's platform included furloughs for men of the first and second divisions who had been in France over a certain length of time and as soon as they could be assured of conscripts to replace them. Well already the promise is broken on the ground of "insufficient means of transport."[15] The very same thing occurred in Australia. I beleive the "Hussys" are feeling very much incensed against it.[16] Now the thing is this. Ships must come to Canada to return with goods essential to England. England is too busy making munitions to be making things for export to Canada. So I figure that the ships must travel light one way at least. The soldiers on furlough would'nt expect a first class passage by any means. When we go to

"Blighty" on leave we are the happiest men on earth to get into an old car without doors or windows. Let them get to Canada on furlough and its up to the Gov. to get 'em back. Doubtlessly they'd find a way. There's not many left anyway who are eligible as the terms were almost prohibitive in the first place.[17] Every politician has his say. I see there are all kinds of ways to escape conscription too for the elegibles. I hear Burns of the boot store has bought his son a farm.[18] I suppose there's all kinds of schemes. Just tell Charlie Wilcox my views on his party's acheivement. I beleive in conscription myself for the duration of this war, voted for it in fact, but if we build up a military party we are just building what we are supposed to be fighting to break down, "Militarism." Its the predominating power in England to-day. They are calling for more & more men, & women to fill men's places. Realizing that they must have a stronger "militarism" than Germany has to be able to beat her. Where will it all end. No one knows, but I'd hate to be at the mercy of a "military" power, German or otherwise. Well, sweetheart, I guess this is'nt of much interest to you You'll probably be full of your own ideas on the subject. Glad to hear of Jim's business acumen. Also Winnie's growing beauty, though I always knew she'd carry enough beauty for the whole family. Take great care of her, hon, she's getting to be a big girl, and inclined to romance already by what I hear of her literary choice. Rather young for that kind of dope yet. Oh, Say I forgot to mention in my recent letters. The last time in the line I met Tom Milgate from Jackson St.[19] He was pleased to see me & we had a great talk about home. Remember me to Gid & Rose, & Rose Mitchell & J. Long. Also the Knotts. No, I never saw any of Stone's boys here. Kiss Mollie for me. And believe me to be yours as always & always sweetheart.
Goodbye for now from Geo.

LETTER 47   *Notes appear on page 180*

France
Feb 3rd [1918][20]

Dear May
    Received two letters & a parcel from you last night. One letter dated Dec 25th, one Dec 31st. Quite a long time getting here you will think. I suppose a little of the delay was due to me being away from the Battn for

10 days again on a course. The way it happened was so nice too. We got a new officer in our platoon. By the way we get them quite often. They generally last one trip in, two at the most. Then down the line. Probably Canada with a story of the war to tell. Well to continue this officer seemed to be a good sort. In fact he's the first one I could get along with. I guess I'm too blunt for most of them. One day when we were out on "rest" he told me to take charge of the bombing. I saw the opportunity right away. I said "I'm not a bomber, sir." He says "you're in charge of the bombers are'nt you"? I said "yes but I'm not a bomber." Consequence 10 days bombing course. I'm not missing anything anyway. I did my spell in the line. When we came out I came to school. By the time my 10 days is finished the Batt goes in again & of course yours lovingly goes also. Anyway I'm having 10 days change & living near civilization. Though not outside the danger zone by any means. Last night we had 5 air raids.[21] Each distinct from the other. Beleive me, I thought he'd get us if he tried much more. Say you wonder why I was so displeased with things in general. Say kid it was just natural perverseness. Coming back to this cursed country after living in England for a spell. You know my old temper. Well the fellows in the line were warning each other not to speak to "old Tim" sure as hell he'll shoot you. That's how bad I felt until I took a tumble to the way I was acting. As for your worries sweetheart they are mostly imaginary. I just wish I was [*page missing*]

I get a chance. Circumstances are much against much writing these days as the billets are always too cold.[22] I am writing this one in a French village estaminet. I got in right the other night by giving the little girl my loose change. Came back with an invitation to dinner. Some dinner, will describe in detail later as I'm feeling lazy after eating so much & being so unaccustumed to much eats for so long. Very pleased indeed to hear about all the presents you got & the good time you all had at Xmas. Hope to God sweetheart I'll be with you next. Love to the kiddies & lots & lots to yourself from yours as always Geo.

LETTER 48   *Notes appear on pages 180-82*

France
Feb 4th 1918

Dear Sweetheart

I wrote a kind of a letter to you on Sunday.[23] This is Tuesday, but as I am off parade this afternoon thought I would write you another one as you don't seem to mind getting them, eh? As I beleive I told you on Sunday I am on a 10 day course at Divn.al [Divisional] School again. Got splashed with some liquid out of a gas bomb which exploded and knocked a sergeant's hand out of commission, and my face is all blotched with "gas" sores. Guess if you could see me now your affection would be terribly tested. Well! sweetheart the only topic, in fact the only thing, in this town, is of course the Training School, so I thought I'd just tell you about that as news of the censor satisfying type are so scarce and I know must be very unsatisfactory to the recipient. In the first place each Division has a separate School of its own. In the school at all times are of course the Instructors.[24] Some of them men who have done their bit up the line & are now enjoying a change. Of course they have to show competence to hold the jobs. Then there are some who don't know what the line looks like but tell the boys who come down on courses how to go about it. All theory of course. Much to the disgust of said boys as you can imagine. Each Battn in the Div sends periodically according to length of course etc. enough men to keep about 4 men on Bombing courses, 4 on some other course, & so on. So that 12 Battns in a Div brings 48 men to a class or a platoon as they are called. Its funny though to see those men getting squared away when they get here together. Take our bunch here now we have been together 8 days. You have 4 companies to a Battn. So that of the 4.18th men (1 man from each company. Compree?) possibly you never set eyes on each other before as each company generally sticks together. Its just the same with all the others. Well you meet at a given point. All bunched indiscriminately together, some just out of the line covered in mud Some clean & neat, just off rest camp or something. I tell you its sure a mixup of humanity. Arrived at school you are shoved into an old barn with mud walls which is to be your home while you stay at the place of instruction. Here comes the funny part of it, to watch the pairing up of the men and their peculiar choices of partners. This time of the year "doubling up" is the rule. The reason is obvious. One blanket down, three over you, a single sleeper can't have less than one down and as each man only has two you will see the advantage of doubling up. One pair in the corner of our particular barn are very illy-assorted according to size but seem to get along very well together. One is a great broad hulk of a chap, slow of movement, deliberate of speech, very dry humor. The other is very small & just bubbling over with high spirits most of the time, sings all the latest songs with a good voice and has an appetite that is alarming, especially in the army where we are surely rationed. As his big friend says he's "a dead loss to the army as what he saves in cloth & shoe leather he makes up & more in what he eats. Honest, last Sunday as I was invited out for dinner I told him he could draw mine if he was hungry. Well he not only drew his own, & mine, but some other fellow's who was sick and could'nt eat it. After he had got outside the three of them he invited his big chum to go and see some people whose acquaintance he had made during the time his Battn was billeted there some little time ago. Only 5 or 6 miles, and he knew the general direction in which it lay so that everything was all right. His chum fell for it all right after being told that there was lots of beer in the trip. They got there all right I guess but I don't know what kind of a time they had as when they got back the big man started telling the story and he says they had'nt gone a mile when "Shorty" had to stop & lie on a bank as he had what the big man called broadly "The Belly-ache," and as he added "It was no ------ wonder, look at the dinner the little runt got away with, and look at the size of him, why I felt like stepping on him and crushing him as I would a cockroach." I could go on telling of these two for an hour, but you'll probably be sick of it; besides but there are some others I want to mention. Over in the other corner is a group of three, oddly enough too, but I suppose it was their own Batt colors that kept them together. Two husky men & noisy, one rather slender and quiet. The two are strangely mixed indeed a bigger contrast it would be hard indeed to find. One an ex-N.S.W. Lancer of S. African war experience testified to by the ribbons he wears on his breast, since that an American Infantryman, seen service in the Phillippines with the American army, since deserted, as he boasts to join a "real" army.[25] His chum is, to use his own vernacular a "Boird from Thoirty-Thoird Street,

Noo Yoirk, USA." A real Bowery Gum shoe man as the ex Lancer calls him.[26]
They quarrel noisily over any old thing, the third party of their combination
first encouraging one & then the other, the only thing real in their quarrels
being their language. Each morning when "cookhouse" sounds you can
see the leather faced old ex Lancer steal out with <u>three</u> mess tins in his
hands and return with 3 breakfasts and looking a little sheepish wake his
two comrades in arms with a roar and a curse and ask them if they think
he's a "blinkety-blink servant of theirs." They look up sleepily, see the mess
tins and smile like cherubs at having attained Lauder's ambition of "Breakfast
in yer bed, etc" but its every morning with these guys.[27] Then we have
representatives of the 22nd Battn the Van Deuxs as they are called. French
Canadians and in spite of public opinion I have still to meet the Van Deux
who would'nt give me anything he had.[28] Last night we had an impromptu
concert and one of the French Canadians, just a kid, surprised us all. Say
he sang French songs, English songs in French, regimental doggerel songs
of their own Battn composition, for about an hour. And his voice was just
perfect. Then we have a huge Indian who wears a big grin all the time. Also
incidentally a "D.C.M.," which he modestly admits he don't know how he
got.[29] After some questioning the story can be wormed out of him, of how,
at Passchendaele he strayed into a pill box which contained 17 Heinies. He
says he did'nt know which party was the more surprised Himself or the
Huns. Anyway he shot one and the others were anxious to accompany
him out to the comparitive safety of the prison cage. All this told in a slow
unemotional voice which convinces the hearers that he means it as he says
it. I could go on all night along these lines, so you see what a fellow will
run into, by way of companionship. Three more days & maybe we'll never
see each other again, but while it lasts [*remainder missing*]

LETTER 49   *Notes appear on page 182*

Say the cherries were good only too many cherries.

Feb 4 1918[30]

Dear little old girl
  I don't know what these fellows would think if they knew I was
describing their mode of living and so on. I'm afraid I'm running an

awful chance. I was going to tell you about the sumptuous dinner I got on Sunday, but last night after Last Post I could'nt sleep for the pain of my face, accelerated by a fierce cough, and it came to me that it would be interesting to just try and describe a few traits of these really wonderful men. So this afternoon I had the oppor: to dodge parade and so took advantage of it. Hope you'll like it. Say I must make a stipulation that I must have a copy of the Re[former], containing the Pass[chendaele] story as I wrote it so disjointedly I'd like to see how it looks.[31] Glad you like it though, hon. Will tell you of my dinner next letter. Say I have'nt the heart to write to anyone but you. I've been badly out of sorts this last week or so. Beleive I'm getting worn out with it all. I have'nt the stamina I thought I had. Wish I could convince the doctor of it though. Guess I'll carry on till I drop at it. Queer! sickness don't count & a scratch from shrapnel which never hurts at all, & down the line for 3 months. *San faire puna.* Roll on the time I'll see you again my sweetheart. Tell Mamie & Annie I'll write sometime Also Rose. Kiss the kids & accept same for yourself from Dad

LETTER 50

France
Feb 6th 1918

Dear sweetheart

Just a line or two to follow the letter I wrote last night. In describing the ex-NSW Lancer I omitted his most peculiar & unexpected talent. Where I wrote about him boasting of his desertion from the Yankee army & joining a real army. Now, please insert with a comma after "army" "Quotes Kipling, Omar Kayyam, Edgar Allan Poe, Service, and all the poets. Can string it off in yards, with expression too." I got a letter from Mary to night & a parcel from mother. She sent me apples, a package of tobacco, 2 boxes of matches, 4 candles, a plum pudding, & a pork pie. I was pleased to get it too, as my rations have been very distasteful these last few days, as I have been feeling pretty rotten. Hope the kiddies are having a good time, and you are all feeling well. Jim seems to be improving very much in his writing & spelling, his grammar is also very good. I was pleased indeed to get his and Winnie's letters. Mollie must be a little dear too. Should be tickled to death to see her I can assure you. Mary says how her baby is getting on, & can walk round now by the chairs. Remember me to Miss McLeod. Lots & lots of love to you & the kiddies from yours as always George.

LETTER 51   *Note appears on page 182*

> France
> Feb. 7th 1918[32]

Sweetheart

Just seems you're in luck, that's if you like my letters. I'm sure out of luck myself, got into a place where there is a little recreation at night and am confined to billets with sores all over my face from gas. Too sensitive to travel around looking like a mangy dog you "compree." Don't know what to write about now I've started even, but recollect that I promised to detail my experience at a Sunday dinner in a French village, with a private family. It all started when I was down here last summer. One Sunday last summer my chum & myself were on pass for about 5 hours and called in this place for a drink of beer. Well we were used so good that we went back every chance we got. We got to be quite chummy with the family. So much so that we exchanged letters 3 or 4 times, but with my limited knowledge of French (I may say very limited) and their limited knowledge of English made it very uninteresting. Its very strange but I have'nt got enough brains or maybe opportunity to pick up the language sufficiently well to converse, altho I can make out by using my hands & head etc so you will see the difficulty in keeping up correspondence. Well anyway, when I got back here my first thought was my old friends, so I slipped off on the quiet without a pass and reached there just as the estaminet opened namely 6 o'clock. I walked in and up to the diminutive bar. Nobody in at all, customers I mean so nobody behind the bar. The door between the bar & the living room opened and the mademoiselle walked in with "business" all over her face, just has one look and screams something in voluble French back into the kitchen and turns to me all smiles & says excitedly 'Cum een "m,sieu." Well you should have seen the greeting I got. It seems when I quit writing, they having written the last letter that passed between us, they thought that I had been killed. Well this was Tuesday and I beat the pickets every night until Saturday and the old lady said to me,

"Sheorch, you dinner to-morrow." They pronounce my name exactly as Fred Hertzel used to. You remember the German that used to work in the Steel Range. To continue. Of course I was tickled to death and accepted with alacrity. Knowing it would be a change from our bully etc. So next day after church parade I slipped off taking the main chance of being caught & missing my dinner altogether Anyway I got away with it I had'nt had much breakfast and the walk is 4 kilometres, nearly 3 miles, so by the time I got there, 12.30, I was feeling hungry enough to eat the old woman & all her family. Well I walked in as usual, ordered a bottle of beer & waited for something to happen. Well the beer of course made me ravenous and still nothing doing. I began to think affectionately and with regret of my bully which I had told some of the boys to get as I, and here my chest expanded to its fullest extent, "As I have friends in town who desire my presence to grace their family dinner table." Well as my appetite got painful I began to wonder if I had been wise and if they really did so desire my presence to such an extent as my vanity had led me to beleive. My anxiety increased as customers all soldiers began to drop in. These, thought I have eaten, and I groaned gently to myself. All the time though I could hear something banging and jingling in the kitchen accompanied by much bustle and vociferation in French & childish screams sounding to my hunger sharpened senses like an air raid. The banging representing the anti aircraft & aerial bombs the children's screams of course taking their proper place in the scheme of things. Well, when my patience was almost exhausted to say nothing of my physical condition, the madame comes into the bar & draws a huge jug of beer, spelled "Biere" here, and calls out in her broken, very much so, English, "Come on" again the atrocious mispronunciation of my very distinguished Christian name. But I assure you I forgave her freely when the meaning of her invitation sunk into my, by now, almost exhausted senses. I arose from my chair with pride glanced round at the company to fully appreciate their looks of envy, understand I had by now arrived at the stage where every letter in the alphabet spelled FOOD, FOOD, FOOD, interspersed with EATS and I imagined these fellows must be feeling as envious of me now as I had been of them what seemed to me as ages ago when they had arrived looking if not well fed, at least, full of something. Arrived in the holy of holies I saw the altar I mean the table loaded down with grub. Large soup plates & a

huge dish of vegetable soup to start. The angel of this sanctuary filled my
dish; I was so hungry my imagination even is running ahead of the story
before she filled my dish of course she sat me at the table on the right hand
of the head the head place being occupied by m,selle, Olga Flore, the only
daughter of five possessed by madame who was home on this occasion.
Well, now I'm getting to the really enjoyable part of the story, she filled
my dish, thats twice she's filled it a'int it?; with clear soup and a dish of
vegetables which had been fished out of the soup on the side of my dish,
she indicating by motions that she did'nt know whether I liked my soup
clear or otherwise, anyway I could suit myself. Bless her heart I did'nt
even stop to explain that I liked mine any old way. I just waded in. In the
dish were leeks; that divine emblem of Wales, onions; oh! sweet perfumed
delicacy; carrots, favored of the Gods as the only vegetable containing
nothing detrimental to the frail human, and some other suspicious looking
product of the earth which I strongly suspected of being sugar beet, but
which I left severely alone. Well there being plenty I went after it in earnest
and did'nt desist until I felt some stronger. By this time my brain began to
clear & I began to think that if I did'nt go easy I'd have no room left for
what I suspected was still to come. Sure enough it came. Boiled beef, and
Brussels sprouts. Talk about war time. The little green spheres of edible
leaves always appealed to me with their seductive sweetness, so I loaded
up again on these, by this time having to call in the assistance of the beer
to what the little boy called "swaller" it. Then I noticed the absence of the
"pomme-de-terre," potatoe in English. Looked funny, too, as the crop here
last year was abundant. By the time the beef & sprouts had begun to be a
back number I felt as though I had'nt a trouble in the world and that
hunger was just an imaginary condition brought on by a sordid mind.
Imagine my pain then, only to be compared to that of the small boy when
he admits he could chew another mince pie, but falters that he don't think
he could swallow it, I say imagine my condition of mind when she slings
on with great pride in her culinary proficiency, the "piece de resistance" in
the shape of a fried rabbit, first boiled then fried in some sweet stuff as I
ascertained from my fair neighbor, for by this time I was feeling sufficiently
disinterested in eats to get interested in the surroundings. Fried rabbit
accompanied by the famous French fried potatoes looking very handsome
in their delicate yellowish brown exteriors and their snowy white "innards"

Again I called on the beer to do its duty. Who said prohibition. Beer in this case was the only friend I could depend on to help me do my duty as a soldier and a man or two. My charming hostess, in spite of her two hundred lbs avoirdupois she sure looked charming to me through the steam of the fried spuds & rabbit, had good reason to be proud of her culinary triumph. It was delicious and this from the unpreduciced mind of a, by this time very well fed man. Surely I thought there will be no more demands made on my holding capacity, but I was doomed to disappointment. Up she comes as fresh as ever with a dish of stewed prunes & raisins, accompanied by Vin, Rouge, <u>alias</u>, red wine, hot & spiced. Ye Gods, what a drink! By this time it was 3 o'clock the estaminent part being closed at 2. I was to use the soldiers term "well away." After the wine came the inevitable black coffee in wee cups. After the coffee I was graciously offered the seat of honor next the stove while "la mere" and "la fille" washed the dishes of which there was quite a pile. After that the mother told me stories of how her husband was a prisoner in Germany & she had to send him food or else as she expressed it, namely, "Him dead." The girl showed me postcards from her "fiancee" in the trenches who was coming home this month maybe & possibly they get married. After le guerre, visit Canada. Good luck to them. They are well worth all that they can get if he's as good as her. You see I'm getting sentimental, man like even after just describing such a good meal in such an unexpected place. Hope you can read this. The candle's bad & the chatter is worse so its likely to appear more or less disjointed George

LETTER 52   *Notes appear on page 182*
[On letterhead bearing the Canadian YMCA logo.]

France
Feb 22nd 1918[33]

Dear girl

Just got a letter from you dated Jan 27th You say its the third you had written since you had received one from me. Say! that's funny I seem to be writing pretty much the same as usual. I wish you would just mention the date of the letters as you get them I would have an idea which ones you got then any way. I never got the parcel yet that you mentioned as

having sent in your letter of Jan 14th, containing those papers etc. I seem
to be unfortunate regarding those papers. All the time I have just received
the one and that the one containing the offending article after I came
back from leave. I got a dandy parcel from the girls a few days ago. Very
opportune too as the rations were down to zero. Guess if this war lasts
much longer we'll all be trained down to live on air all right. Yes! I see Fred
Cooper most days. He is looking FINE.[34] Speaking of being embarassed at
a question listen to this. One morning around Christmas time he says to
me, "Get any mail from home lately." I said "Yes. I got one last night." He
says "Did <u>your</u> wife mention mine." I answered "No, why?" "Somebody has
written and told me she's in hospital and its probable she's dead by this
time, its funny your wife did'nt mention it." I did'nt even know that you
knew his wife, but I'll try and keep you posted as to his health, appearance,
morale etc, especially as news is at a premium. I saw J Darby the other day
as we were going into the line. I had'nt seen him for a long time. I have'nt
run across J Wilson, Winship nor any of that bunch for a long time, though
I would very much like to see them.[35] You say you are having a terrible
winter over there. Well since the end of January its been pretty good here.
Much better than last winter I assure you, its a good thing for us too, as
conditions are poor enough to make it uncomfortable without fighting
excessively cold weather. Beleive me, I'd be glad to be sitting alongside
that range of ours if the weather was 40° below. I'd take a long chance on
freezing to death I'll lay odds. Glad the kiddies got my letters and Winnie
got my birthday card. Bless her little heart, hope she had a good time on
her birthday. I'm glad the doctor fixed up Jim's nose so he looks normal
at least. How's my <u>little</u> girl getting along? Why did'nt you go to Kinton's
dance. You need'nt stay home surely just because I'm not home to take
you. I wrote to Rose Mitchell thanking her for the present to me. Well roll
on spring. We'll have another cut at winning the war then I guess. Hope
we can do it too, so I can get home before I get superannuated. I'm sure
getting more anxious to be back with you all the time. Guess you got my
letters dated Feb 3rd to 6th I beleive they were. I've been feeling pretty sick
since that, but this last two days I'm improving again. Glad of it too, as
this is an awfully poor place to be feeling out of sorts in. The word <u>place</u>
includes any part of the country where the troops are on active service as
you have got to parade to the doctor if he's a mile away no matter how

sick you are, or else you are <u>not</u> sick. By the time you've hobbled you're way to the doctor of course <u>he</u> thinks you can't be sick or you could'nt get that far so there you are <u>Compree</u>. Love from George to you & our kiddies

LETTER 53   *Notes appear on pages 183-84*

Tell Jim & Win. I'll write as
soon as I get a chance. Their
snaps were first class were'nt they?

France
March 19th [1918][36]

Dear sweetheart

Just a line or two to let you know I'm still all right. I got a letter from Jim two days ago. He does fine does'nt he? His letters are quite lucid and full of information. I liked his sarcastic way of handling the article by Mr. Cunningham in the Vindicator concerning his injury I was with Hicks, Spencer, C. Foster, Young Hurst & Logerman from Court St. and am going to see Buck Blackler to night if the rain don't keep up too heavily.[37] We had a little celebration the other night, beleive me. Its the only thing to do, I guess. Hicks rather surprised me. He said he thought I was in Blighty yet Pretty good after me being out here 18 months eh? Guess I'll have to advertise. He also informed me as to what Frank Powell was doing. Making 10 dollars a day in an aeroplane factory and being exempted from military service is pretty soft, what? Hicks is looking pretty good though but like myself he rather envies Frank Powell. I'm thinking that I am as good a man as he is to be making 10 bucks per diem and he has no kiddies, and I have three to be raised yet. It is a little unfair all things considered, I think. If I had had the courage to stay out, they would'nt have touched me probably at all, not for a long time any way. I wrote to Miss McLeod and enclosed a piece of painted canvas which comprised part of the iron cross sign on a German aeroplane which was brought down just behind our support lines.[38] Let me know if she receives it safely. Also a page from a French scholar's arithmetic book. Guess it was a High School pupil at that. I never got the last parcel you mentioned. You remember the one you said little Mollie stoned the raisins for. I have received all the others

though so I guess this one will be along in a couple of days maybe. I heard from mother. She got the money I sent her all right. Guess she'll find it useful too. Also had a letter from Sarah. She tells me that her fiancee was on leave the same time that Harry was on his. Harry is supposed to be in France now.[39] Everything at home was fine. Guess I'll close now for lack of news and with lots and lots of love to you and our children from yours as always
Geo. Timmins

LETTER 54   *Note appears on page 184*

> So good of you, dear to send
> to mother so often. Look after
> yourself first. I will send again
> next pay day. Geo.

France
April 27 [1918][40]

Sweetheart
    I got a letter from you last night dated March 27th It contained Winnies letter & Easter rabbit also the <u>cut</u> of the latest purchase into our household. It looks first rate indeed. I just hope Win proves to be a success at it. Hope I'm home soon to pass an opinion on her progress anyway. Must have cost pretty highly, did'nt it? So Miss McLeod is wondering how she will get along without Mollie for two weeks. Just imagine how I've missed Mollie, Winnie, Jim and also yourself for two <u>years</u>. It just seems this war is going to be perpetual. One side one year in the ascendant, and next year the other side and so on, ad infinitum. Guess they have lost all track of the reasons for it by now. I also got a letter from May Timmins. She says that all the soldiers from Oshawa have been sent over now. Guess we can stand them all right. The other day I saw a fellow out here in an Imperial regiment and I spoke to him in passing. He spoke back and his accent was
[*remainder missing*]

CHAPTER 5

Keep on hoping, sweetheart

MAY–DECEMBER 1918

LETTER 55   *Note appears on page 185*

France
May 17th [1918][1]

Dear sweetheart

I got two letters from you a couple of days ago dated April 14 & 17th.
Was sure delighted to get them too. Got one from May Timmins at the
same time, containing some snapshots. She's getting to be a pretty good
looking girl is'nt she? Very kind of Mr Long to take the bunch out driving.
Say about that trip to Chicago. Take my tip and take the kiddies there
this summer. Don't wait for me as you'll probably have to wait until the
invitation peters out. You seem to think I'll be disappointed in your
appearance when I get home. Don't let that worry you hon, I'm only
anxious to be able to get home to see you. I can't imagine you looking
anything but pretty as a picture as you always were. If the girls follow
their mother they'll have no trouble in getting lots of admirers. If I can
get home I can see myself having a stand-in with all the young fellows
around the burg. Mollie's natural history seems to be at fault a little does'nt
it. Glad to hear Winnie seems to have the musical instinct. Hope she is a
success. I almost forgot to mention that I got a parcel from Sarah, Edith &
Florrie. It was fine too. Didnt get Rose's yet. Expect it any time now though.

Guess my leave to Canada is still some distance away. Never mind, old sweetheart, it will be finished some day. Hope it is'nt too far away. Say! I don't want you to be working this summer like you did last and making yourself sick with the heat & hard work. You are too much to me to do that and take chances of a serious illness especially as the kiddies need you so much. If you do a bit around our own garden you are doing enough for anybody. So I want to insist although its from a distance that you take care of yourself. A little of the old bullying spirit you used to resent so much. I'll never bully any more beleive me, but I want to add my kick to Jim's anent working for small pay for picking berries galore. I'm inclined to socialism. If the war workers get so much why should my boy have to pick fruit at the same old price. You mustnt show him this but just think it over. I'd rather have him loafing down by the creek than working for some measly fruit grower. Tell Miss McLeod to hurry up & send me those snaps of you. Things over here are a little quieter these last few days, but we are expecting something to come off at any time. Things are so uncertain that we are on the look out all the time. Its nerve racking all right. I'm getting so nervous I just jump if I hear a gun go off close at all. The weather has taken a turn for the better. Its terribly hot these last 3 or 4 days but its better than rain & mud. Will write again as soon as I can. In the meantime, sweetheart, beleive me to be loving you & thinking of you all the time. Love to you & the kiddies from yours as <u>always</u> Geo.

P.S. Tell P. Holdaway to rush those pictures of the little kidds.

LETTER 56   *Notes appear on page 185*

France
May 25th [1918]

Dear sweetheart

Guess this is the most leisure I've had for a couple of months so will take the opportunity and try and write a real letter to you, as I fully understand how unsatisfactory it is to get a <u>note</u> when one expects a letter. So I will start at the place I last <u>wrote</u> to you. I told you about meeting Hicks & the rest. We were supposed to be "out" for about 25 days training at that time but man proposes and (in this case) the unspeakable Hun, disposes. He certainly increased the amount of personal animosity of the

18th Battn towards himself by cutting short their period of "training" and
rest, especially as the weather was ideal & we were getting paid regularly
and we were running a "wet" canteen, albeit the price of the beer was high
and sometimes the grade low, but altogether it was paradise to us fellows
fresh from the mud & misery of a winter in the line. Came the news like a
bolt from the blue. "Heinie is attacking in force south of us, has advanced
all along the line. Cut Imperial Divisions to pieces." Well we were the only
bunch in sight that was out doing nothing, so it was "Fall in, full marching
order." Nobody knew where we were going, but we were on our way. We
stopped at a camp somewhere close to the lines & they used us while we
were waiting, to strengthen defences. Defences that were long into disuse.
Old, old trenches, had to be cleaned out and deepened, barbed wire had
to be put up for miles ready to fall back on if the necessity arose and it
sure seemed that it would arise all right. Every day we got news that he
had advanced still further into our lines both in depth & width. We were
being held as an emergency division, a sort of Flying Column, that could
be rushed into any sector, to try and avert disaster.[2] Well the third day I
think it was, really things were happening so often & so suddenly that
nobody was sure of the day or anything else I'm sure, we were again "Fell
in" ready for the road loaded like pack mules. – The man who first thought
of the phrase "Light Infantry" was sure a humorist worthy of note. – As I
was saying we Fell in with everything we owned and got the order to move
off about 9 o'clock at night, destination unknown of course, but Dame
Rumour was busy as usual and we had all sorts of guesses as to where we
were really bound. Anyway everybody's guess was away out. We marched
all night. I say marched but I think after the first three hours it was more
like a stagger. We "carried on" though, grouching, swearing, and staggering.
I don't think a single man dropped out. We finally arrived at our destination
about 4 A.M. Then we were told how well we had done. We had marched
about 28 Kilometers It takes 5 French Kilo to make 3 English miles, so
roughly, we had made 18 miles, over French "roads" in pitch darkness and
raining all the time, carrying full pack, blanket, 170 rounds of ammunition,
rations & other things deemed indispensable to "Light Infantry." We
unloaded at an old barn devoid of doors or windows, even the walls were
in a great state of decay, said decay being partly due to artillery fire. Old as
was the barn it looked pretty good to us, for if it was'nt a shelter it was at

least a destination, something we had been trying to reach all night, & the wet mud floor was soon covered with steaming human forms, sleeping and forgetting in their exhaustion that there was ever such a thing as mud or war. But this state does'nt last long as soon as the first exhaustion wears off the cold & damp creep in and make rising and moving around a very urgent necessity. We "stood to" in this place about 3 more days, listening to the incessant roar of the guns and expecting to be called at any moment to reinforce some ill fated division which had been driven back and suffered so heavily that they had to be withdrawn, but our luck was sure in. We got communiques every 12 hours or so containing the gist of the war news. Something like this "All well in front. Heavy fighting but still holding out"! Beleive me I was'nt a bit anxious to get nearer as the guns were going night & day and I thought someone was likely to be killed if they kept it up. We hung around there called out every few hours to "stand to" expecting to be sent right up, only to be dismissed as the probable new trouble had been safely passed over, our only recreation being to watch the evacuation of the village we were in & the ones close at hand by their native population. It was tragic and yet comical. You'd see an old, old woman, back bent with years of labor in the village she was now leaving behind, like Lot's wife with many a backward glance, accompanied maybe by an old man, and a smart young madame, or possibly a good looking mademoiselle, occasionally dragging a wondering kiddie by the hand, or trundling along a most bewildering assortment of wheeled vehicles, from ancient baby buggies & wheel barrows to huge farm carts drawn by a well fed horse, the said vehicles containing the movable worldly goods of the people pushing them. The worldly goods in most cases being so scanty as to make moving a matter of great simplicity, but always on the top of the load could be seen a huge feather mattress which seemed to be the proudest possession of the poor refugees, except in occasional cases maybe there was a family cow to be led with great care through the crowds of soldiers who infested the village roads, they are too mean to be designated as streets. In cases where there was a cow or calf to be led and in the same family the ill fortune to have children the cow invariably came in for the greatest share of attention as the native mind seems to run in narrow channels which seem strange to us as to the relative value of cows or kids. I mentioned the streets being infested with soldiers. Say it was the biggest mixup I have ever seen. There were soldiers from almost every unit in this sector, who had been separated from their Battns in the drive and were now hopelessly lost until some kind of reorganization should bring order out of chaos and give them establishment in some unit or other. In the meantime they were just hanging on to the edge of things getting fed as best they could and I'm afraid their best was very poor indeed, as our rations were down to the disappearing mark, and we were an organized outfit. Well when we were getting used to this mode of living, and we can get used to any place or thing now in about 3 or 4 days, we were ordered for the road again. We were supposed to be going into some small town near the line to billet in reserve for emergencies still, so this looked good to us. We marched about 14 Kilo's again in the rain until we came to a nice little town although it was badly shattered by shell fire. This was supposed to be our destination, but evidently the orders had been changed en route as we kept right on going even though we saw that our transport was snugly ensconced in decent billets in the place. The men began to wonder if we'd ever get anywhere at all, just kept marching on & on through another shell smashed town until we came to a broad gauge railway. Here we got orders to get our Lewis guns off the limbers also water cans :– ie. old petrol cans used to carry water into the line for the troops to drink – and the next days rations. We did'nt know where we were in the least and when we were led into an old trench in a wide open space, began to think that we were in the support line at least. We were told to dig in and make ourselves comfortable. Ye Gods! just imagine being led into a half finished sewer excavation in Canada, in the middle of the night, and being told to dig in and get comfortable before daybreak. It was raining pretty hard most of the time so you can tell the beautiful condition we were in. Anyway we dug holes in the side of the trench and got some old barbed wire stakes and with our rubber ground sheets made some shelter for ourselves. In the morning we discovered where we were, that is, as far as we could considering none of us had ever seen the place before, but anyway we could see we were still in reserve some distance from Heinie although in imminent danger of being shelled at any moment. He proved this by giving our platoon two casualties before noon. Well having deepened this trench we moved up again that night about 500 yards forward into another old trench here we did the same, and the next night up nearer & did the same, see the scheme, we were improving the defences as well as holding a very critical reserve position. Our third move proved more lucky for us as we stayed there for 2 days making 5 days in all since moving up here. The fifth night we were ordered up to the front line, presumably for 3 days as this was an 8 day trip but it eventually transpired that the first day & night had not counted and so we were billed for 4 days in the front line. We were about to start out just 9 PM. Got lined up on an old road and started across country for the line when an awful barrage opened on our front line as we could see from where we were and then we saw the S.O.S. go up for artillery retaliation and we thought that the Heinie had decided on a night attack in force. Our barrage opened up in grand style, and we being in the open fields spread out into what is called technically "Artillery Formation." That is a series of little groups in diamond shape so as to offer as small a target as possible to gunfire, if, as in this case we expected him to do, he raised his range searching for our guns which seemed from the noise to be all around us. We waited in this formation for some definite order to come through either to go forward to the assistance of the front line or to retire on to our own recently vacated reserve line in case the front line fell back. We got the latter order but the line held and gradually the barrage died away. So we started out again to relieve the men in the line as per schedule. We cut across country and as is usual in such cases got lost in the darkness and while our guides & leaders were debating as to the best way out of the difficulty, Heinie suddenly decided it for us by dropping two shells into the midst of the first platoon. Very fortunately we only got 11 casualties[3] We could easily have had 3 times as many but we were just lucky. We cleaned up the wounded & detailed some men to get stretchers and get them to the nearest dressing station all the time expecting to hear the shriek of another shell coming our way but again fortune favored us & nothing happened. By this time our guides had found out where they had gone wrong and so we retraced our way for almost a mile until we hit the main road & so up to the line. We were passing groups of huts on both sides of the road that had been rest camps only a few days previously now owing to the German offensive they were in close support & being rapidly hammered to pieces by his guns. We came to a place where we had to take a light railway line as our line of march. It was full of shell holes & the rails were blown up and twisted all shapes, warning us that this was'nt a place that could be truthfully advertised as a health resort so we lost no time in covering this bad piece of country. By the time we reached the line, which crossed this track at right angles the battns in the line were getting out their casualties received in the barrage which had held us up as we started out the first time to releive them. They had quite a number and the sight of the bandages on the wounded and some on stretchers who did'nt need bandages, having finished with the war for all time, was not very encouraging to us after what we had just come through and knowing we had to stay in that lovly place for four days, 96 hours I figured mentally. When we got in we were further impressed. The line was a hastily dug trench affording little protection and we had to be on the watch all the time in case he came again as he was expected to do at any time. We dug in in turns & looked over in turns. Dodging shrapnel very frequently but all the time improving our position. The next morning he subjected us to a 3½ hours bombardment with everything he had. Heavies, Whizz bangs & overhead shrapnel, but we escaped with slight casualties thanks to some extent to our industry in deepening our trench. We got reports like this occasionally though Such & such a platoon lost 9 men with one shell, so & so lost 8 with another and so on.[4] The next morning at daybreak we were getting rations from the sergeant. One man from each section going for his section's rations. We were standing in a row in the bay when a shell hit the parapet and of 6 of us there [...] killed [*rest of line illegible*] and one, myself, escaped with a mouth & nose all full of dust & powder smoke. I was sent flying on my back but scrambled up in about 5 seconds and made my way to the heap of dirt & dead as best I could. The wounded I got out & got the stretcher bearers working and then with some assistance got the others dug out & placed on the fire step. All before breakfast too. Our rations were buried but we dug 'em out. A case of eat 'em dirty or starve till next day. Needless to say we ate 'em. The same afternoon another big one landed in our bay but fortunately we all escaped with a shaking up. By this time I was beginning to feel a little shell shocked.[5] To add to our discomfort it rained and the very work we had done on the trench was to our disadvantage here as the water lay there & rose to about 2 feet in depth & the sides of the trench were slimy and everything you touched was covered in nice oozy mud. We were in an awful mess I can assure you. Anyway [*words illegible*] until our time was in but were glad to be releived.

13

crossed this track at right angle
the batt^ns in the line were getting
out their casualties received in
the barrage which had held us
up as we started out the first
time to relieve them.. They had
quite a number and the sight of
the bandages on the wounded
and some on stretchers who didn
need bandages, having finished
with the war for all time, was no
very encouraging to us after ~~what~~ we had
~~just come through and to worse~~
we had to stay in that lovly plac
for four days, 96 hours I figured
mentally. When we got in we were
further impressed. The line was a
hastily dug trench affording littl
protection and we had to be on th
watch all the time in case he can
again as he was expected to do at
any time. We dug in in turns & loot
over in turns. Dodging shrapnel
very frequently but all the time
improving our position. The next
morning he subjected us to a 3½
hours bombardment with everything
he had. Heavies, Whizz bangs &
overhead shrapnel but we escaped

Page 13 of Letter 56, 25 May 1918

with slight casualties thanks to some extent to our industry in deepening our trench. We got reports like this ocasionally though Such & such a platoon lost 9 men with one shell, so & so lost 8 with another and so on. The next morning at daybreak we were getting rations from the sergeant. One man from each section going for his section's rations. We were standing in a row in the bay when ~~the~~ a shell hit the parapet and of 6 of us there and one, myself, escaped with a mouth & nose all full of dust & powder smoke. I was sent flying on my back but scrambled up in about 5 seconds and made my way to the heap of dirt & dead as best I could. The wounded I got out & got the stretcher bearers working and then with some assistance got the others dug out & placed on the fire step. All before breakfast too. Our rations were buried but we dug 'em out. A case of eat 'em dirt or starve till next day. Needless to say we ate 'em. The same afternoon

Page 14 of Letter 56, 25 May 1918

The relief was exciting in the extreme. We had just reached the light railway I mentioned before when his flares must have discovered us and he put a barrage of whizz-bangs right on us. It was a case of run for it as there was no cover I don't know how it happened, but with shells bursting all over and around us we came out with only 3 casualties out of about 25 men in the party. But the run near killed us. We were loaded with wet mud. Clothes soaked with rain besides the ordinary load we had to carry. Then we marched back about 14 miles without a bite to eat and only some water we got at a dressing station on the way to drink. We had to rest every ½ mile or so and we could scarcely drag our feet. As soon as a halt was called down we dropped & went to sleep in the mud of the road. We were releived at 10 P.M. and it was near noon next day when some of the party got to our billet. But a good breakfast of bacon & tea worked wonders & the rest of the day & night to sleep & the next day a bath & scrape off mud & we were feeling pretty fit again. We were only there 4 days and then in the line again. We made the most of our short time out I assure you. As far as we could but there was'nt much in the place we could buy. Guess I'll close now as my envelope will be censored sure as ------ if its too full. Keep this. Will write again soon & shoot a little more <u>bull</u>. Love to you all from yours as always George

LETTER 57   *Notes appear on pages 185-86*

France
June 29th [1918]⁶

Dear sweetheart

I've been back with the Battn six days now. Say! after all its funny the way a man swears at the outfit when he's got to stay with it, but when he gets away for two weeks and comes back and is greeted enthusiastically by the whole bunch it sure alters things a whole lot. You should have seen the welcome I got. The Battn had been out two days, and were bivouaced in some woods, and I had quite a job to find them, when I got in the whole bunch were away at some brigade sports or something so I waited around a while and finally they began to come back in threes & fours. Our platoon nearly shook my arm off. I had been all day with no rations as it was quite a long railway journey from St. Valery. I just said I was hungry and that I had nothing with me <u>and</u> of course no money, and the whole bunch dragged out their grub and invited me to "go to it." It sure does a fellow good to see such good hearted fellows. The next night I was invited to visit a town called Dainville with some of them, one of their number having received a registered letter with five pounds in it. We had a good old drink beleive me as far as its possible on the rotten dope they sell here.[7] Anyway we were highly exhilarated by the time we got back to camp, which was the effect we were trying after. Next day though. Oh! my poor head. That night I did'nt go; just pretended to be asleep when they came looking for me. Well it was a good thing I did'nt as things turned out. They came home uproarious. Some jolly some fighting drunk. But the funny thing about it they all had to come and see me before they would go to bed. One lad was lying outside his "bivvy," and when they tried to get him to bed he just refused to go until they fetched me just so he could see me he said. You see they are all chaps that have arrived since me And they look on me as a kind of a patriarch I think I should grow white whiskers just to look the part. Its sure great though to have the good-will of so many good boys. Boys is right, as they run from about 17 to 23 years of age. Don't get this published as there's been enough rot about how the boys in France drink. Its only once in six months anyway and if those white livered uplifters were here they would probably understand that a <u>good</u> <u>man</u> in khaki can drink and raise ------, and still be a better man than any old thing in mufti. There's a big excuse for them. Just imagine for three straight months we had been in hell. Shelled night & day practically, in the line or out, and now we are out for a month's training. The prospect of a whole month in the comparative safety of a town 12 miles behind the line after the experience of the last 3 months is well worth celebrating.[8] Its only too bad that we can't do it more royally. Enough of this though. I got all my back mail when I came back to the Battn. Three letters from you, one from Edith, one from Sarah, & one from Sarah's fellow, Somewhere in France. Two parcels from you, though one only got here yesterday as it has been down to the Rest Camp. And one from Rose & Gid. They were sure great. The one that went to the Rest Camp was the one that contained the corn cob pipes. Now the peculiar thing about that parcel was that I had company to tea so it came in very opportunely although the cake was badly broken, also the cookies as it had been all over the place trying to catch me up. Bet you could'nt guess who my "company" was. Well knowing how you are getting curious I will tell you. In Sarah's letter she gave me Harry's address. This was the first time I had had it. She said he had written, and said he had a notion that he had been close to us. When we moved I thought I had missed him again. Well yesterday after dinner I was in our billets when somebody started shouting my name saying there's a fellow here wants to see you. Before I could get my shirt on, as I had been busy hunting the festive, (very much so) little louse, who should come in & grab me but your brother Harry. Gee! I was just tickled to death to see him. He is looking just fine. He had walked about six Kilo's from where they are billeted, also for, presumably a month. Well, we sat around in the sun all afternoon and chatted and had tea together, your parcel, as I said before being particularly appreciated. Neither of us having any money it looked like being a terribly dry season, but relief always comes to the deserving. Fred Manning of Oshawa comes up and says he's just bummed five francs from somebody he knew so we had better go and spend it.[9] We did. Anyway we are going to have a night in the near future, if things pan out all right. Speaking of Manning reminds me of something. The night I mentioned that the boys came home exhilarated there was a friend of mine, a sergeant in Manning's platoon came and shook hands with me and with drunken gravity congratulated me. I asked him wherefore. He started giving a speech, as how he had the last time in the line picked up some Oshawa papers, received by Manning. When he reached this stage I tried to stop him suspecting what was coming off, but he would persist in detailing all he had read in a loud voice, dwelling on what he called the extra good paragraphs. He also bragged about how he had read it to the whole platoon as it was too good to be wasted, especially as it was signed by, here he pointed me out, my friend on the left. Gee! I felt cheap. But they all said it was very good, so I had to be content with that, but I sure don't like to see my name shoved in the paper like that. Guess McLeese was just talking when he told you he had written to me. I did'nt get it yet anyway. So glad to hear dearie that you had such a good time May 24th. Do I remember May 24th two years ago? Guess I do. Such events as that are the only ones I let my mind wander back to. You say you are working Saturday nights & holidays. Don't you think its a pretty trying time for you. What happens to the kiddies while you are away? Guess Winnie is quite a capable little girl by now though. Just you let Miss McLeod & all who want to, volunteer for land work, you kindly stay out. You have enough to do at home. I dont want you doing anything like that. You can do your share by staying home & looking after the home & kids. What Hamblin did, was to raise the rent after agreeing with Walter to let it remain stationary until he came back to Canada. Edith expects to be married in Sept. She wants me to try & get leave to be present. I'd like to all right, but I guess its no use. Tell Mollie I guess I dream of her as often as she dreams of me. Poor little girl. I'd just like to be able to comfort the poor little baby. Lots of love to Winnie, Jim & Mollie, not of course forgetting yourself sweetheart from yours as always George

LETTER 58 *Notes appear on page 186*

France
July 6th [1918]

Dear sweetheart

Just received your letter dated June 12th. Poor little old girl, you just did seem to be discouraged with everything Never mind honey, buck up. I guess you are getting a hard time though just the same. Things must be awfully dear over in Canada, by what you say. Guess Stories must have made their pile before venturing on their own, eh? Did they have to get out or just quit on their own accord. Billie Clarke seems to have dropped in right though does'nt he. No, I've never seen Jack Burr yet. Anyway its time he had another go at it. We have some draftees with us already. Things are fine over here at least for us just now as we are on a month's rest The weather is splendid; dry and quite hot. Just great for lying around evenings. How's Alf Gower getting along?[10] Is he still sick? If she has to work to keep him she has'nt got much of a cinch. Why dont you pack up and go with the children to Lake Forest to see Enoch?[11] It would be a great change & a rest for you. Now don't get working too hard nor get the kids doing it either. Beleive me its no good. What you make will probably have to be spent in doctor's bills, then there's all the discomforts which accompany sickness in a home where there's children. I am enclosing a £1 note. Hope you get it safely. It will buy the kids some ice cream anyway. Lots & lots of love to you & the kiddies from yours as always <u>George</u>.

LETTER 59

France
July 13th [1918]

Dear sweetheart

Just taking the opportunity of writing a few lines to you. The last time I wrote I told you we were on <u>at least</u> 4 weeks rest We had 12 days and then the order for a rest was cancelled. We are now moved up again & expect to go in to morrow in a new piece of front too. I hope to hear from you again shortly as my mail is still keeping pitifully small, one letter about every three, sometimes four weeks. I never had the chance to see Harry again. I don't know whether they moved up before us or not. I was sorry too as I had promised myself a good night with him, but we did'nt get paid in time anyway. Is Enoch called up yet? Hope not, as the longer he can keep out the better it will be for him. The old war is still going on as usual. Looks as though its come to stay for ever don't it? God forbid though eh? I've got to get home pretty soon to see you and the kiddies again. How's Tom Knott and family doing? Say! did you ever hear anything of Percy Mitchell? I got a letter from Mary. She says her baby can walk & talk now. He must be a dandy by this time all right. I think we are very lucky that the war is being fought in Europe on that account that our babies can play around and grow fat without getting mixed up with shells & things. I saw an incident about two months ago, which is fixed in my mind by the very tradegy of it. We were in a small town pretty close to the line, in fact close enough for Heinie to shell it every day. Not much you know but every day somebody would get hit. Sometimes as on one occasion, he dropped one right on the road outside our camp and killed about 9 or 10 & wounded a big bunch. You see at this distance he only uses big shells & they being very expensive he don't use many, but when they connect whow! watch out. Well in all these small towns there's always a few people, who for the sake of the money they make by overcharging the soldiers for small things they have for sale take a chance on themselves & families being killed. One night we were sitting by a canteen talking and watching 3 little kiddies playing around just like my little girls used to, when suddenly we heard a "big one" coming. You can hear them coming with a noise like a street car coming through the air. Say those poor little kids just stopped their play and looked up as though they could see it, the two bigger ones about 4 years I should say followed it over in the direction it was travelling with their eyes, (it was fortunately a high one, figuring from where we were, as it landed about 300 yards away from us) but the poor little one that I had picked out for my especial notice, looking as she did so much like my little girl did when I left home, she would be about 2½ maybe. Say! I felt my heart ache for that little one. The look of fear that came into her eyes, she was laughing & trying to chatter to the others when the noise first struck us. She turned around to run into the house when she found it was over us & past, she about turns again & was playing again almost as happily as ever. I say almost, because the look of trouble was still in that poor little ones eyes. God grant that none of mine ever hear a shell coming. War's Hell all right. Don't forget to write. Tell me how you like the photos. I send a card each for the children the other day. Lots of love to you all & may we meet soon is the earnest wish of yours as ever Geo.

LETTER 60   *Notes appear on pages 186-87*

France
July 21st [1918]

Dear sweetheart
    Seems to me like 20 years instead of two since I saw you at Niagara Camp. This is Sunday so its two years ago to-day since you came to see me in camp, and brought the baby. I hope I'll see you again before two more. Do you remember how we used to talk over the possibilities of my being away a long period? We used to gasp almost at the idea of being apart two years, but always agreed that that would be the very extreme. What a rude awakening. We have been moving around again very freely just recently consequently we have had a good chance to see old friends Saw the wonderful Mr Danks the other day.[12] He is with some labor Battn. He tells me he was booked for Canada until Fritz made his drive in March last, and then they were all shot over to France in a hurry. Of course he has practically a safety first job. He is a regular sob artist. Talking about "the old 'ome"; etc. etc. I saw 3 more Oshawa boys that day and the same night on the march out I met George Smith who used to work with Powell and

joined the artillery at Cobourg at Christmas time the same time as Gibby who was killed.[13] He came to our camp yesterday as he heard we were stopping there for a couple of days, & took me over to see Bill Lewis that used to board at Cameron's when they lived in the cottage[14] At night we all came over and found Jack Wilson, Bill & Charlie Burcham, Harry Winship.[15] Jack tells me that Harry Wilson is in Canada by this time with a useless arm. Also that Harry was killed at Passchendael.[16] To crown all this, to day I got a letter from Ernie Miner. Says he's doing fine, and only just missed me by a small margin on our last move.[17] By the way we are moving around and being re-arranged as it were, it looks as though something is coming off.[18] By the time you get this we'll probably be in the limelight again, just note the date. The news is a little more assuring this last week, so maybe we will be able to look forward to a pass this fall or winter All passes of course were cancelled while the worst was on. Needless to say I don't mean a pass to Canada. I got your letter saying about the coal and Dr Kaiser's visit to the house.[19] I'm so sorry sweetheart that you should be placed in such an unenviable position. The people even being able to think suspiciously of you because you did'nt feel it necessary to satisfy their curiosity concerning your affairs. I <u>know</u> you are above suspicion but don't on any account give these scandalmongers a chance at you. Its worried me quite a bit, loving you as I do and being so powerless to comfort you or help you at all. That's the worst thing of all for me to contemplate. You there without anybody to help you a little. Another thing, Winnie must be getting quite a big girl now so just keep an extra look out over her. Sweetheart! I know this advice is needless but I feel much better for giving it. Just forgive me won't you. I get really anxious sometimes as to how they are getting along. I just wish I could get home to love you & try to help you forget all our troubles. Won't we have a good time when the end of this old war comes. Roll on the time. Remember me to everybody who may be interested. Lots of love to you and our kiddies from yours as always George.

LETTER 61   *Notes appear on page 187*

London
Aug 31st Saturday [1918][20]

Sweetheart

Just a line to let you know I'm going on fine. [*words illegible*] out of
my leg on Wednesday and I thought I would be able to get up and hobble
round the ward, but nay! The wound had'nt healed good enough so it was
decreed that I remain in bed.[21] Guess its a week more in bed at least. Never
mind its another week of the war gone I see in the papers that we are still
pushing ahead & the Canucks are doing fine work Such is the peculiar
make-up of a man that often as I have wished myself out of it & knowing
as I do, none better, the horrors of it, I almost find myself wishing I was
into it again. Its so good to feel you are in & winning. Advancing all the
time. Its so different to fighting on the defensive like we were in March &
April. That's what gets your goat. Anyway, kiddie, I suppose I should be
thankful to be lying here in a good warm bed with lots to eat, instead of
being suffering what I know the boys are suffering out there. Its adding to
my chances of eventually getting home again & seeing you all. I often
imagine what it will be like to have you all round me again. Sometimes
squabbling eh? I'll guarantee to be good natured and every other old thing
that goes to make a model husband. I wrote to Esther some days ago but
she was in Scotland. They sent the letter on & by return she sent me a lovly
box of Scottish scones & fresh butter. Just imagine real butter. It was sure
good. I invited the boys & the nurses to participate & beleive me they
were appreciated, especially as there's a bunch of Highlanders in here.
Gordons, Seaforths, Argyll & Sutherland and all kinds of Scotch
regiments represented. I'm getting so anxious to hear from you, but guess
it will be a little while yet, as the letters will have gone to France of course.
But I hope you are all doing fine. I'll write you all about the advance as far
as I was in it as soon as I can get up. Please don't send any parcels for me
to Eng. I'll enclose the shoulder straps off one of my prisoners. I brought
out 5 perfectly healthy, unwounded Germans for about 6 miles. Me being
wounded & almost crippled. I made two of them help me along in turns,
tho the truth is they did'nt want much making. They seemed glad to get
away at any price. They half carried me through the grain fields. Their only

Such is the peculiar make-
up of a man that often as I
have wished myself out of it, &
knowing as I do, none better,
the horrors of it, I almost find
myself wishing I was into it
again. Its so good to feel you
are in & winning. Advancing
all the time. Its so different
to fighting on the defensive
like we were in March & April.
Thats what gets your goat.
Anyway, kiddie, I suppose I
should be thankful to be
lying here in a good warm
bed with lots to eat, instead
of being suffering what I know
the boys are suffering out there

Letter 61, 31 August 1918

anxiety was to make it faster. Honest one almost feels sorry for them, or else contemptuous, for their eagerness to please. Still longing to see you and loving you just as much as ever Yours as always George

P.S. My sentiments concerning being out there again may be criticised so don't show this You, I know understand me just a little Geo

LETTER 62   *Notes appear on pages 187-88*

> I guess they are going to
> leave the metal in my thigh.
> Hope it don't go bad after.[22]

Sept 27th [1918]
London

Sweetheart

I got two letters from you yesterday that had been to France one dated July 17th the other July 23rd, so I'm congratulating myself exceedingly. One also from Miss McLeod Say! we are fortunate indeed in having her for a friend. I only wish I could have received her letter while in France. Its the kind of letter a fellow like me just wants to brace him up. I'm inclined to be ashamed of my letters. I have been so "fed up" often that I have written in anything but a cheerful note, and yet I've tried not to show it and then the longing to hear from you has overcome my reluctance to write when I've felt so babyish, that I've gone ahead and then the wail has crept into my correspondence I'm so sorry, dear, that I caused you to be ever worried, but I always wanted sympathy from you, and never in vain. You need helping more than I do and deserve it more. How I wish I could just get home again soon to show my love and gratitude to you, for all you have done and for the way you have helped me by you courage and cheerfulness while I've been such a poor kind of a fellow. I just wish that you were having a rest now like I am getting. You must be in need of it. Just you wait until I <u>do</u> get back. My wound is getting along well now. Guess I'll soon be getting discharged from hospital. In fact my only kick is that I'm getting well too fast. I like being here fine. Did you get any further news of Harry yet? So pleased to hear that the children are so well. Miss McLeod speaks so highly of them, I'm so proud of them all. When I'm discharged from here, I'm sent to a Military Hosp. for a short time, possibly two weeks, then to a Convalescent Camp, then sick leave, then the depôt again.[23] After that it depends on what happens but I am refusing to think about it yet. Keep on hoping, sweetheart. Lots & lots of love to you & our kiddies from yours as always George.

Please continue to address my letters to Sarah at Cradley

LETTER 63   *Note appears on page 188*

London
Sept 30th [1918]

Dear Winnie

I am sending you a small bag of lavender, which I got from the Sister.[24] I have told her about you all, of course, and she was very much interested, especially in your photos which I have carried for so long. I never got the new ones you promised to send me. When I get on sick furlough I will get one taken of myself, so you will have an idea what your dad really looks like, as I'm afraid those I had taken in France do not flatter me in the least and of course I want to look as well as I possibly can, now you are all growing up, and beginning to take notice of things. Miss McLeod tells me good news about the way you take your music lessons. Say Winnie I'm quite proud of you. Also of Jim. I'll write to Jim when I get up and able to get him something. The news about Uncle Harry must be a mistake as Sarah has had another letter from him since. Be a good girl as I know of course you always have been. Kiss Jim & Margaret for me. Lots of love & kisses for yourself from your proud old dad.

P.S. Guess on second thoughts you had better leave Jim alone and kiss mother twice instead

FRAGMENT 4   *Notes appear on page 188*

[Western Ontario Regimental Depot, Witley Camp][25]
[Christmas 1918]
Second Edition

Dear May

I never opened your parcel until this morning. Was delighted with contents. Plum pudding, cake, pipe, comb, shaving soap, cigarettes, socks to take notice of things.

Miss McLeod tells me good news about the way you take your music lessons. Say Winnie I'm quite proud of you. Also of Jim. I'll write to Jim when I get up and able to get him something. The news about Uncle Harry must be a mistake as Sarah has had another letter from him since. Be a good girl as I know of course you always have been.

Kiss Jim. & Margaret for me.

Lots of love & kisses for yourself from your proud old dad.

P.S. Guess on second thoughts you had better leave Jim alone and kiss mother twice instead

Letter 63 (to Winnie), 30 September 1918

with a letter from Miss McLeod. I divided the plum duff immediately. Say! it was grand. Moist & rich and lovely. I didn't cut the cake yet as its apt to be wasted when it comes in volume like ... now. Gee, whiz! I'm hungry for a look at her, <u>all of you of course</u>, but the littlest the most. You understand don't you. It looks like being a noisy Xmas here. Just 12 hours away and everything seems to be wide open. Peace on earth goodwill towards men, good night!, Christian nations. Edith's letter informed me that Loll had been over on a 10 days pass, but couldn't get back as he was overtaken by appendicitis, and had to undergo an operation [*remainder missing*][26]

Don't forget to write to . Grandpa.

LETTER 64 *Notes appear on page 188*

272 Golf St.
[Oshawa]
Sunday Jan 22/60

Hi: ----[1]

Received your letter of Jan 6. Thanks for your solicitude. Glad to say I am feeling a lot better, tho. owing to the savage cold I have'nt been outside for 5 days. I begin to feel like Bonaparte on his rock ... About your ancestors. They are probably better left alone as they were very ordinary people & would laugh like hell at any suggestion that they were otherwise. However my family tree is something like this. My father's family were hard working, upright people moderately sinful. My mother's were the most picturesque. Her family name was Hollaway. Her father was a gamekeeper on the estate of Lord Lyttleton of Hagley Hall.[2] He in common with all game keepers was wont to poach a little to eke out the family rations. He goes back to around 1804 as he was 87 when he died & I remember I was there when he died. I was 9 years old about 1890. I remember my cousin Mercy weeping fit to die, she had been acting nurse to him in his last illness. Grandmother lived for some after. He left three sons & 3 daughters.

May and George Timmins on a visit to Ottawa in the early 1950s

The boys were Charlie, George, & Joe. The girls were Maria, Sarah, & Mary Anne, the latter being my mother. As the boys grew up the industrial era of Britain was beginning to boom. Railroads were building. Large factorys were being built, but the semi-rural population, like the Hollaways, worked their gardens, and the boys in a way I never found out blossomed into manufacturers in a very small way of course. Charlie & George had somehow got into the business of making by hand what was known locally as Bullheads, but were really railway spikes as we know them. They were such good workmen & demand so great that they became so well known that the purchasers of these commodities used to call at their forge in carriages, which was when George in his self reliance and obstinacy would keep them waiting till he was good & ready to see them & then before discussing business would produce a bucket and demand that the first order of business was to get the bucket filled with beer. This was accomplished by sending the girl who worked for him to the nearest pub for what would be 3 gallons of beer. The girls used to "point" for the forgemen. That is put the point on after the heavy work of forging the head & shank was finished. The high handed way of handling the boss, of course, could'nt last and about the time I left England in 1902 machines were being invented to make nails & spikes & other simple things. George & Joe died about 1905. Something wrong with their livers. When we remember the gallons of beer and the murderous work we cease to wonder why. I suppose there were scores of progeny left. Some particularly handsome girls as I remember All redhaired. This is the low down on the Hollaways. Some time I'll fill you in on the Dunn's grandma's family. Don't forget to write.

Love Grandpa

LETTER 65   *Notes appear on page 188*

[Oshawa]
May 6/65

Hello Joe & Nicole,[3]

Received your letter on Tuesday May 4th. I was in York in 1898. At that time I was working in Middlesborough in a tube works making tube fittings. Yes, the old empire is through, I guess, and about time. There was

always too great a division between the different grades, the classes and
the masses. That's the reason I came over here. I didn't like the touching
of hats to the minister etc. Speaking of your friends trips in to the
industrial midlands. That's the place I left. I remember the long rows of
attached houses, although we lived in a semi-detached. We were a step
or a step & a half ahead of the mob. I hope that you get to see it though
of course it can be totaly changed by this time. Take York as the starting
place. Drive south to Burton-on-Trent, Staffs. That's where the famous
breweries are, then the best way I should think is to hit Dudley city. Then
drive straight south from 'Dudley' thru 'Netherton', to 'Old Hill', then to
'Haden Hill'. That's where I was born, in a village on the outskirts of the
industrial harshness and poverty. About 5 miles from Dudley to Haden
Hill as I remember it. We used to walk to Dudley on Holidays to see the
old famous castle which was blown apart by Oliver Cromwell.[4] When you
get to Old Hill there is a cross, and ancient 'Four Corners', if you turn
right you will hit Cradley Heath in about a mile. That was the heart of
the iron trade. Ships anchors & anchor chain etc. from Blast furnaces to
finished product. Her people were named "Dunn." I imagine they're
mostly passed on now [...]

Love Grandpa

LETTER 66   *Notes appear on pages 188-89*

272 Golf St.
Oshawa Ont.
August 11th [1969]

Dear Nicole,

Received your letter on Aug. 8th Was very pleased indeed to get it. The
8th of Aug is a day I always remember when it comes around.[5] On Aug 8th
1918 I was at Amiens in your beautiful country. That's the day we started
the movement that ended the war. It also ended my participation in
hostilities. It seemed so nice to lie in hospital, with a nurse asking "how's
your health this morning, and reading about the war while you had a hot
breakfast in bed. "Those were the days."[6] [...] I am keeping about the same.
Some days not so good though. Hope that you can read this. My writing
is sure getting to be terrible. I, who used to be the pride of teacher's heart

old to regain health ‘
strength again. Hope
you keep well and
are happy in your
new location. and the
kids grow & are a
pleasure to you both.
They are beauties from
the start – Kiss then
for me.
   Don't forget to write
to   Grandpa.

I'm a poor writer
now. please excuse

Letter 67, 26 August 1974

in the 3rd grade, for my reading, writing & arithmetic. Held up as an example in fact. The very best of everything to you both. From Grandpa

    P.S. Don't forget to write & tell me how things are

Grandpa

LETTER 67   *Note appears on page 189*

August 26 [1974]

Hillsdale Manor

[Oshawa]

Dear Joe and Nicole,

    I received Joe's change of address card. They sure set you a long way off from everybody. So sorry to hear about it as we will not see you & your beautiful youngsters for a long time I guess. I am still suffering with bad legs I take pills & pills for relief but it don't seem to do any good. Guess I'm too old to regain health & strength again. Hope you keep well and are happy in your new location, and the kids grow & are a pleasure to you both. They are beauties from the start – Kiss them for me.[7]

    Don't forget to write to Grandpa

    I'm a poor writer now. please excuse

NOTES

Introduction

1 George Timmins (hereafter cited as GT) to May Timmins (hereafter cited as MT), 31 August [1918].

2 Library and Archives Canada (hereafter cited as LAC), RG 150, accession 1992-93/166, box 9698-43, 3235822 Timmins, George. (Hereafter, all references to military personnel service records found in LAC, RG 150, accession 1992-93/166, are cited by box number, service number, and name.) See also "Operations of the Canadian Corps, 1918, Part II, July 15 to November 11" in Canada, Ministry of Overseas Forces, *Report of the Ministry: Overseas Military Forces of Canada, 1918*, 126-85 (hereafter cited as *Report of the Ministry*); Shane B. Schreiber, *Shock Army of the British Empire: The Canadian Corps in the Last 100 days of the Great War*; David Campbell, "The Divisional Experience in the C.E.F.: A Social and Operational History of the 2nd Canadian Division, 1915-1918," 514-42.

3 On 14 July 1916, the four companies of the 116th were each photographed at Niagara Camp. Copies of these photographs survive in the Oshawa Military and Industrial Museum, 1000 Stevenson Road North, Oshawa, Ontario, L1J 5P5.

4 GT crossed the Atlantic on the RMS *Olympic*. See "116th Reaches England," *Gazette and Chronicle*, 3 August 1916. See also Chap. 1, n. 13. (Hereafter, all references to the *Gazette and Chronicle* are to the paper of that name published in Whitby, Ontario.)

5 Letters could take three to four weeks to arrive. R.B. Fleming, "Introduction," in *The Wartime Letters of Leslie and Cecil Frost, 1915-1919*, ed. R.B. Fleming, 26.

6 Of other ranks (hereafter cited as ORs) of the CEF serving outside Canada, only 20 percent were married. Of the ORs in GT's circle, the figure is over 32 percent. Desmond Morton, *Fight or Pay: Soldiers' Families in the Great War*, 244; Tim Cook, "'My Whole Heart and Soul Is in This War': The Letters and War Service of Sergeant G.L. Ormsby," 51-63; Desmond Morton, "A Canadian Soldier in the Great War: The Experiences of Frank Maheux," 79-89.

7 The men of the CEF had, on average, a grade six education. Desmond Morton, *When Your Number's Up: The Canadian Soldier in the First World War*, 278.

8 See Jeffrey A. Keshen, *Propaganda and Censorship during Canada's Great War*; Ian Hugh MacLean Miller, *Our Glory and Our Grief: Torontonians and the Great War*; Robert Rutherdale, *Hometown Horizons: Local Responses to Canada's Great War*; Peter Liddle, "British Loyalties: The Evidence of an Archive," in *Facing Armageddon: The First World War Experienced*, ed. Hugh Cecil and Peter H. Liddle, 523-38.

9 The parish records of Holy Trinity Anglican Church, Old Hill, are deposited in the Dudley Archives and Local History Centre, Mount Pleasant Street, Coseley, West Midlands, UK, WV14 9JR.

10 GT to Joseph and Nicole Houlden, 6 May 1965.

11 Ibid.

12 Robert Sherard, "The White Slaves of England," in *Into Unknown England 1886-1913: Selections from the Social Explorers*, ed. Peter Keating, 175-76. GT and MT's marriage certificate confirms Esau Dunn's occupation. See also Sydney Allen, "The Chain-makers – in 1914: Old Hill and Lye contingent," *Black Country Bugle*, November 1986. For information on current and historical events in Old Hill and Cradley Heath see http://www.blackcountrybugle.co.uk.

13 GT to Joseph and Nicole Houlden, 6 May 1965.

14 I am grateful to Joseph Houlden for this information.

15 D.S. Hoig, *Reminiscences and Recollections*, 43.

16 M. McIntyre Hood, *Oshawa: "The Crossing between the Waters"; A History of "Canada's Motor City,"* 406; J.E. Farewell, *County of Ontario*, 73-80. In 1909, the Ontario Malleable Iron Works and the Canada Malleable Steel Range Company occupied adjacent lots. GT does distinguish between the two firms, calling the former simply "the Malle" and the latter the "Steel Range" or "Can. Malle." Many friends and acquaintances were employed by both firms. GT's home in 1916, at 460 Albert Street, Oshawa, was located directly across from the factory. See also Thomas Bouckley, *Pictorial Oshawa*, 125.

17 Winnifred died in 1998, Jim in 1993, and Mollie in 1999.

18 GT's employment information comes from his attestation paper, which he signed on enlisting in the 116th Battalion in Oshawa on 21 March 1916. LAC, box 9698-43, 3235822 Timmins, George.

19 GT to MT, 7 January 1918 and 29 June [1918].

20 GT to MT, 30 March [1917].

21 No runs of the two local Oshawa newspapers, the *Ontario Reformer* and the *Oshawa Vindicator*, survive. A few scattered copies exist in the Oshawa Community Museum and Archives, 1450 Simcoe Street South, Oshawa, Ontario, L1H 8S8. All references to these papers come from this rare collection.

22 Joseph Houlden, interview with author, Ottawa, 9 December 1993. In March 1916, 33,960 men volunteered, and a total of 185,887 from October 1915 to May 1916. Morton, *When Your Number's Up*, 60.

23 GT to MT, Monday Night [24 May 1916]. To do one's bit can have the meaning of "making one's contribution to a cause ... especially by serving in the armed forces." Two of the earliest recorded usages with this sense were *Punch*, 12 May 1915, and *Ladies Home Journal*, June 1917. *Oxford English Dictionary* (hereafter cited as *OED*), vol. 2, 227.

24 Rutherdale, *Hometown Horizons*, 52.

25 "A" Company consisted of men from Uxbridge; "B" Company, men from Beaverton; and "C" Company, men from Whitby. See "116th Battalion on Long County Trek," *Gazette and Chronicle,* 18 May 1916. See also Chap. 1, n. 42; E.P.S. Allen, *The 116th Battalion in France;* "The 116th Battalion in the County Town," *Gazette and Chronicle,* 1 June 1916; "Whitby Recruiting Meeting," *Globe,* 24 January 1916. (All references to the *Globe* (Toronto) are from the electronic version at http://proquest.umi.com.proxy. library.carleton.ca.) This method of recruiting and organization echoed the experience of the Pals Battalions of Kitchener's New Armies. See Peter Simpkins, *Kitchener's Army: The Raising of the New Armies, 1914-1916,* 79-103; Martin Middlebrook, *Your Country Needs You: Expansion of the British Army Infantry Divisions,* 63-84. On the value of regimental histories, see Tim Cook, "'Literary Memorials': The Great War Regimental Histories, 1919-1939," 167-90.

26 "116th Battalion on Long County Trek," *Gazette and Chronicle,* 18 May 1916.

27 "County Grants $5,000 for 116th Battalion," *Gazette and Chronicle,* 25 November 1917; "Battalion Supplies: List Necessary for Overseas Battalion Not Supplied by Government" and "Battalion Should Be Helped," *Gazette and Chronicle,* 20 April 1916.

28 "The 116th in the County Town," *Gazette and Chronicle,* 1 June 1916.

29 "Advance Guard of the 116th Come to Town," *Gazette and Chronicle,* 25 November 1915.

30 "Postal Service for Canadian Force," *Globe,* 13 February 1915. Today the Department of National Defence has an electronic message board for members of the Canadian Forces: the means of communications have changed, but the needs and purposes have not. See "Morale by Message Board!" at http://www.forces.gc.ca/site/Community/Messageboard/index_e.asp (accessed 20 May 2008); Cook, "'My Whole Heart and Soul,'" 51.

31 That "absence is easier to endure than separation" is Nigel Nicolson's observation. See Nigel Nicolson, *Portrait of a Marriage,* 217.

32 GT to MT, 17 November 1916. All mail for Canadian troops in the field passed through the hands of the Canadian Postal Corps in London, England. In 1918, it handled 68,174,000 letters, 10,226,100 newspapers, 5,332,670 parcels, and 433,000 registered letters. *Report of the Ministry,* 88, 271-72.

33 GT to MT, [23] November [1916].

34 GT to MT, [23] November [1916]; GT to MT, 29 December 1916; GT to MT, 26 March [1917].

35 GT to MT, 26 September [1916]. For more on pay arrangements, see Chap. 1, n. 37; GT to MT, 6 November [1916]. On 2 March 1916, the rate of exchange for the Canadian dollar was £1 = $4.80; 28 February 1917 $4.78 ¼; 11 November 1918 $4.86 ½. As a rough measure, therefore, £1 = $5 Canadian. £1 = 20s. (shillings) or 240d. (pence); 10s. = $2.50; $1 = 4s. = 48d; 1s. = 12d. = 25¢. See the *Times* daily Money Market column. (Hereafter, all references to the *Times* are to the paper of that name published in London, England, and unless stated otherwise are taken from the electronic version at http://infotrac.galegroup.com.proxy.library.carleton.ca.)

36 GT to MT, 17 November 1916.

37 GT to MT, 17 May [1918].

38 GT to MT, 28 April [1917].

39 GT to MT, 29 June [1918].

40 GT to MT, 25 May [1918].

41 GT to MT, 17 May [1918]; GT to MT, 29 June [1918].

42 An enterprising colleague wrote to everyone he knew in England in the hope of receiving a food parcel. GT to MT, 17 February [1917].

43 GT to MT, 20 December [1916]. May responded by sending tins, an unsustainable expedient. The quality of army food provoked loud complaint. See also GT to MT, 4 February [1917]; *Report of the Ministry*, 74-75.

44 GT to MT, 20 December [1916].

45 For considerations of fair play, and the role of food, see Craig Mantle, *The "Moral Economy" as a Theoretical Model to Explain Acts of Protest in the Canadian Expeditionary Force, 1914-1918*, 18, 25, 55, and Craig Mantle, *For Bully Beef and Biscuits: Charges of Mutiny in the 43rd Battalion, Canadian Expeditionary Force, November and December, 1917*, 1. Links at http://www.cdaacd.forces.gc.ca/cfla/engraph/research/historical_e.asp. For more on soldiers' agency, see Tony Ashworth, *Trench Warfare, 1914-1918: The Live and Let Live System*, and Leonard V. Smith, *Between Mutiny and Obedience: The Case of the French Fifth Infantry Division during World War I*.

46 GT to MT, 2 January [1917]. In letters written on 12 May [1917] and 2 July [1917], GT responded to news from May that two of their acquaintances had acquired automobiles.

47 GT to MT, 19 March [1918]. Sometimes GT was angry and bitter at the unfairness of the world that determined that the services rendered by men from the same community could be so various: GT to MT, 5 June [1917], and GT to MT, 2 August [1917]. On Hicks, see Chap. 4, n. 37.

48 GT to MT, 17 May [1918].

49 GT to MT, 27 January [1917].

50 GT to MT, [23] November [1916].

51 GT to MT, 12 May [1917].

52 GT to MT, 17 May [1918].

53 GT to MT, 5 June [1917].

54 GT to MT, 2 July [1917].

55 GT to MT, [23] November [1916].

56 GT to MT, 21 July [1918]. See also GT to MT, 7 January 1918.

57 GT to MT, [23] November [1916]. See also GT to MT, 15 December [1916].

58 GT to MT, 21 July [1918].

59 GT to MT, 24 December [1916].

60 GT to MT, 10 September 1917.

61 GT to MT, 24 December [1916]. The challenge to be more mindful of the circumstances of a writer and to caution against the tripartite characterization of the war's

phases (from enthusiasm to reality to disillusionment) is borne out in GT's wartime letters. For example, GT to MT, [23] November [1916]; GT to MT, 2 July [1917]; GT to MT, 31 August [1918]; Liddle, "British Loyalties," 523-38.

62 GT to MT, 7 January 1918.

63 GT to MT, [23] November [1916].

64 Ninety-five men from the 116th Battalion were transferred to the 18th Battalion with effect from 5 October 1916: fifty-one from "D" Company, forty-three from "A" Company, and one from "C" Company. See LAC, RG 9, series III-C-3, vol. 4203, folder 1, file 7: battalion orders 116th Canadian Infantry Battalion, 28/09/16-8/12/16, #252.5 Transfers. By the final months of 1916, the original 2nd Division had all but disappeared. During September and October 1916, 289 officers and 5,660 ORs arrived as replacements. Campbell, "Divisional Experience," 242; Tim Cook, *At the Sharp End: Canadians Fighting the Great War, 1914-1916,* vol. 1, 525, 528-29.

65 May submitted as many as three of GT's letters for publication in the *Ontario Reformer* newspaper. Soldiers' letters were frequently published in newspapers. The *Gazette and Chronicle* printed many letters from local soldiers, including: "A Whitby Township Boy in England," *Gazette and Chronicle,* 7 August 1916; "News from Soldier Boys on Overseas Service," *Gazette and Chronicle,* 24 August 1916; "Letters from the Front: Buried Bodies Blown Up," *Toronto Daily Star,* 4 November 1916. The *Times* printed a series entitled "Letters from the Front" between October 1914 and April 1917. GT to MT, 29 June [1918]. (All references to the *Toronto Daily Star* are from the electronic version at http://micromedia.pagesofthepast.ca.proxy.library.carleton.ca.)

66 GT to MT, 31 October [1916]. **Jack Burr:** born Taynham, Kent, England, 1882; moulder; enlisted Oshawa, 116th Battalion, March 1916; living at 67 1st Avenue, South Oshawa; left behind a wife and four children aged between six and twelve; died April 1959. LAC, box 1311-23, 745906 Burr, John Henry. See also Chap. 2, n. 7. Most of the local men mentioned by GT lived in South Oshawa, in the area of the original village of Oshawa, roughly bounded by modern-day Park Road to the west, Ritson Road to the east, King Street to the north, and Bloor Street to the south. The enlistment papers of CEF members are available electronically. For links to these and related resources see http://www.collectionscanada.gc.ca/genealogy/022-909-e.html.

67 GT to MT, 7 December [1916].

68 GT to MT, [23] November [1916].

69 GT to MT, 7 January 1918. **Thomas Milgate:** born Kent, England, 1881; stationary engineer's handyman; enlisted Niagara, August 1915; married and living at 42 Jackson Street, South Oshawa, a short distance from Albert Street. LAC, box 6167-54, 141973 Milgate, Thomas William Alfred. For more on Milgate, see Chap. 4, n. 19.

70 GT to MT, 22 February 1918. **Fred Cooper:** born Bath, England, 1886; moulder and machine hand; enlisted Oshawa, 116th Battalion, December 1915; had served two years in the 46th Regiment Canadian Militia; lived on the same street as GT, at No. 531; sailed on the *Olympic*; left behind a wife, a two-year-old, and a baby of one

month; won the Military Medal. LAC, box 1970-22, 745950 Cooper, Fred Frank. See also Chap. 4, n. 34.

71 GT to MT, 28 April [1917]. Knitting societies, or needle battalions, were often a part of the Red Cross effort in the local towns or district where a battalion was raised. These organizations represented a way in which women could serve. See "A Request from Lt. Col. Sam Sharpe," *Gazette and Chronicle*, 1 November 1917; "Soldiers Comforts Club," *Gazette and Chronicle*, 18 October 1917; "116th Knitting Notes," *Ontario Reformer*, 13 September 1918; W.A. Wilson and Ethel T. Raymond, "Canadian Women in the Great War," "Special Services, Heroic Deeds, etc.," vol. 6, *Canada in the Great War: An Authentic Account of the Military History of Canada from the Earliest Days to the Close of the War of Nations 1918-1921*, 176-78, 207-9.

72 On Captain Hind, Lieutenants Jacobi and Henry, and Sergeant Major Palmer, see Chap. 1, n. 42, and Chap. 2, n. 47. On the intermingling of ranks, see Cook, *At the Sharp End*, 72. One is hard pressed to imagine British ORs in similar circumstances meeting and mingling with their officers.

73 GT to MT, 28 April [1917]. **William Edward Graydon Gibbie:** born Chatham, England, 1893; player piano installer for the R.S. Williams Piano Company, Oshawa; enlisted Coburg, December 1915; Gunner, Canadian Field Artillery; arrived in England April 1916 and embarked for France July 1916; killed in action 25 March 1917, aged twenty-four; buried Highland Cemetery, Roclincourt, Pas de Calais, France. The will in his pay book specified that everything be left to his mother, Mrs. Florence Gibbie. On his gravestone are the words "Sleep on Dear Graydon. Thy Work is Done. Reward Awaits Thee. Mother." See also Chap. 1, n. 62; LAC, box 3488-54, 314661 Gibbie, Graydon; "Marking the Graves of Dead Soldiers," *Gazette and Chronicle*, 17 August 1916. The Commonwealth War Graves Commission is responsible for the records of the war dead of the British Commonwealth. Its casualty database, the Debt of Honour Register, can be found at http://www.cwgc.org (hereafter cited as CWGC) and is searchable by name.

74 GT to MT, 5 June [1917]. **John Wesley McMullen:** born Hastings County, Ontario, 1894; labourer; enlisted Oshawa, 116th Battalion, December 1915; like GT, McMullen joined the 18th Battalion in the field, 22 October 1916; died Vimy, Easter Monday, 9 April 1917; aged twenty-two; buried in Zivy Crater, Thélus. Fifty Canadian dead were placed in the crater by the Canadian Corps burial officer in 1917. Zivy and another crater, Lichfield, just to the north, are the only two Commonwealth War Graves Commission cemeteries in France that are constructed as mass graves. LAC, box 7126-23, 746055 McMullen, J.W.; Norm Christie, *For King and Empire*, vol. 3, *The Canadians at Vimy, April 1917: Arleux, April 28, 1917: Fresnoy, May 3, 1917: A Social History and Battlefield Tour*, 72-73; CWGC.

75 GT to MT, 29 August [1917]. On 15 August at 4.25 A.M., the 18th Battalion along with the rest of the Canadian Corps launched its attack on Hill 70. Total losses for the Canadian Corps 15-25 August were 9,198. G.W.L. Nicholson, *Canadian Expeditionary*

Force, 1914-1919: Official History of the Canadian Army in the First World War, 284-97 (hereafter cited as Nicholson, *C.E.F.*); LAC, RG 9, Militia and Defence, series III-D-3, vol. 4926, reel T-10721, file 398, war diary, 18th Battalion (hereafter cited as LAC, WD, 18th Battalion), August 1917; J.A. Cooper, *Fourth Canadian Infantry Brigade: History of Operations; April 1915 to Demobilization,* 23-25. Numerous important Canadian military histories, including the 1964 edition of *C.E.F.,* are available at the website of the Department of National Defence, Directorate of History and Heritage, http://www.forces.gc.ca/dhh/collections/books/engraph/home_e. asp?cat=6. The battalion war diaries of the CEF are available electronically. For links to these and related resources, see http://www.collectionscanada.gc.ca/genealogy/022-909-e.html.

76 GT to MT, 29 August [1917]. **Harry West:** born Gosport, Hampshire, England, 1886; labourer; enlisted Oshawa, 116th Battalion, February 1916; sailed on the *Olympic;* joined the 18th Battalion on the same day as GT, 22 October 1916; killed on 21 August 1917 by an enemy high-velocity shell, bursting on the road from Bully Grenay amid "D" Company, as the battalion marched into corps reserve following its engagement at Hill 70; the shell burst inflicted 52 casualties, 23 fatal. West is buried in the Aix-Noulette Communal Cemetery Extension, a short distance from the road to Bully Grenay, along which he had marched. The 18th Battalion suffered approximately 220 casualties between 9 and 21 August 1917. LAC, box 10239-28, 746141 West, Harry Charles; LAC, WD, 18th Battalion, 21 August 1917; CWGC. See also Chap. 3, n. 13. Detailed maps of the locations mentioned in the letters and notes can be found at Google Maps.

77 GT to MT, 10 September 1917. **Charles Victor Gibbs:** born Newtonville, Ontario, 1898; moulder; enlisted Oshawa, 116th Battalion, December 1915; joined the 18th Battalion in the field on 22 October 1916; spent a summer camp with the 34th Regiment; slightly wounded in his left hand by a shell on 13 May 1917 but returned to his unit seventeen days later; wounded in the leg June 1918; his wife, May Gibbs, lived in Cedar Dale in East Whitby Township. His brother, **James Gibbs:** born Newtonville, 1892; labourer; enlisted Oshawa, 116th Battalion, February 1916; transferred to the 18th Battalion October 1916; taken ill with a severe case of trench fever April 1918; sent to England. LAC, box 3493-7, 745997 Gibbs, Charles Victor; LAC, box 3494-5, 746001 Gibbs, James.

78 GT to MT, 29 June [1918].

79 GT to MT, 7 January 1918.

80 GT to MT, 25 May [1918].

81 See LAC, WD, 18th Battalion, 22 July 1917; LAC, RG 9, series III-D-1, vol. 4692, folder 51, file 4, 18th Battalion historical records, 12, 14, 22-23. On reconnaissance and scouting, see Campbell, "Divisional Experience," 85-88; Cook, *At the Sharp End,* 277-78.

82 LAC, WD, 18th Battalion, 19 August 1917.

83 GT to MT, 10 September 1917. **Thomas Dougall:** born Middlesex, England, 1897; labourer; enlisted Guelph, October 1914; arrived England April 1915; docked seven

days' pay for being absent without leave, July 1915; gained temporary commission, 18th Battalion, February 1917; awarded the French Médaille Militaire for distinguished service, April 1917. LAC, WD, 18th Battalion, 7 November 1916; 18 November 1916; 16 February 1917; 22 July 1917; 17 August 1917; 19 August 1917; LAC, box 2671-32, 53560 Dougall, Thomas.

84 He died Sunday, 19 August 1917, at No. 6 Casualty Clearing Station, Barlin. A narrative of the attack, northwest of Lens on 15 August 1917, and an account of Dougall's actions and death can be found in LAC, RG 9, series III-D-1, vol. 4692, folder 51, file 10, 18th Battalion, August 1917, battalion narratives, Operations Hill 70; CWGC.

85 GT to MT, 1 November [1917].

86 GT to MT, 1 November [1917]. GT's animus toward these men is clear but, set against their military and medical records, given in Chap. 3, n. 27, his assessment was unfair.

87 GT to MT, 22 October [1917]. In 1917, during the Lens operations, Henry Sinclair Horne commanded the British First Army, of which the Canadian Corps, commanded by Gen. Sir Arthur Currie, formed a part. Robin Neillands, *The Great War Generals on the Western Front 1914-1918,* 327; "Ages of Generals in War," *Gazette and Chronicle,* 12 October 1916.

88 GT to MT, 7 January 1918. In response to depressed conditions after the Panic of 1893, Jacob S. Coxey, a businessman with a social conscience, led a march of unemployed workers to Washington, DC. The authorities were singularly unreceptive; Coxey was arrested for trespassing on the Capitol Hill lawns. See Carlos A. Schwantes, *Coxey's Army: An American Odyssey,* 49-185.

89 GT to MT, 7 January 1918.

90 GT to MT, 14 December 1917.

91 GT to MT, 10 September 1917.

92 GT to MT, 7 February 1918.

93 GT to MT, 7 February 1918.

94 GT to MT, 24 November [1917].

95 GT to Jim, Winnie, and Mollie Timmins [November 1917]. See also Chap. 2, n. 33.

96 GT to MT, 25 November [1917]. On growing food shortages, see Gerard J. DeGroot, *Blighty: British Society in the Era of the First World War,* 210-14.

97 GT to MT, 29 August [1917]; GT to MT, 10 September 1917.

98 This quote is from Virginia Woolf, "Swift's 'Journal to Stella,'" *The Common Reader,* vol. 2, ed. Andrew McNellie, 70.

Chapter 1: "about 35 yds from Fritz"

Letter 1

1 Niagara Camp was the western Ontario district mobilization and training facility, located just outside Niagara-on-the-Lake. By March, a manpower crisis was imminent. In April, enlistments fell, prompted by improved employment opportunities,

higher wages, and the view that the war was a European problem. GT enlisted at the height of the volunteer recruitment drive; in no month after June 1916 did more than ten thousand men volunteer. On 15 May 1916, GT reported to camp as a private with the 116th Overseas Battalion, C.E.F. Keshen, *Propaganda and Censorship,* 41; Morton, *When Your Number's Up,* 60; Rutherdale, *Hometown Horizons,* 52-53, 81-87; Barbara Wilson, *Ontario and the First World War,* xliii-liii; LAC, box 9698-43, 3235822 Timmins, George. Nicholson gives 34,913 enlistments in March 1916 and records only 4,761 voluntary enlistments at the time of Vimy, in April 1917. Nicholson, *C.E.F.,* 212-22.

2 May (Dunn) Timmins: born Cradley Heath, Staffordshire, England, 1883; died in Oshawa, 1955, a few months after celebrating her fiftieth wedding anniversary. GT died in 1974.

3 The 98th Battalion began recruiting in Welland and Lincoln counties, Ontario, under Lt. Col. H.A. Rose, November 1915; 36 officers and 1,050 ORs arrived in England, 25 July 1916; used as a reinforcing unit, it was disbanded as an entity in August 1917. See LAC, RG 9 and RG 24, box 19 (Parts 3, 4, and 5), Guides to Sources Relating to Units of the Canadian Expeditionary Force and the Canadian Militia; Keshen, *Propaganda and Censorship,* 42; Morton, *When Your Number's Up,* 8-10.

4 GT is referring to the many soldiers who were discharged as medically unfit; see Chap. 1, n. 86.

5 May Timmins was the daughter of GT's half-brother, Gideon Timmins, and his wife, Rose.

6 The last request is written on the back of the last page of the letter.

Letter 2

7 The Brotherhood of St. Andrew was an Anglican organization. For more on the brotherhood, see *Handbook of the Brotherhood of St. Andrew in Canada.* Alongside the Catholic Army Huts, the Young Men's Christian Association, and others, it provided servicemen with reading and writing materials, and entertainment, free cigarettes, and chewing gum. See *Report of the Ministry,* 485-514; Charles W. Bishop, *The Canadian Y.M.C.A. in the Great War: The Official Record of the Activities of the Canadian Y.M.C.A. in Connection with the Great War of 1914-1918;* Rev. I.J.E. Daniel and Rev. D.A. Casey, *For God and Country: War Works of Canadian Knights of Columbus Catholic Army Huts;* "Letters from the Boys at the Front Made Possible by the Y.M.C.A.," *Gazette and Chronicle,* 8 February 1917.

8 Lillie Timmins was the daughter of GT's half-brother, Gideon. The *Corona* was a Lake Ontario ferry built in 1896 to carry 310 passengers. Oshawans waiting to see their friends illustrate the success the Department of Militia and Defence's policy of community recruitment. Canada, Parliament, *Sessional Papers* 1917, 21, n. 22, "List of Shipping Issued by the Department of Marine and Fisheries Being a List of Vessels in the Registry Books of the Dominion of Canada on 31 December 1916," 21; Hoig, *Reminiscences and Recollections,* 154-56; Rutherford, *Hometown Horizons,* 87.

9 Church parades were compulsory and generally unpopular. The chaplains were also officers, complicating their relations with the men. GT gave his religious affiliation as Church of England. John Ellis, *Eye-Deep in Hell: Trench Warfare in World War I,* 155-56; Isabelle Diane Losinger, "Officer-Man Relations in the Canadian Expeditionary Force, 1914-1918," 118-27; Cook, *At the Sharp End,* 395-96; Duff W. Crerar, *Padres in No Man's Land: Canadian Chaplains in the Great War.*

10 Perhaps GT was reflecting the first (optimistic) reports of the Battle of the Somme. See the *Toronto Daily Star,* 7 July 1916; Nicholson, *C.E.F.,* 160-200; "116th to Go Overseas in July," *Gazette and Chronicle,* 29 June 1916.

11 Sixteen men of the 116th Battalion were injured and at least one man of the 169th Battalion was killed when an electrical storm struck the Niagara Peninsula on 2 June 1916. Ten thousand troops were on a twenty-four-kilometre route march, and the lightning jumped across the steel bayonets affixed to the men's rifles. Training in local areas was intended to foster local community support and involvement, encouraging the morale of the recruits. "Men of 116th Battalion Injured at Queenston," *Gazette and Chronicle,* 8 June 1916.

12 For information on army pay arrangements, see Chap. 1, nn. 30, 37.

Letter 3

13 GT sailed on the RMS *Olympic,* leaving Halifax with the 116th Battalion on 23 July 1916 and arriving in Liverpool on 31 July 1916. A converted luxury liner, the *Olympic* was the sister ship of the ill-fated *Titanic.* Ironically, in 1914, the White Star Line planned construction of a replacement for the *Titanic* (named the *Germanic*), plans scuttled by the outbreak of the war. In 1911, the *Olympic,* the flagship of the White Star Line, was the world's largest steamship, carrying 1,054 first-class passengers, 510 second-class, 1,020 third-class, and 860 crew. Refitted for wartime service, she carried 6,000 officers and men. Nicknamed *Old Reliable* by the people of Halifax, she transported 70,000 Canadian troops across the Atlantic. "116th Reaches England," *Gazette and Chronicle,* 3 August 1916; Simon Mills, *R.M.S. Olympic: The Old Reliable,* 1, 15, 42-47, 60; Nicholson, *C.E.F.,* 530.

14 Although unrestricted submarine warfare began only on 1 February 1917, by the end of 1916, German U-boats were already sinking a monthly average of over fifty thousand tons of Allied shipping in the English Channel alone. Nicholson, *C.E.F.,* 236; Bruce Cane, *It Made You Think of Home: The Haunting Journal of Deward Barnes, CEF 1916-1919,* 38-39.

15 GT and MT hailed from the Black Country, so-called because of the pollution from the coal and iron industries. See Dianne Pye, "It Was No 'Bed of Roses' for Some," *Black Country Bugle,* 17 November 2005, http://www.blackcountrybugle.co.uk (accessed 29 May 2008).

16 "Pinners" or pinafores were a particularly British fashion and consisted of an apron, usually with a bib. "Collars" were stiff and upright, or turned down, detachable, and worn by the working classes for "good."

17 Social Darwinists and eugenicists had popularized the term "race suicide" to describe what they understood to be the decline of the physical and mental quality of the race, highlighted by Britain's shortcomings in the Second South African War, 1899-1902. See G.R. Searle, *Eugenics and Politics in Britain, 1900-1914.* To social Darwinists and the eugenicists, GT's "thousands" would constitute part of the problem; the "wrong classes" were breeding.

18 MT's father's name, Esau Dunn, appears on a list of thirty-four chainmakers employed by Messrs. John Green of Old Hill at the start of the First World War. John Green and Walker & Sons were Old Hill's leading employers in 1914. See Allen, "Chainmakers"; "Save the mark," originally a mantra to avert an evil omen, had come to be "used (frequently ironically) chiefly in writing to apologise for a preceding or following word or phrase." *OED*, vol. 9, 380.

19 By December 1916, there were 7,240 officers and 128,980 ORs of the CEF in England, with another 2,526 officers and 105,640 ORs in France. The main Canadian camps in England were Bramshott, Witley, Seaford, and Bordon. Nicholson, *C.E.F.*, 224.

Fragment 1

20 In August, GT was at Bordon Camp in Hampshire. The *Gazette and Chronicle* asked readers to note the spelling of the Camp's name, for mailing purposes. See "116th Battalion at Bordon Camp," *Gazette and Chronicle*, 17 August 1916.

21 In early October, battalion orders for the 116th Battalion specified that in the Canadian divisional area, public houses were out of bounds for Canadian troops except between 6 P.M. and 9 P.M. On Sundays, food and non-alcoholic beverages could be purchased at pubs outside those hours. LAC, RG 9, series III-C-3, vol. 4203, folder 1, file 7: battalion orders 116th Canadian Infantry Battalion, 28/09/16-8/12/16, battalion orders for Sunday and Monday, 1 and 2 October 1916, #248.6. The average weekly convictions for drunkenness in England and Wales fell by 86 percent between 1914 and 1918. See Arthur Marwick, *The Deluge: British Society and the First World War*, 62-67; "British Are Drinking Less," *Gazette and Chronicle*, 2 November 1916; Henry Carter, *The Control of the Drink Trade: A Contribution to National Efficiency, 1915-1917.*

22 A pint of bitter was 3d. before the war, 5d. by the end of 1916, 1s. 3d. by September 1917. In August 1916, the *Times* reported that £182 million was spent on drink, £68 million of which went to the state. "Profiteering in Drink," *Times*, 3 September 1917; "The National Drink Bill," *Times*, 18 August 1916; "30,000 Public Houses May Close in Britain," *Gazette and Chronicle*, 22 March 1917.

23 Food prices rose faster than the rate of inflation. For the family of an unskilled man, the cost of living rose 81 percent between 1914 and 1918. John Stevenson, *British History 1914-45*, 80.

24 The first known performance of "O Canada" was in Quebec City on 24 June 1880. The song became very popular in Quebec but was not heard in English Canada likely until the visit of the Prince of Wales in 1901, and then only in an unsuccessful translation.

In 1908, Robert Stanley Weir, a Montreal lawyer, produced a version that won widespread acceptance. GT is probably referring to this version. *Encyclopedia of Canada*, vol. 4, 382-84.

25 Mobilization of the 84th Battalion was authorized on 29 July 1915; raised in Toronto; the 84th (36 officers and 913 ORs) arrived in Liverpool, 28 June 1916; broken up for reinforcements, mainly to the 75th Battalion, but also to the 73rd; ceased to exist September 1916. LAC, RG 9 and RG 24, box 19 (Parts 3, 4, and 5), Guides to Sources Relating to Units of the Canadian Expeditionary Force and the Canadian Militia.

26 For additional accounts of the crossing, see "116th Reaches England," *Gazette and Chronicle*, 3 August 1916; "A Whitby Township Boy in England," *Gazette and Chronicle*, 7 August 1916; "News from Soldier Boys on Overseas Service," *Gazette and Chronicle*, 24 August 1916.

27 The 1911 Census of Canada records 169 Poles in Oshawa. *1911 Census of Canada, Table vii, Origins of People by Sub-Districts*, 234-35. Some Poles were interned under the 1914 War Measures Act as enemy aliens. In 1914, Poland was divided between the Austro-Hungarian, German, and Russian empires. See Henry Radecki, *A Member of a Distinguished Family: The Polish Group in Canada*, 46.

28 Hughes' inspection establishes the date of this fragment as Monday, 25 September 1916. Lt. Gen. Sir Sam Hughes, the controversial Canadian minister of war, was removed from office by Prime Minister Sir Robert Borden in the fall of 1916. LAC, RG 9, series III-C-3, vol. 4203, folder 1, file 7: battalion orders 116th Canadian Infantry Battalion, 28/09/16–8/12/16, Visit of the Minister of Militia and Defence; R.G. Brown, "Sir Samuel Hughes," in the *Dictionary of Canadian Biography Online*, Library and Archives Canada, http://www.biographi.ca.

Letter 4

29 Bramshott Camp, set up in the fall of 1915, a reserve depot for the replacement battalions headquartered at Shorncliffe, the overseas home of the Canadian 2nd Division. Nicholson, *C.E.F.*, 224; "Interesting Letter from Major G.W.P. Every," *Gazette and Chronicle*, 21 September 1916; "The 116th at Bramshott," *Gazette and Chronicle*, 9 November 1916.

30 Canadian troops, better paid than their British counterparts, inevitably drove up prices near their camps. A Canadian private received $1 (4s.) per day, with a field allowance of ten cents per day. Corporals were paid $1.10 per day, with the same field allowance. A British private received only 1s. a day. Among the Dominion troops, only the New Zealanders were better paid than the Canadians. The Dominion soldiers were known by some as the "fuckin' five bobbers" (1 bob = 1s.). Partly as a result of this, in 1916, Ottawa began to hold back half the Canadian soldier's pay. By contrast, the French soldier received the British equivalent of 2½ d. a day and the German 1¾ d. Before the war, Thomas Jeyes, an iron moulder at the Malle in Oshawa, earned $3.50 a day. In Oshawa, in the summer of 1911, the Board of Works

engaged general labourers at 15½¢ an hour and skilled men at 20¢ to 30¢ an hour. Morton, *When Your Number's Up,* 12, 50, 87-88, 235-37; J.G. Fuller, *Troop Morale and Popular Culture in the British and Dominion Armies 1914-1918,* 76; Ellis, *Eye-Deep in Hell,* 147; LAC, box 4837-5, 746025 Jeyes, Thomas; Hood, *Oshawa,* 162-63; J.M. Winter and Jean-Louis Robert, *Capital Cities at War: Paris, London, Berlin 1914-1919;* on the rate of exchange, see Introduction, n. 35. Also see GT to MT, 6 November [1916].

31 In London, in March 1916, there were a hundred bus conductresses, by February 1917, 2,500. Marwick, *The Deluge,* 90-91.

32 Del Monico's was a popular restaurant at the corner of Shaftesbury Avenue and Piccadilly Circus. In 1942, it was reopened as the Rainbow Club for American GIs. John Costello, *Love, Sex & War: Changing Values 1939-45,* 288-89.

33 "Tommy" was short for "Thomas Atkins." Its derivation variously ascribed, the name stood for the archetypal British Army private on army forms from 1815. See Richard Holmes, *Tommy: The British Soldier on the Western Front, 1914-1918,* xv-xvi; John Brophy and Eric Partridge, *The Daily Telegraph Dictionary of Tommies' Songs and Slang, 1914-1918,* 193; Randle Gray with Christopher Argyle, *Chronicle of the First World War,* vol. 1, 333; "'Jack' and 'Tommy': How the British Sailor and Soldier Came by Their Nicknames," *Gazette and Chronicle,* 11 November 1915.

34 In 1914, a Canadian division consisted of three brigades of four battalions apiece, a battalion of eight companies of 125 men apiece, divided into platoons. The British Army shared this structure until 1914, when it adopted the continental model of four companies of 250 men, divided into four platoons, a decision that posed serious organizational, administrative, and training problems for the Canadians. The 4th Canadian Infantry Brigade comprised the 18th, 19th, 20th, and 21st Battalions, all raised in Ontario. See Bill Rawling, *Surviving Trench Warfare: Technology and the Canadian Corps;* Morton, *When Your Number's Up,* 33-34, 159-65; Cooper, *Fourth Canadian Infantry Brigade;* Cook, *At the Sharp End,* 89-93.

35 In early October 1916, the Canadian Corps was involved in heavy fighting around Courcelette, in the battles of Transloy Ridges (1-20 October) and Ancre Heights (1-11 October). The operation cost the 1st and 2nd Canadian Divisions heavy casualties. GT joined the 18th Battalion as one of the replacements for these losses. He remained with the 18th Battalion, 4th Brigade, 2nd Division, CEF for the rest of the war. Nicholson, *C.E.F.,* 167, 180-98; H.E.R. Steele, *Canadians in France, 1915-1918,* 65-87; LAC, box 9698-43, 3235822 Timmins, George.

36 At least twelve Zeppelins raided London and the Midlands on Saturday, 23 September 1916, dropping a total of 371 bombs, killing 40 people (24 men, 12 women, 4 children) and injuring 130. The two Zeppelins downed were new naval airships: the L33 crash landed and was torched by her crew before they surrendered; the L32 was shot down by 2nd Lt. F. Sowsey of 39 Squadron, the Royal Flying Corps. On the night of 25 September, six to nine Zeppelins dropped 127 bombs, killing 43 and injuring 31. In 1916, a total of 311 people were killed and 752 injured in air raids on Britain. British soldiers

nicknamed a meal of sausage and mashed potato "Zeppelin in a cloud." Great Britain, Ministry of Information, *Chronology of the War: 1916-1917*, vol. 2, 112-13, 115. "The Attack on London," *Times*, 25 September 1916; "Zeppelin Crew's Funeral," *Times*, 28 September 1916; Gray, *Chronicle*, vol. 1, 249.

37 GT assigned $20 a month to his wife. In 1914, a Canadian soldier's wife with three children qualified for a $20 monthly separation allowance from the Canadian government, as long as her husband assigned at least one-half of his regular pay to his dependents. LAC, box 9698-43, 3235822 Timmins, George. See also order-in-council, 17 August 1914, P.C. 2264, and order-in-council, 1 April 1915, P.C. 2553, reprinted in A.F. Duguid, *Official History of the Canadian Forces in the Great War, 1914-1919*, vol. 1, appendices and maps, 61-62, http://www.forces.gc.ca/dhh/collections/books/engraph/home_e.asp?cat=6.

Letter 5

38 GT's numerical notation provides an indication of how much of his correspondence has disappeared. It is not known when he began to number his letters or when he stopped.

39 On 29 October 1916, the 18th Battalion, relieved in the front line by the 20th Battalion, went into brigade reserve at Bully. The 18th relieved the 20th Battalion in the front line on 4 November 1916. LAC, WD, 18th Battalion, October 1916, November 1916.

40 Mary Dunn was MT's sister, then living in England. In the 1920s, she immigrated to Canada. She died in Oshawa, September 1975.

41 LAC, box 1311-23, 745906 Burr, John Henry. For more on Burr, see Introduction, n. 66.

42 When GT joined the 116th Battalion, Cptn. A.F. Hind commanded "D" Company, consisting of fellow Oshawans. GT is likely referring to the transfer of some of the men of the 116th, in particular those of "D" Company, to other battalions and their dispatch to France. GT was transferred to the 18th Battalion effective 5 October and joined the 18th in the field on 22 October 1916. That day the 18th Battalion's war diary records the arrival of eighty-two ORs as reinforcements. The battalion went back into the front line at noon the next day. **Alfred Hind:** born 1877, Oxfordshire, England; chief constable of Oshawa; served in the 34th Regiment of Canadian Militia; enlisted Oshawa, 116th Battalion, January 1916; married, with four children; lived on Simcoe Street, South Oshawa; attained the rank of major; mentioned in dispatches; survived the war; died 1930. LAC, WD, 18th Battalion, October 1916; LAC, RG 9, series III-D-3, vol. 4945, reel T-10753, war diary, 116th Battalion (hereafter cited as LAC, WD, 116th Battalion), September 1918; "116th Battalion on Long County Trek," *Gazette and Chronicle*, 18 May 1916; LAC, Hind, Alfred Frederick, Major.

43 Senator cigarettes were manufactured by the B. Houde Co., Quebec, which was acquired by the Imperial Tobacco Company in 1903. Senator was considered a

small-volume brand. Margot Diochon, Corporate Library, Imperial Tobacco Limited, to Y.A. Bennett, 9 September 1994; D. Winter, *Death's Men: Soldiers of the Great War,* 149.

44 **Jack Cash:** born Limerick, Ireland, 1877; farm labourer; enlisted Toronto, November 1914; served with the 20th Battalion September 1915 to May 1917, when he developed tuberculosis; married Mrs. Batten from Oshawa before leaving for Europe; died in Oshawa, January 1967. The Military Medal was instituted on 25 March 1916 to recognize acts of bravery performed by non-commissioned officers and men of British and Dominion forces. LAC, box 1563-8, 57278 Cash, John; "Medals to Men in Ranks," *Gazette and Chronicle,* 31 August 1916; "Bravery in the Field, Awards of Military Medals, Canadian Contingent," *Times,* 22 December 1916 (4 A.M. edition). His service number is incorrectly given in the *Times* as 57378; "More Honours Given Toronto Soldiers," *Toronto Daily Star,* 13 January 1917.

45 **J.W. Bircham:** born West Hartlepool, England, 1882; a carpenter; enlisted Oshawa, October 1914; left for England May 1915; served with the 34th and 20th Battalions; embarked for France September 1915; awarded the Distinguished Conduct Medal January 1917; survived the war and returned to Canada May 1919. **Charles Bircham:** born West Hartlepool, England, 1886; range mounter; brother of J.W. Bircham; also in the 20th; spent four years in France. **Bert Norris:** born Middlesex, England, 1889; machinist; enlisted Toronto, November 1914; served first in the 34th Regiment; sergeant in "B" Company of the 20th Battalion; awarded the Distinguished Conduct Medal in September 1917 "for conspicuous gallantry and devotion to duty"; wounded by a machine-gun bullet through the left thigh at Passchendaele 12 November 1917; died in Canada, 1958. **Albert Wallace** has proven elusive. Cooper, in *Fourth Canadian Infantry Brigade,* reports that the corps commander visited the 4th Brigade at Bully Grenay on Saturday 28 October and presented medals to the men of the 20th Battalion. The 18th and 20th Battalion WDs give the same date. It would appear, therefore, that GT must have confused Saturday with Sunday. See LAC, box 742-39, 57067 Bircham, (James) William; LAC, box 742-36, 58078 Bircham, Charles; LAC, box 7368-7, 57464 Norris, Bert; LAC, WD, 18th Battalion, October 1916; LAC, RG 9, Militia and Defence, series III-D-3, vol. 4930, reel T-10730, file 408, War Diary, 20th Battalion (hereafter cited as LAC, WD, 20th Battalion), October 1916; Chap. 1, n. 77.

46 Widows' pensions were not a right. When the war began, a deserving widow could receive from the Canadian government three-tenths of her husband's pay and an additional one-tenth for each child. These rates increased several times; by the end of 1915, the widow of a private might receive $22 per month, with an additional $5 for each child. No monies were paid to sons and daughters beyond the ages of sixteen and seventeen, respectively. Morton, *When Your Number's Up,* 254; Desmond Morton, "Supporting Soldiers' Families: Separation Allowance, Assigned Pay, and the Unexpected," in *Canada and the First World War: Essays in Honour of Robert Craig Brown,* ed. David MacKenzie, 194-229; Morton, *Fight or Pay.*

47 [the line]: censored but legible.

48 While a unit was on active service, the job of censor fell to the battalion officers, who were generally very strict. Losinger, "Officer-Man Relations," 195-208.

Letter 6

49 The 18th Battalion was in the front line in the Calonne sector 4-10 November. The line was quiet until the night of 7 November when, at 10:30 P.M., an enemy wiring party was spotted. Sergeant Dougall fired a Lewis gun at the enemy, "who were only 30 yards [27 metres] away. Many were heard to cry out." LAC, WD, 18th Battalion, November 1916; Cooper, *Fourth Canadian Infantry Brigade.*

50 Throughout the CEF, the usual pattern of duty saw each battalion in a brigade rotated between front line service, close support, or brigade reserve behind the line. Whole brigades and divisions were similarly rotated to allow time for training and the absorption of replacements. A battalion could expect to spend roughly one-third of its time in the line or in close reserve. The 18th's WD reflects this pattern clearly. See also Cook, *At the Sharp End,* 217-54.

51 GT understated conditions. It had rained on sixteen of the twenty-one days prior to 8 November 1916. Nicholson, *C.E.F.,* 188-92; Gray, *Chronicle,* vol. 1, 258-60.

52 Florence Dunn was MT's sister.

53 Bombers, grenade-throwing specialists, were handpicked and received advanced training. In the 18th Battalion, in November 1917, five non-commissioned officers (NCOs) and forty men were attached to the battalion bombers, the same number found in each of the four companies in the battalion, for a total of twenty-five NCOs and two hundred men. In both the 19th and 20th Battalions, the battalion bombers were carried on the strength of the companies from which they had been drawn, but they came under the command of an officer specially detailed to their command. The company bombers remained under the command of their company's commanding officer. LAC, RG 9, series III, vol. 4115, folder 1, file 12, Establishment. Infantry Battalions, Change in, and Special List of Employed Men of 18th, 19th, 20th, and 21st Bns, November 1917; Rawling, *Surviving Trench Warfare,* 55-58; Cook, *At the Sharp End,* 209-12; Shelford Bidwell and Dominick Graham, *Fire-Power: British Army, Weapons and Theories of War 1904-1945,* 118; for more on grenades, see Chap. 1, nn. 64, 99.

54 Jack Long Sr. boarded at Rose Mitchell's house, next door to the Timmins family on Albert Street.

Letter 7

55 In December 1915, the YMCA distributed 300,000 sheets of paper. Charges for some of its services, especially its canteen services, led to criticism from soldiers. After June 1917, the YMCA distributed non-alcoholic drinks to soldiers gratis. From June to December 1918, its canteens served 270,000 gallons of tea, 62,400 gallons of cocoa, 10,000 gallons of coffee, and 50,900 gallons of cold drink using 5,985 cases

of condensed milk and 280,000 pounds of sugar. Bishop, *The Canadian Y.M.C.A. in the Great War*, 16-17, 39, 47, and 208; *Report of the Ministry*, 508-9. (1 imperial gallon = 4.546 litres; 1 pound = 0.454 kilograms.)

56 The 18th Battalion was in the front line from 4 November to 10 November in Calonne, Sector II (Maroc), and again from 16 November to 22 November when it moved into brigade reserve. LAC, WD, 18th Battalion, November 1916.

57 Sarah was MT's sister. Henry Dunn was her brother. He lived in Ocean Beach, California, and enlisted 1 September 1917. LAC, box 2749-5, 2601823 Dunn, Harry.

58 The standard white loaf both lost its whiteness through the addition first of wheat husks and then other cereals and gained in nutritional value. On the day that GT was writing, the British Board of Trade received extensive powers to curb food waste, control markets, and regulate prices. Rationing was still a relatively limited practice, subject to regional variations and local initiatives. The first Public Meals Order, limiting the number of courses a restaurant could serve, was introduced on 5 December 1916. See Trevor Wilson, *The Myriad Faces of War: Britain and the Great War 1914-1918*, 513-16; Richard van Emden and Steve Humphries, *All Quiet on the Home Front: An Oral History of Life in Britain during the First World War*, 189-219.

59 On wartime knitting societies, see Introduction, n. 71.

60 In the Somme area, the first snow fell on the night of 17 November 1916. Gray, *Chronicle*, vol. 1, 264.

61 The rifle was probably a British Lee-Enfield. The CEF's Canadian-made Ross rifle was replaced (except for those used by sniping specialists) in June 1916. Its serious deficiencies included its intolerance to dirt. Rawling, *Surviving Trench Warfare*, 11-12, 34-35, 63-66, 71-72; Morton, *When Your Number's Up*, 31-32.

62 In fact it was his son, Edward Robert William Gibbie Jr., who was ill. **Gibbie Jr.:** born Chatham, England, 1899; machinist; enlisted 116th Battalion, Oshawa, December 1915; only five feet one and a half inches tall and underage; sailed on the *Olympic* with his father; dangerously ill with meningitis October 1916; hospitalized for five months; hospitalized again September 1917; medical board ruled he should be returned to Canada on grounds of age, small physique, and the severity of the illness experienced, November 1917; returned May 1918; died in Toronto, 1980. **Edward Robert William Gibbie Sr.:** born Stepney, London, England, 1871; boxmaker; enlisted 116th Battalion, Oshawa, December 1915; overage, discharge recommended August 1916 at Bramshott; served in the 238th Canadian Forestry Corps; embarked for Canada October 1917; died 1938. LAC, box 3488-52, 745995 Gibbie, Edward Robert William, Senior; LAC, box 3488-53, 745996 Gibbie, Edward Robert William, Junior. A photograph of Edward Gibbie Sr. can be found in *The Ontario Regiment, R.C.A.C., 125 Years: 14 October-9 December 1990*, Robert McLaughlin Gallery, Civic Centre, Oshawa, Ontario.

63 An ointment to relieve stiff joints, it was used to combat lice. A wartime advertisement boasted that it could cure salt rheum, "eczema, ulcers, abscesses, bloodpoisoning, piles, cold sores, chapped hands, chilblains, eruptions, etc." A box cost

fifty cents. Morton, *When Your Number's Up*, 140; "Zam-Buk Cured in 2 Months," *Gazette and Chronicle*, 3 February 1916.

64   Grenades, small bombs thrown by hand, invented in the mid-fifteenth century, had by the mid-seventeenth century produced grenadiers, only to fall out of use two hundred years later. The Russo-Japanese War, 1904-05, revived military interest in grenades. Kenneth Macksey, *The Penguin Encyclopedia of Weapons and Military Technology*, 156; Bidwell and Graham, *Fire-Power*, 124-25; Cook, *At the Sharp End*, 209-12; Chap. 1, nn. 99, 110.

65   **Henry Winship:** born Gateshead, England, 1880; labourer; enlisted Toronto, November 1914; had served with the 4th Battalion, Durham Light Infantry; served in France with the 20th Battalion; survived the war and returned to Canada May 1919. LAC, box 10497-49, 57536 Winship, Harry.

Letter 8

66   Miss McLeod was an Oshawa teacher and close friend of the Timmins family who wrote regularly to GT. It is not known whether any of this correspondence survives.

67   The green envelope ensured that the writer's own officers, that is, his commanding officer or one of the battalion officers, did not censor the letter, but it was still liable to scrutiny at the base, and infractions were punished. One Canadian sergeant found himself a private after writing that an officer was a "silly bloody ass." Losinger, "Officer-Man Relations," 205.

68   Reserve could mean being as close to the front line as the third line of forward trenches, or anywhere from one to fifteen kilometres behind the front lines. GT was behind the lines but not beyond the sight of German artillery spotters. The 18th Battalion went into brigade reserve on 22 November; it is therefore possible that this letter was written on 23 November 1916. LAC, WD, 18th Battalion, November 1916.

69   Approximately 1.5 kilometres north of GT's position, the model village of Maroc, with houses built on a single pattern, with identical gardens, largely undamaged but deserted. Corrigall, *The Twentieth: The History of the Twentieth Canadian Battalion, Central Ontario Regiment, Canadian Expeditionary Force*, 96.

70   The term "Fritz," a diminutive of "Friedrich," denoted a German soldier or soldiers (*OED*, vol. 6, 205). After 1915, the term was largely replaced by "Jerry" (*OED*, vol. 8, 219). Canadian troops also used "Heinie," a diminutive of "Heinrich" (*OED*, vol. 7, 108), and "Boche," a French term of abuse for Germans. Gray, *Chronicle*, vol. 1, 316.

71   Snipers were an elite band of men who accepted great danger in exchange for considerable independence in the discharge of their duties, rather like bombers. Trench mortars were a kind of "pocket artillery," used mainly against enemy machine-gun nests and observation posts. They had some success cutting barbed wire but were unpopular with the men in the trenches since they often drew retaliatory artillery fire. LAC, WD, 18th Battalion, November 1916; Morton, *When Your Number's Up*, 78; Rawling, *Surviving Trench Warfare*, 10-36, 50-55, 64-65; Ashworth, *Trench*

Warfare, 64-69, 161-65; Nicholson, *C.E.F.*, 155-59; Cook, *At the Sharp End*, 283-90, 314-20.

72 Rains in October and November 1916 postponed some military actions. Gen. Sir Douglas Haig, the commander-in-chief of the British Expeditionary Force, wrote on 21 November 1916: "The ground, sodden with rain and broken up everywhere by innumerable shell-holes, can only be described as a morass." Maj. Gen. Sir David Watson, commanding the 4th Canadian Division, reported to Canadian Corps Headquarters that "the men's clothing became so coated with mud, great coat, trousers, puttees and boots sometimes weighing 120 pounds [54 kilograms] that many could not carry out relief." Nicholson, *C.E.F.*, 197; Robin Prior and Trevor Wilson, "Haig, Douglas, First Earl Haig (1861-1928)," in *Oxford Dictionary of National Biography*, vol. 24, ed. H.C.G. Matthew and Brian Harrison, 456-64, online ed., ed. Lawrence Goldman, May 2008, http://www.oxforddnb.com.proxy.library.carleton. ca/view/article/33633; Brian Bond and Nigel Cave, eds., *Haig: A Reappraisal 70 Years On*; Ashworth, *Trench Warfare*, 1-40.

73 These were sentry positions, usually occupied by two or three men some distance forward of the front line in no man's land. The listening posts could be deliberately constructed as part of the front line system or just convenient shell holes. The objective was to edge as close as possible to the enemy's line, to listen for any sounds that might signal unusual activity, including an attack. Cook, *At the Sharp End*, 281-82.

74 The rubber boots, which looked like fishermen's waders, were issued in late 1915. They were cold, they were treacherous on slick duckboards, and they did not permit feet to breathe, thereby accelerating the onset of trench foot. Ellis, *Eye-Deep in Hell*, 48; D. Winter, *Death's Men*, 26; Cook, *At the Sharp End*, 240-42.

75 The earthworks were likely undermined by rain so that GT and his fellow sentries had to make their way back from the listening post not by way of the connecting sap but overland through no man's land. Barbed wire, a nineteenth-century innovation used on American cattle ranches, was adopted by all the belligerents but especially the French and the Germans. Often fifteen metres deep, in multiple belts with breaks at strategic points guarded by machine-gun nests, the heavier artillery alone could sometimes punch holes in the wire. Martin Van Creveld, *Technology and War: From 2000 B.C. to the Present*, 176; Ellis, *Eye-Deep in Hell*, 24-25; Nicholson, *C.E.F.*, 189; Morton, *When Your Number's Up*, 153; "Barbed Wire in Warfare," *Gazette and Chronicle*, 29 June 1916.

76 The distance between trenches varied enormously from sector to sector. Men in the listening posts feared the gaseous effects of indigestible army rations that might alert the enemy to their location. Ellis, *Eye-Deep in Hell*, 24; Morton, *When Your Number's Up*, 142; Ashworth, *Trench Warfare*, 4-7.

77 Instituted on 4 December 1854 during the Crimean War, the Distinguished Conduct Medal was awarded to non-commissioned officers and private soldiers for gallant

conduct and distinguished service. J.H. De Wolfe, *Our Heroes in the Great War: Giving the Facts and Details of Canada's Part in the Greatest War in History*, 324.

78   Canadian casualties on the Somme in 1916 were 24,029; Rawling gives a total figure of 21,793 Canadian Corps casualties for the period 1 September-20 October 1916. Nicholson, *C.E.F.*, 198; Rawling, *Surviving Trench Warfare*, 239. See also Christopher Duffy, *Through German Eyes: The British and the Somme 1916*.

79   College Hill is an area of Oshawa. **Stan Harrison:** born Topcroft, Norfolk, England, 1891; labourer and moulder; enlisted Niagara, 37th Battalion, June 1915; joined the 18th Battalion 2 June 1916; granted ten days' leave to Blighty 24 September 1917; arrested as an absentee and returned to France under escort 31 October 1917; rejoined the 18th Battalion and court-martialled 9 December 1917; sentenced to ninety days' Field Punishment No. 1; general officer commanding 4th Canadian Infantry Brigade subsequently remitted thirty days of his sentence, substituting a forfeit of twenty-seven days pay; wounded 1 April 1918, multiple shrapnel pieces in the right hand, left thigh, and penis; recovery took four months; absent without leave for four days and fifteen minutes over Christmas 1918, for which he forfeited his pay; spent twenty-three months in France; injury to his hand left him unable to resume his work as a moulder. Hood, *Oshawa*, 234; Hoig, *Reminiscences and Recollections*, 139; LAC, box 4110-45, 409232 Harrison, Stanley Russell.

80   "Jake" was American slang meaning excellent, admirable, fine, okay (*OED*, vol. 3, 181). See Fleming, *Wartime Letters*, 239.

81   The debate over conscription dominated much of 1917; the Military Service Act became law on 29 August 1917. Most of Canada's First World War soldiers were volunteers. De Wolfe, *Our Heroes*, 323-24; Morton, *When Your Number's Up*, 62-70; Thomas P. Socknat, *Witness against War: Pacifism in Canada, 1900-1945*.

82   Between 1914 and 1918, 3,240,984 tons were shipped across the English Channel to provide each man with 4,300 calories a day. Nutritionally sufficient, the front line diet (a fairly steady supply of bully beef, biscuits, and bread), even if it reached the men under fire, still left many feeling perpetually hungry. In the winter of 1917-18, the German U-boats played havoc with supplies. A government campaign urging everyone to "Eat less and save shipping" quickly became "Eat less and save shitting." Food and hunger become persistent themes in GT's later letters. D. Winter, *Death's Men*, 147-49; Ellis, *Eye-Deep in Hell*, 125-33; Morton, *When Your Numbers Up*, 140-43; Gordon Reid, *Poor Bloody Murder*, 129-30, 151-52; Malcolm Brown, *Tommy Goes to War*, 78-83.

Letter 9

83   The 18th Battalion was in brigade support, Calonne, Sector II (Maroc). LAC, WD, 18th Battalion, December 1916.

84   GT is likely referring to Mrs. Louisa May Foster, who was living at 497 Albert Street in February 1917 when her son Charles Foster enlisted with the 182nd Battalion. LAC, box 3226-20, 868434 Foster, Charles.

85 The 18th Battalion's WD records bath and clothing parades at Bully Grenay on 26 November and 17 December. The ideal of a bath once a week was often not achieved; once a month was common. Clothing was sterilized and disinfected, but the lice eggs usually survived to hatch after two or three hours of exposure to body heat. Only in 1918 was it realized that lice excretions were responsible for trench fever, which, in 1917, accounted for 15 percent of all cases of sickness in the British Expeditionary Force. LAC, WD, 18th Battalion, November 1916; December 1916; George G. Nasmith, *Canada's Sons and Great Britain in the World War,* 339-40; "Trench Fever New Malady," *Gazette and Chronicle,* 14 October 1915; Ellis, *Eye-Deep in Hell,* 55-57; Morton, *When Your Number's Up,* 145; D. Winter, *Death's Men,* 146-47, Cook, *At the Sharp End,* 251-53, 385-86.

86 **Paul Williams:** born Dunnington, Warwickshire, 1882; butcher; enlisted Oshawa, 116th Battalion, February 1916; childhood accident left him with deformed right foot and permanent limp; Moore, medical officer of the 116th, passed Williams as medically fit, noting only: "Right foot slightly deformed from accident"; survived basic training and joined the 18th Battalion on the same day as GT; returned to England after only three weeks as could not march more than 1.6 kilometres; conclusion of medical board, Shoreham, November 1916: "This man should not have been enlisted for overseas." Transferred to light duties with the Canadian Army Service Corps; discharged as physically unfit April 1918; died in Toronto, March 1939. At the time of enlistment, Williams was married, with a son of sixteen months. Captain Moore passed several men later deemed unfit for soldiering. In September 1916, the Canadian Militia Department introduced stricter medical requirements. Of the 407,221 men who enlisted up to 31 March 1917, 43,053 were discharged as medically unfit and, of these, 1,478 had already been shipped overseas. See LAC, box 10401-14, 746155 Williams, Paul; "Big Wastage in Canadian Forces: Forty-Three Thousand Have Been Discharged as Medically Unfit," *Toronto World,* 8 May 1917; Ian R. Whitehead, *Doctors in the Great War,* 3-4, 151-80; Sir Andrew Macphail, *Official History of the Canadian Forces in the Great War, 1914-19: The Medical Services,* also available at http://www.forces.gc.ca/dhh/collections/books/engraph/home_e.asp?cat=6.

Letter 10

87 GT was in Cité Calonne, about a kilometre from the enemy line.

88 The Canada Malleable Steel Range Manufacturing Co. of Oshawa went into liquidation in July 1917. "Oshawa," *Gazette and Chronicle,* 26 July 1917.

89 The 33rd Battalion was organized in London, Ontario, January 1915; recruited in London, Windsor, Chatham, St. Thomas, Strathroy, and Goderich; broken up almost immediately upon arrival in England; disbanded on 4 August 1917. LAC, RG 9 and RG 24, box 19 (Parts 3, 4, and 5), Guides to Sources Relating to Units of the Canadian Expeditionary Force and the Canadian Militia. The terms "J. Canuck," "Jack Canuck," and especially "Johnnie Canuck" were used during the Boer War and widely during

the First World War. "Johnnie Canuck" figured in patriotic song and advertising: on 27 April 1916, the YMCA appealed in the *Toronto Daily Star* for funds to make "life more tolerable in the trenches, where Jack Canuck is face to face with both death and the Hun!" "Johnnie Canuck" embodied Canada as "John Bull" embodied Great Britain. *Canadian Encyclopedia*, 2nd ed., vol. 2, 1112c; display advertising, *Toronto Daily Star*, 27 April 1916.

90 A reference to John Bunyan's seventeenth-century Christian allegory, *The Pilgrim's Progress*.

91 Most soldiers keenly anticipated the rum ration. It was intended both to warm the innards and to raise morale. Morton, *When Your Number's Up*, 139; Tim Cook, "'More as a Medicine Than a Beverage': 'Demon Rum' and the Canadian Trench Soldier in the First World War," 7-22.

92 The 18th Battalion moved into brigade support on 3 December 1916, remaining there until 11 A.M. on 10 December, when it relieved the 20th Battalion in the front line. The WD records a good deal of sniper and enemy artillery and aircraft activity. LAC, WD, 18th Battalion, December 1916.

93 The men of the 20th Battalion were also foraging for fuel in the slag heaps of the Calonne sector. Corrigall, *The Twentieth*, 97.

Letter 11

94 The 18th Battalion WD for 15 December 1916 records that "Cpl. Hunt shot one Hun who was observing with Field glasses. Our M.G.s [machine guns] dispersed two wiring parties. Enemy aircraft active." LAC, WD, 18th Battalion, December 1916.

95 GT, now a seasoned veteran, identified with the 18th Battalion. His former battalion, the 116th, did not cross over to France until mid-February 1917.

96 **Joe Wilson**: born Newcastle on Tyne, England, 1892; painter; enlisted May 1915; served with the 37th, the 2nd, and the 15th Battalions; wounded in the right leg 8 October 1916, in the left leg 11 April 1917, and in the right wrist 19 August 1917. LAC, box 10464-28, 47979 Wilson, Joseph. **Pooke** has proven elusive.

97 On 12 December, Germany issued a Peace Note through Neutral Powers. The Note had the support of the Pope. The Allies rejected the proposals, believing the Note to be a ruse to unsettle Allied public opinion, shore up popular support in Germany for the war, and curry favour with neutrals. See David Stevenson, *The First World War and International Politics*, 162-69.

Letter 12

98 The 18th Battalion was in brigade reserve at Bully. The WD for 20 December 1916 observes: "Enemy seems to have very much water in his trenches." LAC, WD, 18th Battalion, December 1916.

99 In the fall of 1916, Lieutenant General Byng initiated a program of instruction to improve and standardize training, and to foster a centralized Canadian Corps training doctrine. In several letters, GT reports that he was sent for training. An article

in the *Gazette and Chronicle* described some of the finer points of bomb throwing: "Baseball pitching is exactly the wrong motion. The bomb is too heavy for pitching and the jerkiness of the motion is dangerous. The British sportsman had an easy time in learning, because bomb throwing is exactly the same as bowling in cricket." A skilled thrower could lob a bomb 36.5 metres. Campbell, "Divisional Experience," 279-327; "The Art of Hurling Bombs," *Gazette and Chronicle,* 23 August 1917; Rawling, *Surviving Trench Warfare,* 55-58.

100 French author Alexandre Dumas was probably best known for *The Count of Monte Cristo* (English translation 1846).

101 Thousands of estaminets appeared in farmhouses and homes behind the Allied lines. Usually limited to one room, estaminets were a cross between a tavern and a café. Here men could get inexpensive (and weak) beer, wine, and coffee, and meals of fried egg and chips. Morton, *When Your Number's Up,* 239; Cane, *It Made You Think of Home,* 102-3; Cook, *At the Sharp End,* 386-87.

102 The Sons of England was a patriotic benevolent society. See John S. King, *The Early History of the Sons of England Benevolent Society.*

103 Tear gas or xylyl bromide. The other gas to which GT refers was chlorine gas, which caused asphyxiation. Chlorine gas was first used against Canadians (and Algerians) at Second Ypres in April 1915. Tim Cook, *No Place to Run: The Canadian Corps and Gas Warfare in the First World War;* Nathan Greenfield, *Baptism of Fire: The Second Battle of Ypres and the Forging of Canada, April, 1915;* L.F. Haber, *The Poisonous Cloud: Chemical Weapons in the First World War.*

Fragment 2

104 The fragment has been placed here since the references to winter and the Malle seem to indicate that it was written around the same time as Letter 13. The paper of Fragment 2 matches that of Letter 13.

105 **Arthur Day:** born London, England, 1872; labourer; enlisted Oshawa, January 1916; joined the 18th Battalion 6 October 1916; within days accidentally injured both feet in training; at Shoreham Camp, in late October 1916, he could hardly walk; embarked for Canada 4 August 1917. A small report in the *Ontario Reformer* of 21 September 1917, under the heading "Items of Interest," notes that Day "came home last week." It incorrectly identifies him as a member of the 116th and refers to him as the first man in that battalion to be wounded. The report correctly records a bayonet jab in the foot, but there is no mention of a training accident. LAC, box 2376-9, 745975 Day, Arthur Leonard.

Letter 13

106 On 24 December 1916, the 18th Battalion was in the front line in Calonne, Sector II (Maroc). LAC, WD, 18th Battalion, December 1916.

107 Edith was GT's youngest sister, by two years.

108 GT probably is referring to the 116th Battalion, which was still in Bramshott.

109 On 9 November 1916, the *Gazette and Chronicle* published a letter from Pte. Thomas Newman of Whitby detailing the kind of food the battalion received: "A typical breakfast included porridge, fried bacon, bread, butter, tea. Dinner – lentil soup, boiled beef, carrots, potatoes, bread, butter, tea, pudding. Supper – bread, butter, tea, stewed peaches, cake." It is possible that this piece was also published in the *Oshawa Vindicator*. **Thomas Newman:** born Stevenage, Hertford, England, 1874; farm labourer and bricklayer; enlisted Whitby, January 1916; served eight years in India and four in Burma with the Royal Scots Fusiliers; went overseas with GT on the *Olympic*; placed on permanent garrison duty in Bramshott; discharged as physically unfit and overage, returned to Canada May 1918. In 1916, Newman was a married man with six children; died in 1959, in his ninety-fourth year. "The 116th at Bramshott," *Gazette and Chronicle,* 9 November 1916; LAC, box 7295-28, 745697 Newman, Thomas.

110 On 11 November 1915, the *Gazette and Chronicle* published a letter from Pte. J.W. Lynde: "I am in the Bomb Throwers," he wrote, "so if there's any excitement going, I will be connected with it. The Machine Gun Section and the Bomb Throwers are the two branches of the 'Suicide Club.'" All five men with the last name "Lynde" listed in the LAC "Soldiers of the First World War" database appear to have been related and to have hailed from the Whitby area. "J.W. Lynde" is perhaps Pte. Jabez Nathan Lynde, who enlisted on 16 November 1914. "Another Letter from the Front Ranks," *Gazette and Chronicle,* 11 November 1915; Rawling, *Surviving Trench Warfare,* 24, 124; Bidwell and Graham, *Fire-Power,* 124-25; Morton, *When Your Number's Up,* 128-29; LAC, box 5811-38, 79210 Lynde, J.N.; Cook, "'My Whole Heart and Soul,'" 58-59.

Letter 14

111 The 18th Battalion was in brigade support in Calonne, Sector II (Maroc). LAC, WD, 18th Battalion, December 1916.

112 Men on light duty (often men who had reported sick) usually had responsibility for fatigues, though others, too, were expected to take a turn carrying rations, peeling potatoes, or cleaning the billets. Bombers, like stretcher-bearers, snipers, machine gunners, and trench mortar specialists, were usually exempt from fatigues. Brophy and Partridge, *Tommies' Songs and Slang,* 144, 180; Ellis, *Eye-Deep in Hell,* 40-41.

113 "Plum pudding" was also one of the nicknames given to the early trench mortars, which fired round shells also known as "Footballs," "Flying Pigs," and "Toffee Apples." Brophy and Partridge, *Tommies' Songs and Slang,* 196.

114 The *Gazette and Chronicle* carried an article on 6 December 1917 on "War-Time Christmas Cakes." It provided readers with a recipe for the cake called Soldier's Cake, made in Great Britain and sent to soldiers at the front. There were also recipes for "Canadian Trench Cake," "Prisoner's Bread," "Red Cross War Cake," "Camp Cake," and "Wartime Scones."

115 Lomey Town was the local name for the Lower High Street in Cradley Heath. The Beech Tree Colliery was one of the town's most important employers. GT was likely referring to one of its slag heaps that overlooked the community. "Cradley Heath's Lomey Town – as Old as the 12th Century?" *Black Country Bugle,* 22 February 2007, http://www.blackcountrybugle.co.uk; Christine Cartwright, "The Pit That Cried Itself to Death," http://www.cradleylinks.co.uk/beechtree.htm.

116 It rained on Christmas night. LAC, WD, 18th Battalion, December 1916; Corrigall, *The Twentieth,* 99.

117 The battalion WD records a minor operation being carried out at 9 P.M., but this does not appear to be the skirmish to which GT refers. The next day, on 27 December, the artillery did shell the enemy wire. LAC, WD, 18th Battalion, December 1916.

118 GT originally wrote "keep us awake all they could by running over you while you endeavour to sleep & by eating your grub." He corrected himself, however, using "us," "we," and "our." He added a notation at the bottom of the fifth page of the letter, where this correction was made, observing that "my grammar is going the way of my table manners it seems." The comment is placed at the end of this letter. "Rats in Trenches," *Gazette and Chronicle,* 20 January 1916.

119 There is no mention of either incident in the battalion WD, which notes for 27 December that the "enemy very nervous. Using m.gs [machine guns] frequently." LAC, WD, 18th Battalion, December 1916.

Letter 15

120 On 30 December 1916, the 18th Battalion was in brigade support in Calonne. LAC, WD, 18th Battalion, December 1916.

CHAPTER 2: "HE WAS KILLED BY MY SIDE"

Letter 16

1 The day Great Britain went to war, the Chancellor of the Exchequer, Lloyd George, used the phrase "business as usual" in a speech to businesspeople, probably in an effort to avoid economic panic. The phrase passed into common usage. On 22 August 1914, the *Times* reported that a firm of printers and engravers had produced a stamp for use by the business community: "It shows warships maneuvering and bears the words, 'Business as usual during alterations to the map of Europe.'" See "Items of War News," *Times,* 22 August 1914; DeGroot, *Blighty,* 54-78.

2 The 18th Battalion WD records that at 9 P.M., 26 December 1916, a raiding party of the 18th bombed a number of enemy dugouts, "but no Bosches were seen." According to D.J. Corrigall, trench mortars and Stokes guns were used for seven consecutive days, 28 December-3 January, to damage the enemy's wire. The 18th was relieved by the 20th on 28 December and moved into brigade support. There was still considerable danger: on 1 January 1917, five soldiers of the 18th Battalion were wounded on

a working party. LAC, WD, 18th Battalion, December 1916 and January 1917; Corrigall, *The Twentieth*, 100.

3 GT to Winnie, 30 December 1916.

4 During 1914 and 1915, the Canadian economy recovered from the pre-war recession, and real wages rose as manufacturers competed for skilled workers. By the fall of 1916, however, commodity prices began to increase; in 1917, the inflation rate was 18 percent and, in 1918, 13.5 percent. Robert Bothwell, Ian Drummond, and John English, *Canada, 1900-1945*, 162.

Letter 17

5 The 18th Battalion went back into the line, relieving the 20th in Calonne, Sector II (Maroc), on 3 January 1917. The 20th and 21st Battalions were scheduled to carry out a raid on the night of 17 January. In preparation, the 2nd Canadian Division artillery shelled the enemy front line, 3-16 January. On 9 January 1917, the 18th Battalion WD records that the Canadians fired 987 shells and 57 trench mortars in their sector during the day. Enemy guns also fired on Allied patrol planes. Artillery fire did extensive damage to enemy trenches, but the wire entanglements were not sufficiently broken up. Several more days of continuous artillery bombardment ensued, and at 11:30 P.M., 17 January, the 20th and 21st Battalions staged a raid, while the 18th Battalion held the front line. One hundred prisoners were taken, and the third line of enemy trenches was entered. The 18th Battalion had fourteen men wounded in the action out of a total of thirty-six killed and seventy-three wounded. On 18 January, the 18th Battalion moved into reserve in billets at Bully Grenay and, on 19 January, to the Canadian Training Area and billets at Haillicourt. On 20 January, GT had his first bath and change of clothes since 17 December. He was in Haillicourt on 27 January. Raids, like that of 17-18 January 1917, were unpopular. The main purpose of the raids was to obtain information on enemy dispositions, morale, and preparedness, and any other intelligence information of value, by capturing enemy prisoners and documentation. They were also intended as a means of inflicting damage on the enemy and keeping Allied troops on their mettle by combating the "live and let live" mentality that permeated some sectors of the front line. LAC, WD, 18th Battalion, January 1917; Rawling, *Surviving Trench Warfare*, 47; Ellis, *Eye-Deep in Hell*, 76-79; Ashworth, *Trench Warfare;* Cook, *At the Sharp End*, 291-302.

6 On 17 January, it snowed, and on the next day there was a blinding snowstorm in the Bully Grenay area, with snow continuing on 19 January. The weather turned bright on 21 January but was extremely cold and remained that way for much of February. Corrigall, *The Twentieth*, 102-7.

7 **Jack Burr:** wounded in the head and neck at Calonne, Sector II (Maroc), 17 January 1917; wounds dressed by stretcher bearers; admitted to the No. 22 General Hospital, Camiers, 18 January 1918; hospitalized three weeks; evacuated to England, still complaining of neck pains; the bullet lodged in his neck was found and removed

at the military hospital in York 9 April 1917; sent to the 4th Reserve Battalion 19 April 1918; to the 98th Battalion at Witley June 1918; back to the field, 8th Battalion, 14 August 1918; wounded by shrapnel in the left hand September 1918; index finger amputated. LAC, box 1311-23, 745906 Burr, John Henry.

8 "Blighty" is a corruption of "bilaik," Hindustani for "foreign country," especially England. A "Blighty" or "Blighty One" meant a wound sufficiently grave to send its recipient back to England for treatment. Superficial or non-life-threatening wounds were treated in France, hence GT's expression of empathy and regret. Brophy and Partridge, *Tommies' Songs and Slang*, 85-86; Randle Gray with Christopher Argyle, *Chronicle of the First World War*, vol. 2, 1917-1918, 316; "War-Made Words," *Gazette and Chronicle*, 22 November 1917.

9 GT appears to be referring to Billy Clarke, mentioned in Letter 9.

10 The words "We're still resting ... resting is right" have been censored in the original but are still legible.

11 The 18th Battalion and the remainder of the 4th Brigade were out of the line for several weeks. GT's battalion did not go back to the front until 19 February, but the period of "rest" was scarcely one of inactivity. One Canadian trench newspaper, the *Listening Post*, commented that "rest" was a "refined period of torture for infantry." GT and his fellow soldiers experienced days filled with gruelling physical drill, company drill, platoon drill, bayonet fighting, battalion training, route marches, battalion inspections, company inspections, and specialist training. See, for example, the 18th (Western Ontario) Canadian Battalion Syllabus of Training – three weeks (3 June-29 June 1917) in LAC, WD, 18th Battalion, June 1917; *Listening Post*, 28 September 1917, quoted in Fuller, *Troop Morale*, 78.

Letter 18

12 On 30 January 1917, the battalion had paraded in full marching order to billets at Auchel, via Marles-les-Mines and Lozinghem. On Sunday, 4 February, the 18th was in rest billets at Auchel. LAC, WD, 18th Battalion, January 1917.

13 On 17 January 1917, no man's land was "white with snow." Corrigall, *The Twentieth*, 102-6.

14 An article entitled "Prevention of Coal Shortage" in the *Gazette and Chronicle*, 8 March 1917, observed that the winter of 1916-17 had seen a "coal famine," attributable to both the severe weather and the increased demand for exports to fuel the booming American economy. It was suggested that some of the undeniable suffering that had occurred over the winter could be avoided in future if coal was purchased in the summer or autumn, because "coal famines," the article predicted, would occur at shorter intervals in the future.

15 William Colgate began his business in New York in 1806. The company established its first international subsidiary in Canada in 1914. See http://www.colgate.com/app/Colgate/US/Corp/History/1806.cvsp.

16 As GT indicates, billets were often poor. One widely used photograph of Canadians housed in a barn, "Canadians at Villers au Bois, 1917," Imperial War Museum Collection, is reproduced in Brown, *Tommy*, 65. Dugouts were by no means uniform in terms of the security of shelter or comfort they afforded. Those in the front lines tended to be rudimentary, often no more than hollows in the walls of the trenches. Ellis, *Eye-Deep in Hell*, 16-19; Cook, *At the Sharp End*, 217-35; Corrigall frequently comments on the conditions of Canadian billets in *The Twentieth*.

17 In February 1917, the commanding officer of the 18th Battalion was Lt. Col. Gordon F. Morrison, formerly of the 19th Battalion. He succeeded Lt. Col. H.L. Milligan in the fall of 1916; Morrison returned to Canada in April 1917 and was replaced by Maj., later Lt. Col., L.E. Jones, of the 18th Battalion, who remained the 18th's commanding officer for the rest of the war. Cooper, *Fourth Canadian Infantry Brigade*, 16, 22.

18 **Lt. Gen. the Hon. Sir Julian H.G. Byng** (1862-1935): British Army cavalry officer; served in the Boer War; commanded the Cavalry Corps 1915; appointed commander of the Canadian Corps May 1916; full general in command of the British Third Army June 1917; Governor General of Canada 1921-26. On 5 February 1917, Byng inspected the 18th Battalion and presented medals; accompanied by Maj. Gen. Sir H.E. Burstall, who commanded the 2nd Canadian Division for most of the war. See Cooper, *Fourth Canadian Infantry Brigade*, 18; LAC, WD, 18th Battalion, February 1917; Corrigall, *The Twentieth*, 105; Nicholson, *C.E.F.*, 540; Cyril Falls, "Byng, Julian Hedworth George, Viscount Byng of Vimy (1862-1935)," Rev. Jeffery Williams, in Matthew and Harrison, *Oxford Dictionary of National Biography*, vol. 9, 318-22; Campbell, "Divisional Experience," 271-78.

19 The extensive training, repeated drills, frequent inspections, and new equipment were to prepare the Canadian Corps for the assault on Vimy Ridge in April 1917.

20 Soldiers considered not to have cared properly for their equipment were charged for it. For example, on 11 March 1917, GT's old battalion, the 116th, moved into trenches at the foot of Vimy Ridge and into mud over their knees. Some "old soldiers" suggested shortening the length of their coats, "in accordance, not with the orders of the 9th Brigade, but with the depth of the mud encountered." Approximately two hundred men found themselves on charge for "destroying Government property." This was the first experience of the front line for the 116th. One soldier charged was Pte. Albert Alroy Cooke: on 5 April 1917, he was placed under stoppages of one dollar per pay for "whilst on active service 'mutilating Govt. property' (cutting great coat)." Cooke died April 1935 at the age of forty-three. LAC, box 1936-15, 745955 Cooke, Albert Alroy; Allen, *116th Battalion*, 18.

21 The type of gas helmet to which GT is referring at this time was probably a thick flannel hood, with a mica eyepiece impregnated with phenol. Attempts to improve this design succeeded only with the invention of the small box respirator late in 1916. Although gas helmets and masks were as unpopular as they were uncomfortable, they worked. Tim Cook, *No Place to Run*, 42-45, 87-89; Morton, *When Your*

Number's Up, 133, 199; Tim Cook, "Through Clouded Eyes: Gas Masks and the Canadian Corps in the First World War," 4-20.

22 The adjutant of the 116th Battalion noted that the village of Auchel (where GT was resting) was regarded in the spring of 1917 as the "Queen of billets in the Corps area." Allen, *116th Battalion,* 40.

23 In June 1917, three-fifths of the French army mutinied, a primary grievance being scarcity of leave. Reforms gave the *poilu* seven (extended later to ten) days' leave every four months. Canadian soldiers usually received ten days' leave every twelve months; officers were granted leave four times a year. See Leonard V. Smith, *Between Mutiny and Obedience;* Fuller, *Troop Morale,* 72; Morton, *When Your Number's Up,* 234.

24 The French government, acutely conscious of the country's falling birth rate, which hit an all-time low in 1916, pursued an aggressive pronatalist policy. A French soldier's leave was widely advertised as an opportunity to serve the nation through the procreation of future military cohorts. Marie-Monique Huss, "Pronatalism in Wartime France," in *The Upheaval of War: Family, Work and Welfare in Europe, 1914-1918,* ed. Richard Wall and J.M. Winter, 329-67.

Letter 19

25 On 12 February, the 18th Battalion marched from Auchel to Haillicourt; on 13 February it moved to divisional reserve at Ecoivres, engaging in battalion, company, and platoon drills, and specialist instruction. On 19 February, the 18th relieved the 20th Battalion in the front line of the Thélus Sector, not far from the village of Neuville St. Vaast. LAC, WD, 18th Battalion, February 1917; Nicholson, *C.E.F.,* 233.

26 **Walter Stone:** born London, England, 1881; labourer; enlisted Oshawa, 116th Battalion, January 1916; sailed on the *Olympic* with GT; transferred to 18th Battalion 6 October 1916; gassed May 1917; admitted to No. 4 Stationary Hospital, Arques, 20 May; transferred to No. 7 Convalescent Depot, Boulogne, 23 May and to No. 3 Rest Camp, Marlborough, England, June 1917. Married, with two children aged eight and eleven, living in South Oshawa, 1916; died in Toronto, 1968. LAC, box 9357-3, 747995 Stone, Walter.

27 When the 116th arrived in England, some of its number (including GT) were transferred to other battalions in the field, principally, it seems, to the 18th and also to the 2nd, the Central Ontario Regiment, which belonged to the 1st Brigade, 1st Canadian Division. It was not until 11 February 1917 that the remainder of the 116th Battalion (reinforced by new recruits) arrived in France. By this time, GT had spent almost five months in the trenches. The 116th, untested in the front line, visited it only briefly in the second week of March 1917. For most of the period between February and July 1917, the 116th supplied working parties, reconstructing roads and trenches and consolidating positions – not quite the easy task GT claims. The 116th Battalion's WD reveals a daily toll of casualties from enemy shelling. The 116th was in the unenviable position of having been selected (after much lobbying by Col. Sam Sharpe, who fought to prevent the breakup of the 116th) to replace the

60th Battalion of the 3rd Division. The 60th was disbanded, despite its solid reputation as a fighting unit, because its recruiting pool in Quebec had run dry. Bitter at the decision, some of the men erected a memorial to the 60th close to the village of Vimy: "In memory of the 60th Battalion. 1915 – Raised by Patriotism. 1917 – Killed by Politics." Viewed as inexperienced usurpers who performed lowly tasks since coming to France, the 116th was unpopular with the 9th Infantry Brigade and the 3rd Division. Allen, *116th Battalion,* 13, 17, 28; "116th Broken Up," *Gazette and Chronicle,* 26 October 1916; LAC, WD, 116th Battalion, February-July 1917; Desmond Morton, "The Short Unhappy Life of the 41st Battalion CEF," *Queen's Quarterly* 81, 1 (1974):70-80; Kenneth Radley, *We Lead, Others Follow: First Canadian Division, 1914-1918.*

28 Censored but legible.

29 On 20 February 1917, the 18th Battalion's WD notes of the trenches read: "This sector [Thélus] in very muddy condition, necessitating continuous works by the Battalion to keep in repair." LAC, WD, 18th Battalion, February 1917.

Letter 20

30 March 1, 1917, was the couple's twelfth wedding anniversary.

31 These official cards allowed a man to select a message from a limited range of options (e.g., "I am quite well," "I have been admitted to hospital"). The sender was permitted to add only the date and his signature. Cook, *At the Sharp End,* 248.

32 This sentence is censored but legible. The 18th Battalion WD records that 22-28 February 1917 two ORs were killed and six ORs wounded. LAC, WD, 18th Battalion, February 1917.

33 MT and GT's nephew, John Thomas Carter, was born 20 January 1917, the son of Mary Ann Carter (MT's sister) and John Edward Carter. The Carters migrated to Canada after the war and settled in Oshawa. John was killed 9 June 1942 in Carsdale, Manitoba, four days after qualifying as a navigator with the Royal Canadian Air Force. He was twenty-five years old. He is buried in the same cemetery as GT. A photograph of him can be found in the Book of Remembrance in the main branch of the Oshawa Public Library.

Letter 21

34 On 6 March, the 18th Battalion was in divisional reserve at Mont St. Eloy, preparing for the attack on Vimy Ridge. The size, scope, and organization of the logistical support for the assault were essential to its success. Old roads and tramways had to be repaired and new ones built to carry forward ammunition, rations, and other stores. Signallers buried 21 miles (34 kilometres) of cable 7 feet (2 metres) deep and paid out 66 miles (106 kilometres) of unburied wire. Almost four miles (6.5 kilometres) of electrically lit tunnels were created to house telephone cables and water mains, and to permit troops to move to and from the front in relative safety. The

area had previously been quarried for chalk, leaving caves for stores and munitions, and medical and administrative space. On 8 March 1917, half the 18th Battalion were engaged in fatigues, mainly loading and carrying ammunition. LAC, WD, 18th Battalion, March 1917; Nicholson, *C.E.F.,* 249-57; D.E. Macintyre, *Canada at Vimy,* 63.

Letter 22

35 On 26 March 1917, the 18th Battalion was in billets at Bois des Alleux. For three weeks the weather was wet and misty, and the enemy active: much of the work of the 18th Battalion was limited to the hours of darkness. On 13 March 1917, a German raiding party of about thirty attacked an 18th Battalion outpost manned by a sergeant, six bombers, and three Lewis gunners, all of whom managed to escape, although subsequent enemy shelling killed three and wounded fourteen. Aerial activity was significant. LAC, WD, 18th Battalion, March 1917; Nicholson, *C.E.F.,* 250-51; Macintyre, *Canada at Vimy,* 68-69.

36 On 23-24 March, the 18th Battalion staged a raid to destroy dugouts and trench mortar emplacements. The enemy positions were well manned. The action cost the 18th one officer and three ORs wounded and missing, and seven ORs wounded. Similar raids had been made along the line. On 20 March, the 19th Battalion had sent out a party of four officers and sixty-three ORs: they bombed enemy dugouts and captured five prisoners at the cost of only three slight casualties. But between 20 March and 9 April, the Canadian Corps suffered as many as 1,400 casualties. LAC, WD, 18th Battalion, March 1917; Macintyre, *Canada at Vimy,* 70-71; Nicholson, *C.E.F.,* 234; Cooper, *Fourth Canadian Infantry Brigade,* 18.

Letter 23

37 On 30 March 1917, the 18th Battalion marched to Estré-Cauchee (called "extra-cushy" by the men) from their billets in Bois des Alleux. Between 25 March and 29 March, the battalion focused upon training, using the new platoon organization, which became the backbone of the battalion. A platoon numbered approximately thirty-six men, but not fewer than twenty-eight, and each platoon had four specialist sections: bombers, Lewis gunners, riflemen, and rifle grenadiers. There still remained four platoons to a company and four companies to a battalion. The firepower of the battalion rose from four machine guns to sixteen Lewis guns. On 31 March, the battalion began intensive training over a taped replica of the enemy's lines so that each soldier knew his allotted task and had a clear picture of his place in the operation. The replicas were based on aerial photographs and updated by using the intelligence gathered during raiding, reconnaissance patrols, and regular patrols in no man's land. Meticulous preparation of this sort was crucial to the success of the Canadians at Vimy, and to reducing their losses. LAC, WD, 18th Battalion, March 1917; Morton, *When Your Number's Up,* 160-61; Rawling, *Surviving Trench Warfare,* 97-98, 100-101.

38 The news that reached GT was inevitably limited, but the general public's view of events was also refracted through the lens of censorship and propaganda. In March 1917, there was much to report. On 14 March, the Germans began a strategic retreat to a new defensive line, the Hindenburg Line. This was a series of formidable fortified areas. The Germans employed a vigorous scorched earth policy, moving civilians and resources, and destroying or booby-trapping anything that might be of value to the Allies. Although the operation continued throughout March, it was not until 25 March that the British became aware of it. At the time, the media reported that German forces had been forced to withdraw because they had been significantly weakened. This news may account for GT's guarded optimism at the end of this letter. Today, the German withdrawal is understood to have been a sound strategic move that shortened their line and released thirteen German divisions into a much needed reserve. The February Revolution in Russia caused the Allies grievous concern on the Eastern Front. Prime Minister Borden was in London in March 1917 to discuss strategy. The *Times* published various articles in March 1917 on this topic. See Stephen Pope and Elizabeth-Anne Wheal, *The Macmillan Dictionary of the First World War*, 17, 229-30; Keshen, *Propaganda and Censorship*, 47; Norman Stone, *The Eastern Front, 1914-1917*; Holger Herwig, *The First World War: Germany and Austria-Hungary, 1914-1918*; J.L. Granatstein, "Conscription in the Great War," in MacKenzie, *Canada and the First World War*, 62-75; John English, "Political Leadership in the First World War," in MacKenzie, *Canada and the First World War*, 76-95.

Letter 24

39 By 24 April 1917, the 18th Battalion had moved into brigade reserve. Desultory enemy shelling of the reserve areas escalated on 25 April to heavy shelling of the defences and lines of communication. The 18th was relieved by the 24th Battalion on 26 April and moved into rest camp at Roclincourt.

40 "Whizz-bang" was also the name used to refer to a light shell, usually the German 77 millimetre. Brophy and Partridge, *Tommies' Songs and Slang*, 204.

41 On Easter Monday, 9 April 1917, the Canadians took Vimy Ridge. The previous day, at 7:45 p.m., the 18th began to move toward its battle position. The battalion, composed of twelve platoons totalling approximately six hundred men, moved into the line at one-hundred-yard (ninety-one metre) intervals in the early hours of Monday morning. At zero hour, 5:30 a.m., the 18th advanced, together with the 19th, in the first wave of the attack. The advance took place in a heavy snowfall, across cratered and swampy ground. Opposition was stiff. One member of "C" Company of the 18th identified the location of a machine gun "holding up his company and doing considerable damage. Lance Sergeant Sifton, single-handed, attacked the Gun crew and bayoneted every man, but was unhappily shot by a dying Boche." Sifton was awarded the Victoria Cross for his heroism. He was twenty-five years old. The 18th and 19th Battalions reached their objectives forty-five minutes after zero hour and, by mid-afternoon, it was clear to the Canadians

that the ridge had been taken. Vimy cost Canada 10,602 casualties, 3,598 of them fatal. LAC, WD, 18th Battalion, April 1917; Nicholson, *C.E.F.*, 233-68; Morton, *When Your Number's Up*, 168; LAC, box 8896-45, 53730 Sifton, Ellis Wellwood. The last page of the 18th Battalion's WD for June 1917 carries Sifton's citation: LAC, WD, 18th Battalion, June 1917.

42 In fact, things were not going well for the Allies. The Canadians had to fight hard to consolidate their position on Vimy Ridge. The early successes of the Battle of Arras (of which Vimy was undoubtedly the most signal) were checked by dogged German resistance. On 16 April, the French launched the Nivelle offensive (Second Battle of Ainse) along a 25-mile (40 kilometre) front, which resulted in a 600-yard (550 metre) advance at the cost of 100,000 casualties instead of the planned 6-mile (9.5 kilometre) advance at the cost of 15,000 casualties. At the same time, the Russian army was disintegrating and Allied and neutral shipping experienced the worst losses for any month in both world wars: 373 ships were sunk (873,754 tonnes). Gray, *Chronicle*, vol. 2, 38-45.

43 Not only was the weather atrocious but, on 10 April, the 18th Battalion relieved the 1st Royal West Kent Regiment, which had a well-established reputation as an aggressive battalion – a measure of the degree to which the advance was contested and a reflection also of the fighting ability of the 18th Battalion. Ashworth, *Trench Warfare*, 21; LAC, RG 9, series III-D-1, vol. 4692, folder 51, file 4, SQMS Hodges, Record Office Overseas Military Forces of Canada, London, History of the 18th Canadian Infantry Battalion; LAC, WD, 18th Battalion, April 1917; Brereton Greenhous and Stephen J. Harris, *Canada and the Battle of Vimy Ridge 9-12 April, 1917*.

44 **Alfred Gower**: born London, England, 1888; moulder and stove mounter; enlisted Oshawa, 116th Battalion, March 1916; joined 18th Battalion in the field 22 October 1916; wounded 17 January 1917; returned to unit on 6 March 1917; wounded 9 April and admitted to No. 114 General Hospital, Wimereux, 10 April 1917, then to Tooting Military Hospital, London, 12 April 1917. Although medical records confirm that Gower walked to the 9th Field Ambulance CEF for treatment, he was, in fact, severely wounded in the head by a shrapnel fragment, which had pierced his steel helmet. He spent a total of 216 days in hospitals before being found medically unfit for service. In May 1918, Gower's home address was given as 531 Albert Street, Oshawa. LAC, box 3687-24, 746162 Gower, Alfred Henry; see also Chap. 5, n. 10.

45 Esther was GT's half-sister. Felix Timmins, born 1847, was sixty years old when this letter was written. Joseph Houlden, interview with author, Ottawa, 9 December 1993.

Letter 25

46 GT may have misdated this letter since the 18th Battalion was relieved on 26 April 1917. LAC, WD, 18th Battalion, April 1917.

47 **Morley Jacobi**: born 1894; accountant; commissioned lieutenant, 116th Battalion, July 1916; sailed to England with GT on the *Olympic*; embarked for France, February 1917; mentioned in dispatches; contusion in right ankle caused by a shell casing

August 1918 leading to discharge (at the rank of captain) October 1918; died in Oshawa, 1934. The *Ontario Reformer* of 2 June 1916 notes that Jacobi was a member of the McLaughlin office staff and a star hockey player of Oshawa; the Oshawa *Daily Reformer* of 30 June 1927 carries an advertisement, with a photograph of Jacobi, as vice-president of Moffat Motor Sales of Oshawa. **Russell Henry:** born 1896; university student; commissioned lieutenant, 116th Battalion, July 1916; served with the 34th Regiment and the 116th Battalion; sailed with GT on the *Olympic* in July 1916; embarked for France February 1917; ill with "flu" but found to be trench fever, or PUO (pyrexia of unknown origin), May 1917; invalided back to England; attached to the 2nd Reserve Battalion September 1917; suffered two relapses and declared unfit for General Service January 1918; returned to Canada February 1918. **Fred Palmer:** born Ireland, 1883; sanitary inspector; enlisted Oshawa, 116th Battalion, December 1915; lived at 145 Albert Street; previously served one year with the 34th Regiment and two years with the 24th Mounted Rifles; served in the 116th as regimental sergeant major and warrant officer, class I; returned to England from France for officer training December 1917; temporary lieutenant in the 2nd Central Ontario Regiment March 1918; subsequently assigned to the 8th Reserve Battalion; sent to study public health and sanitation at the Royal Sanitary Institute; demobilized March 1919 and returned to Oshawa. LAC, box 4760-40 Jacobi, Morley Rice, Lieutenant; LAC, box 4276-65 Henry, Russell Clifford, Lieutenant; LAC, box 7547-6, 745907 Palmer, Frederick Charles. On Hind, see Chap. 1, n. 42.

48   On Gibbie, see Introduction, n. 73.

49   See "More Honours Given Toronto Soldiers," *Toronto Daily Star,* 13 January 1917.

50   **Jack Darby:** born Essex, England, 1884; moulder; enlisted Oshawa, October 1914; army medical, Toronto, November 1914; assigned to the 20th Battalion, arrived in France September 1915; awarded Military Medal July 1917; promoted to corporal August 1917 and to sergeant November 1917; wounded in the left thigh and right knee 9 May 1918 and evacuated to England; wounds healed quickly but contracted "flu" June 1918; sent to the 12th Reserve Battalion September 1918. Darby gave as his next of kin Mrs. Burder of Albert Street, likely Mrs. Lillie Emily Burder, of 135 Albert Street, Oshawa, wife of Francis Henry Burder. Burder and his brother William (also of the same address) both enlisted in the 116th Battalion on 7 April 1916 and were transferred with GT to the 18th Battalion October 1916. Like Darby, the Burders came from Essex. LAC, box 2293-20, 57390 Darby, John Frank; LAC, box 1270-14, 746187 Burder, Francis Henry; LAC, box 1270-15, 746186 Burder, William George. See also "Wins Military Medal," *Toronto Daily Star,* 22 June 1917: the article notes that "two of his [Darby's] chums, Pte Cash and Corp Bircham, have also received the Military Medal."

51   Few of GT's souvenirs have survived, but one that has is the photograph of the young German soldier. In ballpoint pen in what appears to be GT's hand, on the original envelope containing the photograph from a photographer's shop in Berlin, are the words: "Taken from dead German soldier." In translation, the envelope bears

the address: L/Corp. Siegfried Schulze, 1st Battery, Field Artillery Regiment No. 63, Fifth Division, and is postmarked Berlin, 27 September 1916. Bombadier James Logan, 9th Battery, Canadian Field Artillery, commented: "A German prisoner once said, 'The Frenchman fights for his country, the Englishman fights for his King, the American fights for his flag and the Canadians fight for souvenirs.'" Reid, *Poor Bloody Murder*, 161; Jonathan Vance, "Tangible Demonstrations of a Great Victory: War Trophies in Canada," 47-56. A photograph of Canadian soldiers with their souvenirs is found in Nicholson, *C.E.F.*, opposite page 258.

52 Probably **Frederick Thomas George Burley**: born Plumstead, Kent, England, 1884; enlisted Oshawa, 116th Battalion, December 1915; joined the 18th Battalion, October 1916; shrapnel wound in the abdomen on 25 March 1917 – the battalion was in billets at Bois des Alleux, cleaning arms and equipment, when the enemy shelled the billets; rejoined the 18th, 11 September 1918; lightly wounded 15 September; more seriously wounded 12 October 1918; survived the war and returned to Oshawa. In 1916, he left behind a wife and two children, one six months old and the other two years. GT describes Burley as "little fellow." He was five feet two inches tall. GT was five feet six inches tall. The average height of the soldiers mentioned in GT's letters is approximately five feet eight; the shortest was five foot one and the tallest, six foot one. The CEF average was five foot five. LAC, box 1290-9, 745927 Burley, Frederick Thomas George; LAC, box 9698-43, 3235822 Timmins, George; Morton, "A Canadian Soldier," 79.

Letter 26

53 The 18th Battalion had gone into the line, in front of Vimy Ridge and to the north of the village of Fresnoy, on 6 May 1917. Fresnoy had been captured by the Canadians on 3 May and the Germans were determined to recapture the position. Every evening, the Germans included poison gas and tear shells in the barrage, making necessary the wearing of the cumbersome gas respirators, which further exhausted the troops and made the work of ration parties extremely hazardous. The Canadians were bombarded without respite – approximately 100,000 shells between the evening of 6 May and the morning of 8 May – when the Germans launched a successful counterattack. During the offensive, all three lines of the 18th Battalion (front, support, and reserve) were subjected to intense artillery fire. On the night of 7 May, 5 ORs were killed and 13 wounded. On 8-9 May, communications broke down, forcing the 18th to use runners and pigeons to re-establish contact with other battalions. On the night of 10 May, the 18th Battalion was relieved by the 21st and moved into brigade reserve. Between 12 May and 13 May, the 18th lost 1 officer and 1 OR, while 13 ORs were wounded; on 13 May, the 18th was relieved by the 24th Battalion and moved to the reserve camp at Neuville St. Vaast. Between 1 May and 15 May, the 4th Canadian Infantry Brigade lost 12 officers killed, with 13 wounded; 93 ORs were killed, 339 wounded, and 21 missing. LAC, RG 9, series III-D-1, vol. 4692, folder 51, file 4, SQMS Hodges, Record Office Overseas Military Forces of Canada, London,

History of the 18th Canadian Infantry Battalion; LAC, WD, 18th Battalion, May 1917; Cooper, *Fourth Canadian Infantry Brigade*, 22-23; Nicholson, *C.E.F.*, 274-78; "Pigeons in Warfare," *Gazette and Chronicle*, 9 December 1915.

54 The type of shelter to which GT is referring, also known as a cubby-hole, consisted of a hole dug either into the wall of the trench or its floor. "Funk-hole" could refer to a dugout or any other type of shelter, safe place, or task. The term was in general use in the British Expeditionary Force by December 1914. Although "funk" was British slang for showing cowardice, "funk hole" did not carry any negative connotations about its occupants. See Brophy and Partridge, *Tommies' Songs and Slang*, 125; Gray, *Chronicle*, vol. 2, 346.

55 The 18th Battalion was approximately 800 yards (730 metres) west of the village of Acheville, which lay just to the north of Fresnoy. The position at Fresnoy was very exposed, with the Germans holding trenches to the north and south. The sunken roads in the plain between Vimy and the German lines afforded the troops a modicum of protection. Low-flying enemy aircraft machine gunned the Canadian troops, leading Cooper, in *Fourth Canadian Infantry Brigade*, to observe that "it was a distressing period." LAC, WD, 18th Battalion, May 1917; Cooper, *Fourth Canadian Infantry Brigade*, 22.

56 See "Birds Like War Sounds: Have Accustomed Themselves to the Noise of Explosives," *Gazette and Chronicle*, 9 March 1916.

57 On souvenirs, see Cane, *It Made You Think of Home*, 234 and 291.

Letter 27

58 At 5 P.M. on 19 May, the 18th Battalion relieved the 27th Battalion of the 6th Brigade and, over the course of the next six days, worked on completing the Ridge Line Trench. LAC, WD, 18th Battalion, May 1917.

59 The ammunition limber is the detachable part of a gun carriage, consisting of two wheels, axle, and ammunition box.

60 On 9-10 May, the 18th Battalion WD records that "during the whole of this tour considerable difficulty was experienced in the bringing up of rations owing to the enemy use of Poison Gas and Tear Shells." LAC, WD, 18th Battalion, May 1917.

61 Corduroy roads, consisting of logs laid across unmetalled road surfaces, were a Canadian specialty. They prevented the road from disintegrating under the combined assault of rain and heavy traffic, or helped restore a passable surface to an area churned up by artillery fire. Nicholson, *C.E.F.*, photograph on unnumbered page between pages 306 and 307.

62 According to the 18th WD, Byng "expressed surprise that, considering the heavy fighting and hardships passed through during the last month, it was possible for the men to turn out so clean and in such fine condition." Byng awarded ten Military Medals to men of the 18th Battalion. Byng was a widely liked figure, not least for his reputation of not using his soldiers like so much cannon fodder. GT's comment, however, strikes a rather bitter note and one that escaped censorship. Maj. D.J.

Corrigall writes of Byng's inspection: "We were on parade from 8 a.m. when we formed up on the Battalion parade ground until 1:30 p.m." He adds no further comment. Corrigall, *The Twentieth*, 128; Losinger, "Officer-Man Relations," 14-18; LAC, WD, 18th Battalion, May 1917.

63 On GT's nephew, John Thomas Carter, see Chap. 2, n. 33.

Letter 28

64 On 5 June at Barlin, GT enjoyed his first bath since 14 May. The battalion was to remain "at rest" here until 3 July. LAC, WD, 18th Battalion, June and July 1917.

65 On 27 May, after relieving the 28th Battalion in the Mont Foret Quarries area, the 18th Battalion endured a day of heavy artillery fire. At 1 A.M. on 28 May, a heavy enemy barrage opened, and two large raiding parties, of fifty to sixty men in all, were spotted nearing the Canadian positions. The 18th had a wiring party out at the time consisting of one non-commissioned officer and six men. A search party was sent out to look for them but failed to find three of the men, although two rifles were found in a shell crater. LAC, WD, 18th Battalion, May 1917.

66 GT was unaware that the *Toronto Daily Star* ran a banner headline on 10 April 1917 proclaiming that "Canadians Hold Vimy Ridge Securely." The paper also printed an excellent map of the area on its front page. On civilians' knowledge of the conflict, see Miller, *Our Glory and Our Grief*; Eric F. Schneider, "What Britons Were Told about the War in the Trenches, 1914-1918."

67 On Henry (Harry) Dunn, see Chap. 1, n. 57.

68 On Walter Stone, see Chap. 2, n. 26.

69 The 182nd Canadian Infantry Battalion was raised in Whitby, Ontario; a draft of 75 was sent to the 116th and 125 men to other units, July 1916; on arrival in Liverpool, the 182nd was quickly broken up and fed into reserve battalions, providing reinforcements for the Canadian Corps in the field. Members of the 182nd were the "esteemed rivals" of the 116th. See LAC, RG 9 and RG 24, box 19 (Parts 3, 4, and 5), Guides to Sources Relating to Units of the Canadian Expeditionary Force and the Canadian Militia; "Interesting Notes about the County Battalions," *Gazette and Chronicle*, 27 April 1916; "The 182nd Battalion in Old England," *Gazette and Chronicle*, 5 July 1917. GT's news about the 182nd was a month ahead of the announcement in the *Gazette and Chronicle*.

70 On John McMullen, see Introduction, n. 74

71 For details on burial, see Cane, *It Made You Think of Home*, 90-91.

CHAPTER 3: "I'M STILL FINE"

Letter 29

1 GT was in Barlin on 2 July when the Canadian Corps sports day was held at Chamblain l'Abbé. The 18th Battalion team won the soccer final 2-0. The next day, the 2nd Canadian Division moved from rest into the line, taking over from the British

46th Division in the Lens-Laurent sector. The 4th Brigade moved into divisional reserve with its headquarters in Bully Grenay. The battalion was billeted in huts at Bovigny Woods. Although out of the front line, the men were not out of danger. A week after GT wrote this letter, on 9 July, a shell fired by an enemy long-range gun hit one of the billets, killing nine men and wounding thirty-five. By contrast, when the 18th Battalion went into the front line on 10 July, relieving the 26th Battalion, the WD records there was practically no shelling. On the night of 12 July, the men were moved into brigade support in the Laurent sector and billeted in the well-fortified cellars in Cité Saint-Pierre, which had been occupied by the Germans. The weather was hot, and the 18th Battalion spent the next several days moving ammunition to the front line. On the night of 16 July, the battalion moved back into the front line, in the Lens sector, to find the enemy trench mortars active and support lines systematically shelled at night. On 22 July, the battalion returned to billets in the village of Bovigny. LAC, WD, 18th Battalion, July 1917.

2 On the Hill 70 operation, see Cooper, *Fourth Canadian Infantry Brigade,* 23-25; Nicholson, *C.E.F.,* 269-97; Campbell, "Divisional Experience," 315-19; Cook, *No Place to Run,* 125-32.

3 For centuries, soldiers have made decorative as well as practical objects and souvenirs out of the everyday materials of war that surrounded them. See Jane A. Kimball, *Trench Art: An Illustrated History.* A photograph of such a piece can be seen in Fleming, *The Wartime Letters,* 301. The Canadians in the Fresnoy area were continually harassed by enemy aircraft. "Our airmen were not sufficiently numerous to hold the enemy planes in check," observed Cooper. By the end of the war, the British had lost approximately 4,000 aircraft in combat (but 15,000 in training), the French 3,000, and the Germans 3,128. In 1917, the British produced 14,832 aircraft, the French 14,900, and the Germans 19,400. Cooper, *Fourth Canadian Infantry Brigade,* 22; Gray, *Chronicle,* vol. 2, 53-55, 283, 290.

4 The 1st and 6th Battalions of the Royal West Kent Regiment fought with the Canadians at Vimy. The 18th Battalion relieved the West Kents on 10 April. On 11 April, the battalion war diarist commented: "This proved to be a very difficult and trying tour, the enemy constantly shelling our defences and putting up frequent barrages." LAC, WD, 18th Battalion, April 1917.

5 The *Toronto World,* 12 May 1917, carried official photographs of the Canadians at Vimy; Peter Robertson, "Canadian Photojournalism during the First World War," 37-52.

Letter 30

6 To relieve pressure on the French forces after their collapse in June 1917, Haig decided on a major assault in Flanders and, as a screen for that assault, an attack by the Canadian Corps on the French mining town of Lens, approximately six kilometres to the north of Vimy Ridge. Arthur Currie, who had assumed command of the

Canadian Corps in June 1917, had serious misgivings about the plan. The Germans held two important vantage points, hills to the north and to the east of Lens, as well as the ruins of the town itself. He persuaded his superiors that tactical interests would be best served by an attack on Hill 70 (seventy metres above sea level), two kilometres to the north of Lens. On 2 August 1917, the 18th Battalion was billeted in the village of Bovigny. For three days, heavy rains had forced the cancellation of all training. On 4 August, however, the battalion relieved the 28th Battalion and moved into brigade support in Cité Saint-Pierre; for the next three days, 350 men of the 18th were assigned the job of carrying trench mortars to the front line to prepare for the attack on Hill 70. The assault was meticulously planned, in the manner of Vimy, with repeated rehearsals over taped mock-ups of the German positions. On 9 August, men from the 18th joined others from the 20th and 21st Battalions in a raid on the German front line trenches to gather information about enemy wire and positions. This action had the effect of confusing the Germans, who thought at first that the raid was the anticipated real attack. The 18th managed to penetrate a hundred yards (ninety metres) into enemy lines at the cost of 4 men killed and 24 wounded. The 18th was subsequently taken briefly out of the line for a rest, which included a bath and a change of clothes (the first since 25 July), returning to the front line on the night of 13 August. In the attack on Hill 70, which began on the morning of 15 August, the 18th Battalion not only attained its objective but captured 65 prisoners. In the afternoon, the Germans launched the first of several heavy counterattacks, which produced three days of bitter fighting. In all, they counterattacked twenty-one times in seventy-two hours and used mustard gas against the Canadians. The Germans sustained almost 20,000 casualties in three days. The Canadians lost over 6,000, including eighteen-year-old Pte. Harry Brown of the 10th Battalion, a recipient of the Victoria Cross, one of six awarded in the Lens action. Nicholson, *C.E.F.*, 284-97; LAC, WD, 18th Battalion, August 1917; Cooper, *Fourth Canadian Infantry Brigade*, 23-25; Corrigall, *The Twentieth*, 131-47; Rawling, *Surviving Trench Warfare*, 139-42; Cook, *No Place to Run*, 125, 129-32.

7 GT is referring to Christ's feeding of the five thousand (Luke 9:12-17). Groups of soldiers formed "trench households," communal arrangements that in clearly defined areas such as food, and rations, broke down the distinction between individual and collective ownership. Ashworth, *Trench Warfare*, 155.

8 Enoch Dunn was MT's brother who lived in Lake Forest, a suburb of Chicago.

9 "Sid & Soaf" refers to MT's sister Sophie and her husband.

Letter 31

10 On 29 August, the 18th Battalion was in Le Pendu Huts, near Villers-au-Bois. Here the men were undergoing specialist training. GT does not mention that on 27 August, Haig inspected the 18th Battalion and the remainder of the 4th Brigade. Col. W.W. Murray, author of the *History of the 2nd Canadian Battalion*, observes that the 2nd

Battalion WD "is curiously uncommunicative about this." LAC, WD, 18th Battalion, August 1917; Cooper, *Fourth Canadian Infantry Brigade,* 25; W.W. Murray, *History of the 2nd Canadian Battalion,* 205.

11 Will Ford has proven elusive.

12 "Boche" was French slang for "German"; for more information, see Brophy and Partridge, *Tommies' Songs and Slang,* 88. "What 'Boche' Means," *Gazette and Chronicle,* 30 August 1917.

13 There is a tribute to West in the *Ontario Reformer*: "In sad but loving memory of Harry C. West, who was killed in action on August 21st 1917. Inserted by his friends, Mr. and Mrs. Wm. Hayes, Burke St., and his chum Jack Bone." "In Memoriam," *Ontario Reformer,* 23 August 1918. In the *Oshawa Vindicator,* the relationship between Mr. and Mrs. Hayes and Harry West is explained: "Mr. and Mrs. Hayes received word this week that Private Harry West of Oshawa, had been killed in action. Pte. West came to Oshawa from England about seven years ago and made his home at Mr. and Mrs. Hayes ... He was employed at the Steel Range Company's works and was among the first to enlist with the Ontario County Battalion, the 116th, going overseas with that unit." "Roll of Honour," *Oshawa Vindicator,* 21 September 1917. **Jack Bone**: born Gosport, Hampshire, England, 1886; labourer; enlisted Oshawa, February 1916; attached to 51st Battalion, Bramshott (Garrison Duty Battalion); discharged as medically unfit March 1917; returned to Canada April 1917. Bone had flat feet: "Evidently this man has been unable to walk any distance for many years." Like West, Bone worked for the Steel Range and earned an average of $2.50 a day prior to his enlistment. The two men had signed up on the same day. It was characteristic of the members of the Second Contingent to have strong links to places of employment. This largely reflects GT's experience, although in his case the neighbourhood community also seems to figure prominently. The majority of men mentioned in GT's letters came from a small geographical area. LAC, box 871-4, 745917 Bone, John. See also Introduction, n. 66, and Rutherdale, *Hometown Horizons,* 52.

14 McCleese appears to have been a reporter with the *Ontario Reformer* newspaper.

15 The nature of GT's father's illness appears to have been psychiatric. See GT to MT, 10 September 1917.

Letter 32

16 GT was at Villers Camp, Villers-au-Bois. On the original pencilled letter there is a large X mark between "5 or 6 letters" and "We are," which has been made by a heavy, thick pencil lead, quite different from GT's. There are further editorial marks and changes to the text in this letter, likely made by McCleese to prepare the letter for publication in the *Ontario Reformer.*

17 The reference is to Lens.

18 On Charles and James Gibbs, see Introduction, n. 77.

19 On Horne, see Introduction, n. 87; Don Farr, *The Silent General: Horne of the First Army.*

20 By 1917, the Canadians had gained a reputation for shooting surrendering German soldiers. Comments like this suggest that their reputation may have been deserved. See Tim Cook, "The Politics of Surrender: Canadian Soldiers and the Killing of Prisoners in the Great War," 637-65; Cane, *It Made You Think of Home,* 215-16.

21 For more on Thomas Dougall, to whom GT is referring, see Introduction, n. 83. On patrolling and scouting, see Cook, *At the Sharp End,* 277-78; Campbell, "Divisional Experience," 85-87.

22 La Bassée was in the Artois region of France, approximately thirteen kilometres north of Lens, and eight kilometres north of Loos. It was an area that had seen much heavy fighting. On 16 April 1917, the *Toronto World* announced: "Good Progress Made in Move to Turn Enemy out of La Bassee," but La Bassée itself was not to be liberated until 1918.

Letter 33

23 On 22 October, the 18th Battalion was in Frevillers, in the Ourton area. Since 10 September, the 18th Battalion had undergone a period of intensive training and several rounds of inspections, parades, and sports. On 14 September, the battalion marched from Villers Camp (Villers-au-Bois, ten kilometres north of Arras) to trenches in front of Avion, crossing Vimy Ridge under cover of darkness to relieve the 1st Canadian Mounted Rifles. The next few days were spent constructing dugouts and putting out wire. On the night of 19 September, one officer and ninety-two ORs put out no less than 600 yards (548 metres) of wire in front of Toronto Road trench. On 20 September, however, the 18th was relieved and returned to Villers Camp, and then to Vimy Ridge on the night of 2 October for further fatigues and a stint in the front line before being moved back to billets by light rail. On 15 October, the 18th Battalion, together with the remainder of the 4th Brigade, moved to the Ourton area where, for a week, the 18th Battalion underwent platoon training and company parades, while bombers, Lewis gunners, and grenadiers were given specialist training. LAC, WD, 18th Battalion, September and October 1917; Cooper, *Fourth Canadian Infantry Brigade,* 25.

24 The word removed by the censor is probably "resting." The 18th Battalion had spent a week in Frevillers. GT was to march on 24 October to Ligny-St. Flochel, where the battalion boarded trains for Godewaersveldt and a final march to a new camp at Caestre, to the east of Cassel, as the 18th Battalion, together with the remainder of the corps, moved northward toward the battlefield of Passchendaele. LAC, WD, 18th Battalion, October 1917; Cooper, *Fourth Canadian Infantry Brigade,* 25-26; Nicholson, *C.E.F.,* 323; Corrigall, *The Twentieth,* 153-65.

25 The issue of the burden carried by Canadian soldiers had been raised a few months earlier by Lt. Col. W.W.O. Beveridge, who pointed out that many men serving in the army did not have a good physique but were required to carry a load that "amounts to about 80½ lbs" (36 kilograms). He also noted that a combination of mud and water could increase the load to 114 pounds (almost 52 kilograms), while a wet

overcoat could weigh over 20 pounds (9 kilograms). Another memo by Lieutenant General Maxwell, the quartermaster general, noted that articles shown in the field service manual weighed 59 pounds 6¾ ounces and that to this total had been added a steel helmet, with chain curtain, weighing 2 pounds 10 ounces, giving a total weight of 68 pounds ¾ ounce (30.8 kilograms). Maxwell concluded, however, that nothing could be discarded, save perhaps the groundsheet, which could be conveyed by transport, at least in the summertime. W.W.O. Beveridge, A.D.M.A.S. Sanitation, "Memorandum on the Weight Carried in Relation to the Health of Soldier," 26 January 1917; R.C. Maxwell, First Army, "Weight Carried by Soldier," 27 February 1917 in LAC, RG 9, series III, vol. 384 HQ A&Q, folder 59, files 25-27; for information on full marching order, see Brophy and Partridge, *Tommies' Songs and Slang*, 148.

Letter 34

26 The Third Battle of Ypres, or Passchendaele, essentially consisted of three assaults. The first began at 3:50 A.M. on Tuesday, 31 July 1917, with the attack by nine British divisions and six French divisions along a twenty-four-kilometre front east of Ypres, after a ten-day preliminary bombardment by 3,091 guns firing 4.25 million shells at the cost of £22,211,389.14s.4d. The immediate objective was to drive the Germans off Pilckem Ridge, which commanded Ypres and thus laid the way open for Haig's major assault on Flanders. Heavy rains fell on 31 July, and the intense shelling shattered the drainage system in what was a low-lying area. By the third day, the British had managed to advance to a maximum depth of 2,743 metres at the cost of 31,850 casualties. On the fourth day, the assault ended. Rain fell heavily on 8 August and again so heavily on 14 August that British plans for a second assault had to be postponed for two days. By 25 August, the ground had turned into a quagmire; British losses mounted to 68,010; by 5 October, they stood at 162,768. Two days later, with the rain falling steadily, Haig rejected a request to end the Ypres offensive, a request Currie supported. Currie estimated that the 2,500 metres that still lay between the Allies and their final objective would translate to 16,000 Canadian casualties. In his diary, he wrote: "Passchendaele is not worth one drop of blood." However, on 9 October, Haig ordered the Canadian Corps to Ypres. Nicholson, *C.E.F.*, 304-30; Martienson, *We Stand on Guard*, 169-73; Gray, *Chronicle*, vol. 2, 68, 72; Dean Oliver, "The Canadians at Passchendaele," in *Passchendaele in Perspective: The Third Battle of Ypres*, ed. Peter Liddle, 255-71; Daniel Dancocks, *Legacy of Valour: The Canadians at Passchendaele*.

27 GT has misspelled "Rorabic's" name. **Henry Rorabeck:** born Prince Edward County, Ontario, 14 June 1870 or 1873; patternmaker; enlisted Niagara, 76th Battalion, August 1915, giving 1873 as year of birth; discharged as medically unfit October 1915; successfully enlisted Oshawa, 116th Battalion, December 1915, giving 1870 as year of birth; sailed on the *Olympic* with GT; assigned to garrison duty, England; conduct

and military character were described as good by the authorities; discharged because of physical unfitness and age; returned to Oshawa September 1917. On enlistment, lived at 411 Albert Street; married, with ten children, aged one to twenty-four; died 1949. **Pankhurst:** probably Samuel Edward Pankhurst, born College Hill, South Oshawa, 1872; labourer; enlisted Oshawa, 116th Battalion, April 1916; sailed with GT on the *Olympic*; transferred in October 1916 to the 2nd Battalion; hospitalized with myalgia and poor circulation May 1917; received medical discharge after eight months in France; returned to Canada September 1917; in 1915, he was a married man, with two children aged seventeen and nineteen. **Reuben Northey:** born Oshawa 1896; machinist; enlisted Oshawa, 116th Battalion, December 1915; transferred to the 2nd Battalion; arrived in France October 1916; served four months in the trenches; developed trench foot January 1917 – both feet were affected, but the right foot had also been badly frozen; onset of gangrene led to the amputation of all the toes 30 March 1917; hospitalized until July 1917; discharged as unfit for military service and invalided back to Canada; died in Oshawa, 1971. Trench foot was frequently blamed on the soldier, rather than the cold and wet conditions that caused it. In Northey's case, authorities deemed that neither intemperance nor misconduct was responsible. LAC, box 8453-32, 141992, 746092 Rorabeck, Henry; LAC, box 7556-30, 747994 Pankhurst, Samuel Edward; LAC, box 7375-40, 746067 Northey, Reuben Walter. For more on trench foot, see also Morton, *When Your Number's Up*, 199; Ellis, *Eye-Deep in Hell*, 48-51.

28 **Charlie Danks:** born Marylebone, London, England, 1877; tanner; enlisted Oshawa, 116th Battalion, December 1915; transferred to the 18th Battalion December 1916. Blown up by a shell and buried alive in a trench; suffering from nervous shock, spent five days in a dressing station March 1917; admitted to the 4th Canadian Field Army Hospital with trench fever and dysentery April 1917; evacuated to England May 1917; discharged from the 18th Battalion to the 4th Reserve Battalion July 1917; granted good conduct stripe, Bramshott, December 1917; in 1919, a medical board concluded that Danks suffered from myalgia and war neurosis; died 1955. On enlistment, Danks was living at 31 Jackson Street, Oshawa, a few doors from Tom Milgate, and a short distance from Albert Street; he was married, with five children. LAC, box 2289-60, 745963 Danks, Charles Frederick; Brophy and Partridge define the term "swung the lead" as "malingering: or otherwise evading duty." See *Tommies' Songs and Slang*, 189.

29 GT was appointed lance corporal on 7 May 1917. "'Issue' serg" was a term of derision. The adjective "issue" was used to denote anything officially supplied to the men. LAC, box 9698-43, 3235822 Timmins, George.

30 Earlier experience had shown that the soldier in the field needed extensive knowledge of his whereabouts and objectives for a reasonable chance of success. The training courses, using clay models, aerial photographs, and full-scale mock-ups, proved to be effective. Rawling, *Surviving Trench Warfare*, 98-100.

31 Known as pillboxes because of their shape, these strong points were made of reinforced concrete and were invulnerable to almost anything but a direct hit by heavy
artillery. The pillboxes, which housed machine gunners and riflemen, were so arranged as to provide overlapping arcs of machine-gun fire: troops attacking one
strong point found themselves exposed to fire on their flanks from the neighbouring
strong points. German tactical developments meant that the Allies had to rethink
their own tactics, which hitherto consisted – as at Vimy – of taking the front line
trenches and then using fresh troops to pass over these positions to attack and
capture the second line of defence and so on until the final objective was secured.
Marteinson, *We Stand on Guard*, 169-70; Rawling, *Surviving Trench Warfare*, 144-45;
Nicholson, *C.E.F.*, 239-41, 316-18; Paddy Griffith, *Battle Tactics of the Western Front:
The British Army's Art of Attack 1916-18.*

32 In his letter to MT, GT imitated an old-fashioned script to write the name "Ye Olde
Bulford Arms."

33 Lice tended to congregate in the seams of shirts and undergarments. The seams
could be run quickly over an open candle flame, a skill that required good timing
and much practice to kill the lice while avoiding scorching the material; lice could
also be cracked between the thumbnails. Morton, *When Your Number's Up*, 139;
Brophy and Partridge, *Tommies' Songs and Slang*, 98-99, 109; Ellis, *Eye-Deep in Hell*,
55-57. Leslie Frost, Ontario premier from 1949 to 1961, also refers to "reading" his
shirt when hunting for lice. See Fleming, *The Wartime Letters*, 252, 274, n. 51.

Letter 35

34 On 7 November 1917, the 18th Battalion was based at a reserve camp in Potijze on
the Ypres-Menin Road. For several days, it was employed on fatigues, grading the
bed for the light railway, burying communication lines, and carrying materiel to
forward points. The work was gruelling, the shell fire continuous, and the mud
often waist deep. LAC, WD, 18th Battalion, November 1917. A photograph of Potijze
can be found in Fleming, *The Wartime Letters*, 223. Comparatively little has been
written about the organization and work involved in creating the necessary infra-
structure (buildings, roads, railways, trenches, gun emplacements, and power
sources) to fight the war successfully and about the troops specially raised and
organized for these purposes. Nicholson's *C.E.F.* devotes only a few pages to the
Canadian Corps of Engineers, including tramway and tunnelling companies, the
Corps of Canadian Railway Troops, the Canadian Forestry Corps, and the pioneer
battalions. See Nicholson, *C.E.F.*, 485-503; W. Tait, *1st Canadian Pioneers C.E.F.: Brief
History of the Battalion France and Flanders, 1916-1918;* Michael Ryan, "Supplying
the Material Battle: Combined Logistics in the Canadian Corps, 1915-1918"; K.W.
Mitchinson, *Pioneer Battalions in the Great War: Organized and Intelligent Labour.*

35 **George Alexander Sisson:** born Cavan, Ontario, 1895; telephone installer; enlisted
Oshawa, 116th Battalion, March 1916; transferred to the 18th Battalion with GT
October 1916; wounded in left hand by a shell 11 April 1917; hospitalized for 81 days;

rejoined the 18th on 11 December 1917; wounded again February 1918 by shrapnel in right leg; earlier hand wound developed a septic ulcer, hospitalized for 123 days; pronounced fit July 1918; returned to Canada January 1919; died in 1922. Burr was still in hospital and was not to return to the field until 14 August 1918. LAC, box 8952-55, 746166 Sisson, George Alexander; LAC, box 1311-23, 745906 Burr, John Henry.

36 During the night of 8 November, the 18th Battalion took over the front line, relieving some men of the 22nd and 25th Battalions of the 6th Canadian Infantry Brigade. The weather was poor, and the front line and supports, subjected to continuous shelling, were in bad condition. For the period 9-12 November, the 18th Battalion WD records that supplies reached the 18th, which was in the front line, by means of a series of tracks made by laying down trench mats or duckboards. Rations and supplies could be moved only by mules and men along the tracks (which consequently were subjected to repeated shellfire) since the depth of mud precluded the use of any other route. The 18th Battalion WD records: "During the whole of this tour, the officers and men held this part of the line under the most severe conditions possible." The total casualties for the tour were forty-five ORs killed in action, six officers and sixty ORs wounded, and one officer and twenty-five ORs gassed. The WD also records the death of a mule "which fell off the duckboard tracks and owing to the depth of the mud, had to be shot." LAC, WD, 18th Battalion, November 1917; John Singleton, "Britain's Military Use of Horses, 1914-1918," 179-203.

Letter 36

37 The 18th Battalion moved by bus from close to Ouderdom to Robecq on 15 November, then to Auchel on 16 November, and by motor truck to Villers-au-Bois on 17 November. LAC, WD, 18th Battalion, November 1917. The use of motorized transport in war was an innovation. Buses and trucks came into use commercially for the first time in the 1890s, and, by the outbreak of the war, the British had numerous three-tonne-capacity trucks among its fleet of a hundred vehicles. Mechanization revolutionized the logistics of war, allowing ever greater forces to be mobilized. The artillery barrage that preceded the first attack of the Passchendaele offensive would have been impossible without rail and motor transport. The latter, in particular, aided the artillery, which had an insufficient number of animals to deliver the ammunition from railheads to the front. The British Army ended the war with sixty thousand trucks. Van Creveld, *Technology and War*, 160-61; J.M. Roberts, *Europe 1880-1945*, 267.

38 GT received his "Blighty pass" on 24 November 1917. LAC, box 9698-43, 3235822 Timmins, George.

Letter 37

39 The long letter, which GT refers to in Letter 37, relating his experiences at Passchendaele has not survived. Letter 38 indicates that GT wrote several letters on the subject. The 18th Battalion WD makes clear why GT's letter of 7 November was a short one.

On 6 November, elements of the 1st and 2nd Canadian Divisions took Passchendaele Village at the cost of 2,238 casualties, 734 of them fatal. In this action, two Victoria Crosses were won. Finally on 10 November, in heavy rain, the 1st Canadian Division launched an assault to secure the remaining high ground still in enemy hands to the northeast of Passchendaele. The Canadians prevailed, but at a cost of 1,094 casualties, 420 of them fatal. Total 2nd Division casualties, 1-15 November, were 2,649; total Canadian casualties, 26 October-15 November, were 12,000. In the Third Battle of Ypres (31 July-15 November), the total Allied casualties were approximately 275,000, the German 200,000. LAC, WD, 18th Battalion, November 1917; Nicholson, *C.E.F.*, 304-30; Campbell, "Divisional Experience," 329; Robin Prior and Trevor Wilson, *Passchendaele: The Untold Story*, 179, 186. See also Chap. 3, n. 36.

40 Small Heath is a suburb of Birmingham. This letter was written from 170 Haden Cross, Old Hill, Staffordshire, the home of GT's mother.

41 It is clear that the mud and knee-deep – sometimes waist-deep – water that the 18th Battalion had encountered at Passchendaele were responsible for GT's condition. It sufficed for a soldier to have had his feet soaked and not to have taken off his boots for twenty-four hours for trench foot to set in. In all, 74,711 British troops were hospitalized in France with trench foot or frostbite. GT's gas sores may have been caused by limited exposure to mustard gas or Yperite, which was designed to attack moist parts of the body, such as the eyes, armpits, and crotch, raising excruciatingly painful blisters and sores. Mustard gas was fatal when breathed into the lungs, causing internal blistering of the bronchial tubes and removal of the mucous membrane. Difficult to detect, mustard gas also took as long as twelve hours to produce symptoms. Cook, *No Place to Run*, 119-20, 149-54; Nicholson, *C.E.F.*, 291; Ellis, *Eye-Deep in Hell*, 66-67; D. Winter, *Death's Men*, 122-24; T.J. Mitchell and G.M. Smith, *Medical Services: Casualties and Medical Statistics of the Great War*, Macphail, *Official History of the Canadian Forces*.

Letter 38

42 On GT's nephew, John Thomas Carter, see Chap. 2, n. 33.

43 On growing food shortages, see DeGroot, *Blighty*, 210-14.

Letter 39

44 GT's caution hints that, free of censorship, he had written openly to May from England about his experiences at Passchendaele. Just five months later, on 15 April 1918, General Plummer evacuated five divisions of the Second Army from Passchendaele under the weight of the German Spring Offensive, and, on 16 April, the German Fourth Army reoccupied Passchendaele. Partly on account of this, and partly because of the appalling losses and suffering of the troops in the Passchendaele offensive, the battle became the subject of intense debate. Nicholson, *C.E.F.*, 304-30; Gray, *Chronicle*, vol. 2, 72; Oliver, "The Canadians at Passchendaele"; Prior and Wilson, *Passchendaele*.

Letter 41

45 Winnie's locket and photograph of her father have survived.

46 1917 was a difficult year for the Allied powers. The Russian war effort faded, and in early December the Bolsheviks began peace talks with Germany. In the fall of 1917, the Italian army suffered a catastrophic defeat at Caporetto. On 29 November, Lord Lansdowne, the former British foreign secretary, called for a compromise peace with Germany. In Britain, in November 1917, half a million days were lost to strikes. By February 1918, the head censor at Calais reported that concerns among the troops about food supplies and shortages at home were serious and that the men were writing to their relatives in terms of "them" and "us." Birmingham, only a few miles from where GT was spending his leave, was one of the cities worst hit by food shortages. GT's phrase "they say we are winning" carries overtones of class division. The formation of the Ministry of Information in early 1918, under the Canadian Lord Beaverbrook (Max Aitken), was a direct outgrowth of government concern regarding working-class discontent over food shortages and general war weariness. See DeGroot, *Blighty,* 119; Wilson, *The Myriad Faces of War,* 529-30; Brock Millman, *Managing Domestic Dissent in First World War Britain*; George Robb, *British Culture and the First World War.*

Chapter 4: "Its hell, kiddo, hell"

Letter 42

1 "Outside the dairy shops ... in some parts of London women begin to line up for margarine as early as 5 o'clock on Saturday morning ... in Walworth Road in the south-eastern side of London the queue was estimated to number about 3,000. Two hours later 1,000 of these were sent away unsupplied." "Workers' Demand for Rations," *Times,* 17 December 1917.

2 Soldiers on leave were often distressed by the contrast between life on the home front and that of the combat soldiers and their families. Comprehensive surveys of British wartime society can be found in Trevor Wilson, *The Myriad Faces of War,* and DeGroot, *Blighty.* See also Susan R. Grayzel, *Women and the First World War.* For a discussion of the economic impact of the war in the Canadian context, see Douglas McCalla, "The Economic Impact of the Great War," in MacKenzie, *Canada and the First World War,* 138-53, and Adam Crerar, "Ontario and the Great War," in MacKenzie, *Canada and the First World War,* 230-71.

Letter 43

3 The Canadian Corps, reunited with the First Army on 20 November in its old territory of Lens and Vimy, had been repairing trenches and putting out barbed wire at night. On 3 December, the 18th relieved the 19th in the front line in the Acheville section near Fresnoy, and, on 14 December, the 18th Battalion was in suburban camp near Villers-au-Bois. LAC, WD, 18th Battalion, December 1917.

Letter 44

4 The 18th Battalion WD reads: "Christmas Day. No training today. A Christmas Dinner of Turkeys & Pork was arranged for all men of the Battalion, and everything was done by the officers to make the men comfortable for this, occasion." LAC, WD, 18th Battalion, December 1917.

5 On 19 December, the 18th Battalion moved to a rest area at Febvin-Palfart. The soldiers, billeted in village houses and nearby barns, spent their days in parades and training. Election polls opened for Canadian soldiers on 11 December. GT's first comments on the election appear in his letter of 7 January 1918. LAC, WD, 18th Battalion, December 1917.

6 GT had made four such cross-outs up to this point.

7 GT is possibly referring to Cptn. (Acting Maj.) W.J. Gander of Hamilton, Ontario. On 4 January 1918, the *Toronto Daily Star* reported that Maj. W.J. Gander had a foot amputated in London, England. The 18th Battalion WD indicates that he rejoined the battalion from hospital on 29 October 1917 but was wounded again ten days later carrying out a relief on the night of 8 November 1917. LAC, WD, 18th Battalion, October and November 1917; "Canadian Wounded," *Toronto Daily Star*, 4 January 1918.

8 Stone transferred to the YMCA on 24 November 1917. LAC, box 9357-3, 747995 Stone, Walter.

9 Sisson, and Judd rejoined the 18th Battalion in the field on 11 December 1917. On Sisson see Chap. 3, n. 35. **Arthur Judd:** born Dunton Bassett, Leicestershire, England, 1896; piano tuner; enlisted Oshawa, 116th Battalion, March 1916; transferred to the 18th Battalion October 1916; wounded in left forearm 13 March 1917; transferred to England, 3rd Southern General Hospital, Oxford; discharged from hospital 4 May 1917; transferred to 4th Canadian Reserve Battalion; rejoined 18 December 1917. LAC, box 4985-47, 746177 Judd, Arthur, Sergeant.

Letter 45

10 Winnie celebrated her twelfth birthday on 28 January 1918.

Letter 46

11 On 7 January 1918, the battalion was in Febvin-Palfart, its days taken up by training and by inspections, including one by Currie on 12 January. LAC, WD, 18th Battalion, January 1918.

12 Returned soldiers, and women such as May Timmins, were mobilized to participate in rallies and political meetings in support of conscription and the Union government. On polling day, 17 December 1917, the Union government prevailed but at the expense of dividing the country. The division, Keshen observes, "hardly seemed worthwhile considering that only 24,132 conscripts made it to France." Barbara Wilson, *Ontario and the First World War*, liv-lvii; Morton, *When Your Number's*

Up, 64, 67, 245; Keshen, *Propaganda and Censorship*, 46-50; J.L. Granatstein, "Conscription in the Great War," in MacKenzie, *Canada and the Great War*, 62-75; "Officers from the Front Address Whitby Audience," *Gazette and Chronicle*, 18 October 1917.

13 GT's comments concerning Jeyes are not supported by Jeyes' medical records. **Thomas Jeyes**: born Woolwich, England, 1875; iron moulder; enlisted Oshawa, 116th Battalion, August 1915; sailed on the *Olympic* with GT; transferred to 18th Battalion October 1916; almost immediately hospitalized with influenza and bronchitis at No. 39 General Hospital, Le Havre; not discharged to reinforcements until 3 February 1917; wounded by a shell in left hip, Neuville St. Vaast, 8 April 1917; sent to 22nd General Hospital, Camiers, followed by hospitals in Stoke-on-Trent, Newcastle, and Buxton; in August 1917, medical board recommended discharge; Jeyes was pronounced "somewhat lame," Bramshott, October 1917; returned to Canada October 1917; died July 1968, in his ninety-third year. At the time of enlistment, Jeyes was employed by Malleable Iron Works, earning $3.50 a day and paying $10.00 a month in rent. In 1916, he was married and had three children, aged between two and fifteen years. LAC, box 4837-12, 746025 Jeyes, Thomas.

14 On "Cox's army," see Introduction, n. 88.

15 About 90 percent of soldiers supported Borden, not least because of his promise of three months' furlough in Canada for "Old Originals." The promise was not kept. Just 838 furloughs were granted, because the army was loath to lose experienced soldiers. Keshen, *Propaganda and Censorship*, 49, 232; Barbara Wilson, *Ontario and the First World War*, lxvii; "Officers from the Front Address Whitby Audience," *Gazette and Chronicle*, 18 October 1917; Terry Copp, "The Military Effort, 1914-1918," in Mackenzie, *Canada and the Great War*, 35-61.

16 GT probably meant "Aussys." The terms "Aussie," "Aus," and "Digger" were used to refer to the Australians. Conscription had become an issue for Australians in October 1916, when they voted against it, as they did again in December 1917. Keshen, *Propaganda and Censorship*, 49; Fuller, *Troop Morale*, 170; Gray, *Chronicle*, vol. 2, 119; Pope and Wheal, *The First World War*, 44; John Snow, ed., *Collins Australian Encyclopedia*, 710; *Official History of Australia in the War of 1914-1918*.

17 Privates J.J. Bennett of 201 Albert Street, David Farrer of Eldon (now Banting) Avenue, and George Hobson of Queen Street were among the men who did come home on leave; also Cptn. (Dr.) James Moore in November 1917. See "Three More of the 'Originals' Home on Furlough," *Ontario Reformer*, 26 April 1918; "Dr. Moore's Lecture at St. George's Hall," *Ontario Reformer*, 30 November 1917; Morton, *When Your Number's Up*, 66, 244-45; Keshen, *Propaganda and Censorship*, 46-50.

18 The *Ontario Reformer* of 30 November 1917 carries a notice that the Whitby tribunal granted exemption to William George Burns of the Shoe Store, Oshawa, until 10 January 1918. The government had pledged that agricultural workers would be exempted from service. Nicholson, *C.E.F.*, 344.

19   **Thomas Milgate:** passed through four battalions before ending up as an army cook with the 21st Canadian Infantry Battalion, 4th Infantry Brigade (to which the 18th Battalion belonged), April 1917; sentenced to fourteen days' Field Punishment No. 1, for "Contravention of G.R.O. 1661. Purchasing wine during prohibited hours," April 1918; wounded in the eye and face 14 August 1918; admitted to No. 41 Stationary Hospital, Amiens, 12 September 1918; returned to Canada March 1919; died aged sixty-nine in June 1950. LAC, box 6167-54, 141973 Milgate, Thomas William Alfred; see also Introduction, n. 69; "How Khaki-Clad 'Chefs' Carry Out Their Work," *Gazette and Chronicle*, 14 October 1915. On Field Punishment No. 1, see Morton, *When Your Number's Up*, 84; Ellis, *Eye-Deep in Hell*, 188.

Letter 47

20   On 15 January, after a twenty-five-day stay in the rest area at Febvin-Palfart, the battalion moved to Auchel, marching on 16 January from Auchel to Chamblain l'Abbé. From here they were marched to reserve at Hills Camp, Neuville St. Vaast, relieving the 47th Battalion in the front line of the Avion sector on 18 January. Downpours throughout most of the three-day march compounded the damage done by shell fire to the trenches they were to occupy. On one tour in night support, 24-28 January, they did nothing but clean and improve trenches in the battalion's area. On Sunday, 3 February 1918, the 18th Battalion was in billets at Chamblain l'Abbé, not far from Mont St. Eloy; Divine Service was at 10 A.M. in the cinema hut. LAC, WD, 18th Battalion, January 1918.

21   On 1 December 1917, the Royal Flying Corps had a record 4,338 serviceable aircraft on the Western Front. Aerial activity over Britain also increased notably in January and February 1918. On 28 January 1918, 8,100 pounds (3,675 kilograms) of bombs were dropped on London, killing 67 and injuring 166. Two days later, 14,200 kilograms of bombs were dropped on Paris, in the space of thirty minutes, by thirty Gotha bombers. In all, 49 people were killed and 206 injured. On 16 February, the German airship R39 dropped the largest bomb of the war on London, 2,204 pounds (1,000 kilograms). Soldiers wryly called bombs dropped by aircraft "air pills." Gray, *Chronicle*, vol. 2, 113, 129, 137, 339.

22   In January 1918, the River Seine froze over for the first time in 120 years. Ibid., 123.

Letter 48

23   It seems likely that GT has got his days muddled. In 1918, 3 February fell on a Sunday; the following Tuesday would have been 5 February 1918.

24   Canadian soldiers and the British New Armies at the beginning of the war received rudimentary training at best. Because Canada's pre-war permanent force was so small, there were only eighty experienced instructors to train 25,000 men. On the training schools organized by the Canadian Corps and divisional schools, like the

one GT was attending, see Campbell, "Divisional Experience," 279-327; Morton, *When Your Number's Up*, 31, 118-19, 164-65, 172; Rawling, *Surviving Trench Warfare*, 68-69, 136; Cook, *No Place to Run*, 72-73, 121-23.

25 A squadron of the New South Wales Lancers was in England training with regular British forces at Aldershot when the Boer War broke out, in the fall of 1899. It was decided to send the Lancers to the Cape. "Departure of the New South Wales Lancers," *Times*, 11 October 1899.

26 The Bowery was an area of New York City known for its beer halls and cheap entertainment. "Bowery boy" in the mid-nineteenth century referred to a rough and rowdy man noted for his vulgarity. The gumshoe, invented by Goodyear in the late nineteenth century, quickly came to refer to something carried on quietly and surreptitiously. See Mitford M. Matthews, *A Dictionary of Americanisms*, 173, 759.

27 Harry Lauder (1870-1950) was a renowned Scots music hall comedian. In November 1917, he was in Canada on a tour promoting Victory Bonds. The *Toronto Daily Star* recorded that his concert at Massey Hall on 29 November 1917 resulted in the sale of $25,000 worth of bonds; by 1 December 1917, the figure reached almost a million dollars. An advertisement in the *Star* on 30 November 1917 touted him as "the Highest Salaried Entertainer in the World." One of the 12-inch records advertised for sale, at $1.50, on the Victor label, was "Breakfast in Bed on Sunday Morn." The Lauders' only child, Cptn. John C. Lauder, was killed on 28 December 1916, at age twenty-five. Of his death Lauder wrote: "For me there was no past and there would be no future." On stage he wore a tam-o'shanter with a feather. The 91st Battalion Canadian Militia – the Argyll and Sutherland Highlanders of Canada – were known as "The Harry Lauders" on account of their headdress. Fuller, *Troop Morale*, 125; D. Winter, *Death's Men*, 256-57; Harry Lauder, *A Minstrel in France*; CWGC; "Harry Lauder Sells Near Million in Bonds," *Toronto Daily Star*, 1 December 1917. In November and December 1917, there were numerous references to Harry Lauder in the *Star*. Some of Lauder's recordings can be found on YouTube, at http://www.youtube.com.

28 The 22nd Battalion, 5th Brigade, 2nd Division, was a French-Canadian unit organized under Col. F.M. Gaudet and mobilized in St. Jean, Quebec. From the time the battalion arrived in France in September 1915 it distinguished itself in every major engagement involving the Canadian Corps. Maj. Georges Vanier, future Governor General of Canada, served with the 22nd. Cpl. Joseph Kaeble (aged twenty-six) and Lt. Jean Brilliant (aged twenty-eight) of the 22nd both won posthumous Victoria Crosses. See Jacques Castonguay, "Brilliant, Jean" and "Kaeble, Joseph" in the *Dictionary of Canadian Biography Online*, http://www.biographi.ca; John A. Sweetenham, ed., *Valiant Men: Canada's Victoria Cross and George Cross Winners*. Harry Lauder commented of French Canadian soldiers: "I was not aware that there were any hyphenated Canadians. The true red blood in the French-Canadians is fighting

as a Canadian soldier to-day. Their deeds speak for themselves." "Harry Lauder Sells Near Million in Bonds," *Toronto Daily Star*, 1 December 1917.

29   Over one-third of the 11,500 eligible Aboriginal men enlisted in the Canadian Expeditionary Force, several serving as snipers. One, an Ojibwa, Frank Pegah-magabow, killed 368 of the enemy and was awarded the Military Medal and two bars. Morton, *When Your Number's Up*, 78.

Letter 49

30   This was GT's second letter of the day.

31   No known copy of this issue of the *Ontario Reformer* survives.

Letter 51

32   This letter was edited for publication. The letter is crossed out from "France Feb. 7th 1918" down to and including "but I recollect that." The last part of the letter, immediately after "Good luck to them," has also been deleted.

Letter 52

33   On Friday, 22 February 1918, the 18th Battalion was in Vancouver Camp at Chateau de la Haie, the day devoted to company parades and inspections. On 2 February 1918, the 18th Battalion had left Hills Camp, Neuville St. Vaast, moving by way of Mont St. Eloy to billets at Chamblain l'Abbé. On the night of 8 February, the troops had moved again via Mont St. Eloy to Neuville St. Vaast, and then over Vimy Ridge to the Méricourt sector as the 4th Brigade relieved the 5th Brigade. From 9-15 February, the 18th Battalion worked on fatigues and salvaging material, including 439 reels of barbed wire, 816 iron stakes, and 2,301 wooden ones. The work was danger-ous: "Sentries must be alert, NO MAN'S LAND constantly patrolled during hours of darkness, allposts [sic] strongly wired in, and every preparation made to repulse him with loss ... Care must be taken that men do not proceed alone, or in very small parties, along stretches of trenches in the Front Line, which are not occupied asit [sic] has been known for the enemy to crawl through our wire and way-lay them." The defensive preparations undertaken by the Canadian Corps were extensive: on 26 February, the men of the 18th Battalion tested their box gas respirators by moving through real gas clouds. The anticipated German Spring Offensive was much feared, as the Germans were able to concentrate all their men and resources on the Western Front following the Peace of Brest-Litovsk between Germany and Russia on 3 March 1918. LAC, WD, 18th Battalion, February 1918.

34   Like GT, Cooper had transferred to the 18th Battalion in the fall of 1916. He was hospitalized at the end of January 1917 with trench fever; lightly wounded by shrapnel in the arm in August 1917. LAC, box 1970-22, 745950 Cooper, Fred Frank. For more on Cooper, see Introduction, n. 70.

35   On Wilson, see Chap. 1, n. 96.

Letter 53

36 On 19 March 1918, the 18th Battalion was in Bois des Alleux. After it had entered the front line in the Lens sector on the night of 27 February, it suffered a number of killed and injured as a result of enemy artillery activity along the whole front. Relieved by the 20th Battalion on the night of 4 March, the 18th returned to support, repairing trenches and preparing positions for the anticipated German assault. Currie employed the interim to bring the fighting efficiency of the corps to the highest level possible. The 18th received some reinforcements, including, on 15 March, ninety-one ORs from the 5th Canadian Division. LAC, WD, 18th Battalion, March 1918; Arthur Currie, "Interim Report on the Operations of the Canadian Corps during the Year 1918," *Report of the Ministry,* 99-108.

37 **Frederick Hicks:** born Birmingham, England, 1883; sheet metal worker; enlisted Whitby, 182nd Battalion, April 1916; arrived England May 1917; transferred to the 116th Battalion February 1918, then to 3rd Battalion Canadian Machine Gun Corps on May 1918; wounded in right forearm by shrapnel, reducing the grip of his right hand by approximately 40 percent, July 1918; did not report his injury at the time; shell shocked after "a severe shelling," which produced trembling and "a general nervousness," August 1918. Hicks was married and living in South Oshawa in 1916. **Joseph Spencer:** born Newcastle, Ontario, 1887; stove mounter; spent three summer camps with the 46th Ontario Regiment (1906-08); enlisted Oshawa, 182nd Battalion, May 1916; sailed for England May 1917; served with 116th and 2nd Battalions; wounded in face 8 August 1918. He was married and lived at 483 Albert Street, Oshawa, in 1916. **Charles Foster:** born Oshawa, 1892; tire finisher; enlisted Oshawa, 182nd Battalion, February 1917; arrived England May 1917; passed through four battalions before taken on the strength of the 116th Battalion February 1918; killed in action 19 April 1918. His photograph can be found in the Book of Remembrance in the Oshawa Public Library, Main Branch. It is not known how Charles Foster died, but he is buried in Aix-Noulette Communal Cemetery Extension, thirteen kilometres south of Bethune, in the same cemetery as Harry West (see Introduction, n. 76). Foster lived with his widowed mother, Mrs. Louisa Foster, at 497 Albert Street (see Chap. 1, n. 84). **Blackler:** probably Leonard Blackler, born Oshawa 1895; painter; enlisted Kingston, in the Royal Canadian Horse Artillery, November 1915; left for England March 1916; to France July 1916; driver, 3rd Divisional Ammunition Column; returned to Canada March 1919. **Orville Hurst:** born Oshawa, 1896; patternmaker; served one year in Coburg Battery, one year in 24th Regiment Grey's Horse; enlisted Port Hope, 39th Battalion, February 1915; sailed for England June 1915; transferred to the 26th Battalion June 1916; to 116th Battalion September 1917. Suffered shell shock, 1916; blown up by a shell, burned by a high-explosive shell, won Military Medal, 1917; gassed, 1918. **Logerman** [sic]: Paulus Logeman, born Amsterdam, Holland, 1888; stove mounter; enlisted Oshawa, 182nd Battalion, April 1916; arrived England May 1917; passed through several reserve battalions, transferred to the 116th, .

February 1918. Logeman was married, with two children (one year, and one day old on 2 April 1917). He lived in College Hill on Mill Street, in South Oshawa. His younger brother, George John Logeman, enlisted and served in England. Their mother, Mrs. W.M. Logeman, lived on Court Street, Oshawa. LAC, box 4324-14, 868164 Hicks, Frederick William; LAC, box 9190-42, 868126 Spencer, Joseph; LAC, box 3226-20, 86843; Foster, Charles; LAC, box 748-6, 348399 Blackler, Leonard; LAC, box 4647-40, 412601 Hurst, Orville; LAC, box 5717-14, 868125 Logeman, Paulus; LAC, box 5717-13, 2161318 Logeman, Geo. John; "Ontario County's Heroes Return from World War," *Ontario Reformer*, 4 April 1919.

38   Late February 1918 saw much aircraft activity in the vicinity of the front held by the 4th Canadian Infantry Brigade. On 25 February, an Allied reconnaissance plane forced an enemy machine down behind the Allied lines, possibly the plane to which GT refers. In retaliation, the next day six German scouts attacked a British reconnaissance plane, shooting it down. Corrigall, *The Twentieth*, 111.

39   GT's intelligence information, or his intuition, was very good. Gunner Henry Dunn arrived at the French port of Le Havre on 15 March 1918. LAC, box 2749-5, 2601823 Dunn, Harry.

Letter 54

40   The Michael Offensive (less commonly referred to as the Second Battle of the Somme or the *Kaiserschlacht*), which began on 21 March 1918, sought to drive a wedge between the French and British defensives zones before substantive American support could arrive in Europe. The German army was able to concentrate more of its divisions in the west (30 percent of its strength between November 1917 and March 1918). Allied losses of 1917 (a 25 percent decline in manpower over the preceding eight months) dictated the maintenance of a defensive stance. The uncertainty, high tension, and anxiety of the period are reflected in GT's surviving letters and vividly captured in the 18th Battalion's WD. The end of March 1918 saw the 2nd Division just south of Arras, in the line at Neuville-Vitasse. The next three months brought sustained and intense military activity. On 2 April 1918, the 18th Battalion's war diarist records that there was no shelter available to the men in the trenches and the enemy artillery fire had so disrupted communications that runners had to be used, even in broad daylight, in full sight of the enemy, traversing "ground continually swept by M.G. [machine gun] fire." On 6 April, when the 26th Battalion relieved the 18th in the front line, the men of the 18th were instructed to hand over any unused bandoliers of ammunition so as to augment the reserves of those going into the front line. Throughout April and May, artillery and aircraft of both sides were fully deployed, while the infantry were engaged in improving defences, patrolling the lines, reconnaissance, and trench raiding. LAC, RG 9, Militia and Defence, series III-D-3, vol. 4926, reel T-10721, file 399, War Diary, 18th Battalion, March 1918 (hereafter cited as LAC, WD, 18th Battalion, file 399); Gray, *Chronicle*, vol. 2, 144-54; Nicholson, *C.E.F.*, 366-76; Pope and Wheal, *The First World War*, 264-65; Campbell,

"Divisional Experience," 382-97; Mark Connelly, *Steady the Buffs! A Regiment, a Region and the Great War,* 162-82.

Chapter 5: "Keep on hoping, sweetheart"

Letter 55

1 During May 1918, the 18th Battalion continued the work, begun in April, of building and repairing dugouts and trenches, by day and by night, under frequent and sometimes intense artillery fire. Both sides relentlessly pursued trench raiding and patrolling. Letter 55, like Letter 56, bears a distinct fingerprint, perhaps that of GT. LAC, WD, 18th Battalion, file 399, May 1918.

Letter 56

2 Confirmation of GT's explanation of his employment, and that of the 2nd Division around Arras, can be found in Nicholson and in Campbell. The 2nd Canadian Division was transferred briefly to X Corps and then to VI Corps. In the ninety-two days they helped to hold the line, the 2nd Division lost 21 officers and 336 ORs killed; 97 officers and 2,277 ORs wounded; 2 officers and 34 ORs missing. Campbell points out casualties for the remainder of the Canadian Corps, over the same period, were 185 officers and 2,556 ORs killed, wounded, or missing. Nicholson, *C.E.F.,* 384; Campbell, "Divisional Experience," 382-98.

3 GT is almost certainly referring to an incident on the night of 3 April 1918 when two men were killed and Lt. R.E. Lawrance and seven other men were wounded. **Reginald Ernest Lawrance:** born in Middlesex England, 1877; served for almost nine years with the 2nd Dorset Regiment; member of the 108th Regiment, Waterloo County; enlisted October 1914; married and living in Berlin Ontario. LAC, box 5464-7, Lawrence [sic], Reginald Ernest, Lieutenant; LAC, WD, 18th Battalion, file 399, April 1918.

4 Six men were killed and fifteen wounded, 5 April 1918; one man killed and three wounded, 3 April 1918; three men killed and thirty-one wounded, including one officer, twenty-two-year-old Lt. G.N. Tucker, 2 April 1918. LAC, WD, 18th Battalion, file 399, April 1918; LAC, box 9809-18, Tucker, Gilbert Norman, Lieutenant.

5 On shell shock, see Tom Brown, "Shell Shock in the Canadian Expeditionary Force, 1914-1918: Canadian Psychiatry in the Great War," in *Health, Disease and Medicine: Essays in Canadian History,* ed. Charles G. Roland, 308-32; Peter Leese, *Shell Shock: Traumatic Neurosis and the British Soldiers of the First World War.* In January 2000, a special issue of the *Journal of Contemporary History* was devoted to a discussion of shell shock.

Letter 57

6 The battalion went into divisional reserve on the night of 21 June and was billeted in Wailly Woods. On 27 June, the 18th was relieved by the Princess Patricia's Canadian

Light Infantry and moved to "exceptionally good" billets in Lattre-St-Quentin. The afternoon of 29 June was taken up with recreational training. LAC, WD, 18th Battalion, file 399, June and July 1918.

7 Five pounds was a considerable sum for a private: a glass of weak beer could be purchased for one pence, a glass and a bottle of wine for about two shillings. Morton, *When Your Number's Up*, 239.

8 On 1 July, Dominion Day, a Canadian Corps sports day at Tinques was attended by almost fifty thousand Canadian troops. Aircraft provided protection for the gathering. See Nicholson, *C.E.F.*, 384; LAC, WD, 18th Battalion, file 399, July 1918; William Hayes, "In Fighting Trim: Canada Teaching Her Soldiers to Play in Order to Fit Them for Fighting," 277-88.

9 **Fred Manning:** born Oshawa, 1886; enlisted Oshawa, 116th Battalion, January 1916; sailed on the *Olympic* with GT; joined the 18th Battalion October 1916; wounded in left arm 15 August 1917; discharged from hospital September 1917; rejoined the 18th Battalion 23 November 1917; returned to Canada May 1919. LAC, box 5897-22, 746058 Manning, Frederick Charles.

Letter 58

10 After spending seven months in English hospitals, Alfred Gower spent a further four months in hospital in Canada following his return in February 1918. He died in January 1958, in his seventieth year. At the time of enlistment, he and his wife, Henrietta, had a ten-month-old son, George Alfred. LAC, box 3687-24, 746162 Gower, Alfred Henry. For more on Gower, see Chap. 2, n. 44.

11 Enoch was MT's brother.

Letter 60

12 On Danks, see Chap. 3, n. 28.

13 Graydon Gibbie had enlisted on 24 December 1915 (see Introduction, n. 73). At least two men from Oshawa named George Smith enlisted in December 1915 but neither of them in the artillery. One was a coremaker, born London, England, 1893; enlisted 116th Battalion, 11 December 1915; died 1972. LAC, box 9044-40, 746103 Smith, George. The other was a bricklayer, born Toronto, 1882, but living in Oshawa; enlisted 116th Battalion, 28 December 1915; died 1922. LAC, box 9047-42, 746107 Smith, George James.

14 **William Lewis:** born London, England, 1891; moulder; enlisted Toronto, Overseas Canadian Army Service Corps, Training Depot, December 1915; driver, 10th Canadian Infantry Brigade Headquarters, July 1916; absent without leave for 46.5 hours, resulting in seven days' Field Punishment No. 1 and forfeit of two days' pay, January 1919. Lewis paid $15 a month to Miss Jennie Smith of 379 Albert Street. He died in 1979. LAC, box 5632-17, 510471 Lewis, William James.

15 On Bill (J.W.) and Charlie Burcham [sic], see Chap. 1, n. 45; on Harry Winship, see Chap. 1, n. 65.

16 **Jack Wilson:** one of three brothers, born in Newcastle on Tyne, England, serving with the CEF. All three were painters. Jack, who was married, enlisted in the 20th Battalion on 1 March 1915. Harry signed up on 22 September 1914 and Joseph on 28 May 1915. In his letter, GT appears to have confused the names of the brothers. (Robert) Henry Wilson of the 2nd Battalion died of wounds received in action on 7 November 1917 and is buried in Lijssenthoek Military Cemetery. His brother, Joseph Wilson, was wounded three times. Jack might have believed that Joseph was back in Canada, but according to Joseph's military records he did not return until February 1919. LAC, box 10462-11, 58068 Wilson, John George; LAC, box 10472-16, 8392 Wilson, Robert Henry; LAC, box 10464-28, 47979 Wilson, Joseph; CWGC. For more on Joseph Wilson, see Chap. 1, n. 96.

17 **Ernie Miner:** probably E.J. Miners, born Oshawa, 1898; shipper; enlisted Coburg, Coburg Heavy Battery, February 1917; gunner 10th Brigade, March 1918. LAC, box 6236-6, 2001060 Miners, Ernest John.

18 The 2nd Division was being readied for the Battle of Amiens, which began on 8 August. On the first day, the Canadian Corps advanced 9.6 kilometres and reclaimed twelve French villages, capturing 5,033 prisoners of war and 161 guns. See Nicholson, *C.E.F.,* 402; Gray, *Chronicle,* vol. 2, 200.

19 Dr. Thomas Erlin Kaiser graduated from the University of Toronto Medical School in 1890, setting up his medical practice in Oshawa. He was the town's mayor from 1907 to 1908 and its Member of Parliament from 1925 to 1930. He was also the inspiration behind Oshawa's War Memorial in Memorial Park, patterned after the one in Evesham, Worcestershire, England. The sculptor was Alfred Howell. Amanda Kesek, "Dr. T. E. Kaiser," Historical Information Sheet, Oshawa Historical Society, 6 May 1999; "116th Make History," *Ontario Reformer,* 8 March 1924; "Magnificent, Lasting Tribute to Oshawa's Heroic Sons," *Oshawa Daily Reformer,* 30 June 1927.

Letter 61

20 This letter was written from the 4th London General Hospital, Denmark Hill. LAC, box 9698-43, 3235822 Timmins, George.

21 On 8 August 1918, GT received his "Blighty" wound; his medical report noted: "Shrapnel ball 8.5 cm. anterior to articulation of left femur." He also had two wounds in the right forearm. LAC, box 9698-43, 3235822 Timmins, George.

Letter 62

22 GT was clearly concerned about infection. His medical records indicate that his wounds had turned slightly sceptic at the beginning of September and on 28 September there was still "puffy granulation tissue over centre of scar." LAC, box 9698-43, 3235822 Timmins, George. The *Ontario Reformer* reported on GT's wounding: "Pte George Timmins, whose wife and three children live on Albert St., who has been overseas since the war began, was wounded for the first time the past week, by gunshot in the hip. His many friends in Oshawa, as well as his family hope that his

wounds may not prove serious, but his family can hardly be blamed for hoping that it will be sufficient to open the way for him to come home." The report was, of course, not entirely accurate: GT had not been overseas since 1914. "Local and Personal Items," *Ontario Reformer,* 23 August 1918.

23   GT convalesced at Woodcote Park, Epsom, Surrey; he was discharged on Armistice Day, 11 November 1918. LAC, box 9698-43, 3235822 Timmins, George.

Letter 63

24   On Canada's nurses, see G.W.L. Nicholson, *Canada's Nursing Sisters;* Susan Mann, ed., *The War Diary of Claire Glass, 1915-1918;* Bill Rompkey and Bert Riggs, eds., *Your Daughter, Fanny: The War Letters of Frances Cluett, VAD.*

Fragment 4

25   On 28 December 1918, GT was transferred to the 4th Canadian Reserve Battalion and, on 9 January 1919, moved to Kinmel Park Camp, Rhyl, North Wales. He returned to Canada on the *Aquitania* on 18 January and disembarked in Halifax on 24 January 1919. A few weeks later, Kinmel Camp witnessed riots over delayed sailings that saw five men killed and twenty-three injured. Nicholson, *C.E.F.,* 532; Desmond Morton, "'Kicking and Complaining': Demobilization Riots in the Canadian Expeditionary Force, 1918-19," 334-60.

26   "Loll" was probably GT's sister Edith's fiancée.

Epilogue: "Don't forget to write to Grandpa"

Letter 64

1   GT to his grandson Joseph Houlden.

2   On the Lytteltons, see Dianne Pye, "The Lytteltons of Hagley Hall," *Black Country Bugle,* 20 April 2006, http://www.blackcountrybugle.co.uk.

Letter 65

3   Nicole (nee Spohr) Houlden was born in Rouhling, Moselle, France.

4   For more on Dudley Castle, see "Introducing Dudley Castle and Its Environs to Visitors to the Black Country – 150 Years Ago!" *Black Country Bugle,* 20 October 2005, and "The Great Fire of Dudley Castle – 1750," *Black Country Bugle,* 29 July 2004, http://www.blackcountrybugle.co.uk.

Letter 66

5   Over the last two decades, historians have sought to examine critically the memories and subsequent representations of the war, in juxtaposition to the immediate reality recounted in letters like those of George Timmins. One result of these inquiries has been the growth of professional disquiet over the influence of popular representations of the war (its "Blackadderization") on both ongoing historical analysis and

our collective memory of that conflict. See, for example, Jonathan Vance, *Death So Noble: Memory, Meaning, and the First World War*; Mark David Sheftall, "The Glory and the Sadness: Shaping the Memory of the First World War in Great Britain, Canada and Australia, 1914-1939"; Liddle, "British Loyalties," 523-24; Brian Bond, *The Unquiet Western Front: Britain's Role in Literature and History*; Belinda Davis, "Experience, Identity, and Memory: The Legacy of World War I," 111-31; Janet S.K. Watson, *Fighting Different Wars: Experience, Memory, and the First World War in Britain*; Stephen Heathorn, "The Mnemonic Turn in the Cultural Historiography of Britain's Great War," 1103-24; Dan Todman, *The Great War: Myth and Memory*; J.M. Winter and Antoine Prost, eds., *The Great War in History: Debates and Controversies, 1914 to the Present.*

6 The Welsh singer Mary Hopkin had released her international hit "Those Were the Days" on the Apple label in 1968.

Letter 67

7 GT is referring to his great-grandchildren, Kim and Curtis.

BIBLIOGRAPHY

ARCHIVAL MATERIAL

Dudley Archives and Local History Centre, Coseley, West Midlands, UK
  Holy Trinity Anglican Church, Old Hill Parish Marriage Records
Library and Archives Canada
  RG 9, Militia and Defence
  RG 150, Ministry of the Overseas Military Forces of Canada
Oshawa Community Museum and Archives, Oshawa, Ontario
  Oshawa Daily Reformer, Ontario Reformer, Oshawa Vindicator
Oshawa Military and Industrial Museum, Oshawa, Ontario
  Military and Photographic Collections

PRINTED SOURCES

Allen, E.P.S. *The 116th Battalion in France.* Toronto: Hunter-Rose, 1921.
Ashworth, Tony. *Trench Warfare, 1914-1918: The Live and Let Live System.* London: Macmillan, 1980.
Barnett, L. Margaret. *British Food Policy during the First World War.* Boston: Allen and Unwin, 1985.
Bidwell, Shelford, and Dominick Graham. *Fire-Power: British Army, Weapons and Theories of War 1904-1945.* Boston: Allen and Unwin, 1985.
Bishop, Charles W. *The Canadian Y.M.C.A. in the Great War: The Official Record of the Activities of the Canadian Y.M.C.A. in Connection with the Great War of 1914-1918.* N.p.: National Council of Young Men's Christian Associations of Canada, 1924.
Bond, Brian. *The Unquiet Western Front: Britain's Role in Literature and History.* Cambridge: Cambridge University Press, 2002.
Bond, Brian, and Nigel Cave, eds. *Haig: A Reappraisal 70 Years On.* Barnsley, UK: Leo Cooper, 1999.
Bothwell, Robert, Ian Drummond, and John English. *Canada, 1900-1945.* Toronto: University of Toronto Press, 1987.
Bouckley, Thomas. *Pictorial Oshawa.* Oshawa, ON: Alger Press, 1975.
Brophy, John, and Eric Partridge. *The Daily Telegraph Dictionary of Tommies' Songs and Slang, 1914-1918.* London: Frontline Books, 2008.
Brown, Malcolm. *Tommy Goes to War.* London: Dent, 1978.

Campbell, David. "The Divisional Experience in the C.E.F.: A Social and Operational History of the 2nd Canadian Division, 1915-1918." PhD diss., University of Calgary, 2003.

Canada. Ministry of Overseas Forces. *Report of the Ministry: Overseas Military Forces of Canada, 1918.* London: H.M. Stationary Office, 1919.

Canadian Encyclopedia. 2nd ed. Edmonton: Hurtig Publishers, 1988.

Cane, Bruce. *It Made You Think of Home: The Haunting Journal of Deward Barnes, CEF 1916-1919.* Toronto: Dundurn Press, 2004.

Carter, Henry. *The Control of the Drink Trade: A Contribution to National Efficiency, 1915-1917.* London: Longmans, 1918.

Cecil, Hugh, and Peter H. Liddle, eds. *Facing Armageddon: The First World War Experienced.* London: Leo Cooper, 1996.

Christie, Norm. *The Canadians at Vimy, April 1917: Arleux, April 28, 1917: Fresnoy, May 3, 1917: A Social History and Battlefield Tour,* Vol. 3, *For King and Empire.* Winnipeg: Bunker to Bunker Books, 1996.

Coleman, Terry. *The Liners: A History of the North Atlantic Crossing.* London: Allen Lane, 1976.

Connelly, Mark. *Steady the Buffs! A Regiment, a Region and the Great War.* Oxford: Oxford University Press, 2006.

Constantine, Stephen, Maurice W. Kirby, and Mary B. Rose, eds. *The First World War in British History.* London: Edward Arnold, 1995.

Cook, Tim. *At the Sharp End: Canadians Fighting the Great War, 1914-1916.* Vol. 1. Toronto: Viking, 2007.

–. *Clio's Warriors: Canadian Historians and the Writing of the World Wars.* Vancouver: UBC Press, 2006.

–. "'Literary Memorials': The Great War Regimental Histories, 1919-1939." *Journal of the Canadian Historical Association* 13, 1 (2002):167-90.

–. "'More as a Medicine Than a Beverage': 'Demon Rum' and the Canadian Trench Soldier in the First World War." *Canadian Military History* 9 (2000):6-22.

–. "'My Whole Heart and Soul Is in This War': The Letters and War Service of Sergeant G.L. Ormsby." *Canadian Military History* 15, 1 (2006):51-63.

–. *No Place to Run: The Canadian Corps and Gas Warfare in the First World War.* Vancouver: UBC Press, 1999.

–. "The Politics of Surrender: Canadian Soldiers and the Killing of Prisoners in the Great War." *Journal of Military History* 70 (2006):637-65.

–. *Shock Troops: Canadians Fighting the Great War, 1917-1918.* Vol. 2. Toronto: Viking, 2008.

–. "Through Clouded Eyes: Gas Masks and the Canadian Corps in the First World War." *Material History Review* 47 (1998):4-20.

Cooper, J.A. *Fourth Canadian Infantry Brigade: History of Operations; April 1915 to Demobilization.* London: Charles and Son, n.d. (printed for private circulation).

Corrigall, D.J. *The Twentieth: The History of the Twentieth Canadian Battalion, Central Ontario Regiment, Canadian Expeditionary Force.* Toronto: Stone and Cox, 1935.

Costello, John. *Love, Sex and War: Changing Values 1939-1945.* London: Collins, 1985.

Crerar, Duff W. *Padres in No Man's Land: Canadian Chaplains in the Great War.* Montreal: McGill-Queen's University Press, 1995.

Dancocks, Daniel. *Legacy of Valour: The Canadians at Passchendaele.* Edmonton: Hurtig Publishers, 1986.

Daniel, Rev. I.J.E., and Rev. D.A. Casey. *For God and Country: War Works of Canadian Knights of Columbus Catholic Army Huts.* N.p.: Knights of Columbus, Catholic Army Huts, 1922.

Davis, Belinda. "Experience, Identity, and Memory: The Legacy of World War I." *Journal of Modern History* 75, 1(2003): 111-31.

DeGroot, Gerard J. *Blighty: British Society in the Era of the Great War.* London: Longman, 1996.

De Wolfe, J.H. *Our Heroes in the Great War: Giving the Facts and Details of Canada's Part in the Greatest War in History.* Ottawa: Patriotic Publishing, 1919.

Duffy, Christopher. *Through German Eyes: The British and the Somme 1916.* London: Weidenfeld and Nicolson, 2006.

Duguid, A.F. *Official History of the Canadian Forces in the Great War, 1914-1919.* Ottawa: King's Printer, 1938.

Ellis, John. *Eye-Deep in Hell: Trench Warfare in World War I.* Baltimore: John Hopkins University Press, 1989.

Emden, Richard van, and Steve Humphries. *All Quiet on the Home Front: An Oral History of Life in Britain during the First World War.* London: Headline, 2003.

Encyclopedia of Canada. Toronto: University Association of Canada, 1936.

Farewell, J.E. *County of Ontario.* Belleville, ON: Mika Publishing, 1973.

Farr, Don. *The Silent General: Horne of the First Army.* Solihull, UK: Helion, 2007.

Farrar, Martin J. *News from the Front: War Correspondents on the Western Front, 1914-.* Thrupp/Stroud/Gloucestershire, UK: Sutton Publishing, 1998.

Fleming, R.B., ed. *The Wartime Letters of Leslie and Cecil Frost, 1915-1919.* Waterloo: Wilfred Laurier University Press, 2007.

Fuller, J.G. *Troop Morale and Popular Culture in the British and Dominion Armies 1914-1918.* Oxford: Clarendon Press, 1990.

Gazette and Chronicle. Whitby, Ontario.

Globe. Toronto, Ontario.

Gray, Randle, with Christopher Argyle. *Chronicle of the First World War.* 2 vols. New York: Facts on File, 1990.

Grayzel, Susan R. *Women and the First World War.* London: Pearson Education, 2002.

Great Britain. Ministry of Information. *Chronology of the War: Issued under the Auspices of the Ministry of Information.* 3 vols. London: Constable and Co., 1919.

Greenfield, Nathan. *Baptism of Fire: The Second Battle of Ypres and the Forging of Canada, April, 1915.* Toronto: Harper Perennial, 2007.

Greenhous, Brereton, and Stephen J. Harris. *Canada and the Battle of Vimy Ridge 9-12 April, 1917*. Ottawa: Minister of Supply and Services, 1992.

Griffith, Paddy. *Battle Tactics of the Western Front: The British Army's Art of Attack 1916-18*. New Haven, CT: Yale University Press, 1994.

Haber, L.F. *The Poisonous Cloud: Chemical Weapons in the First World War*. Oxford: Clarendon Press, 1986.

Handbook of the Brotherhood of St. Andrew in Canada. Toronto: Office of the Council, [1911?].

Harris, J.P. *Douglas Haig and the First World War*. Cambridge, UK: Cambridge University Press, 2008.

Hayes, William. "In Fighting Trim: Canada Teaching Her Soldiers in Order to Fit Them For Fighting," *Outing* 69 (1916):277-88.

Heathorn, Stephen. "The Mnemonic Turn in the Cultural Historiography of Britain's Great War." *Historical Journal* 48, 4 (2005):1103-24.

Herwig, Holger. *The First World War: Germany and Austria-Hungary, 1914-1918*. London: Arnold Publishers, 1997.

Hoig, D.S. *Reminiscences and Recollections*. Oshawa, ON: Mundy-Goodfellow Printing, 1933.

Holmes, Richard. *Tommy: The British Soldier on the Western Front, 1914-1918*. London: HarperCollins, 2004.

Hood, M. McIntyre. *Oshawa: "The Crossing between the Waters"; A History of "Canada's Motor City."* Oshawa, ON: McLaughlin Public Library, 1968.

Hopkins, J. Castell. *The Province of Ontario in the War: A Record of Government and People*. Toronto: Warwick Bros. and Rutter, 1919.

Kaiser, T.E. *Historic Sketches of Oshawa*. Oshawa, ON: Reformer Printing and Publishing, 1921.

Keating, Peter, ed. *Into Unknown England 1886-1913: Selections from the Social Explorers*. Manchester: Manchester University Press, 1976.

Kesek, Amanda. "Dr. T.E. Kaiser." Historical Information Sheet. Oshawa, ON: Oshawa Historical Society, 6 May 1999.

Keshen, Jeffrey A. *Propaganda and Censorship during Canada's Great War*. Edmonton: University of Alberta Press, 1996.

Kimball, Jane A. *Trench Art: An Illustrated History*. Davis, CA: Silverpenny Press, 2004.

King, John S. *The Early History of the Sons of England Benevolent Society*. Toronto: Thomas Moore Brothers, 1891.

Lauder, Harry. *A Minstrel in France*. Toronto: McClelland, Goodchild and Stewart, 1918.

Leese, Peter. *Shell Shock: Traumatic Neurosis and the British Soldiers of the First World War*. New York: Palgrave, 2002.

Liddle, Peter, ed. *Home Fires and Foreign Fields: British Social and Military Experience in the First World War*. London: Brassey's Defence Publishers, 1985.

–. *Passchendaele in Perspective: The Third Battle of Ypres*. London: Leo Cooper, 1997.

Losinger, Diane. "Officer-Man Relations in the Canadian Expeditionary Force, 1914-1919." MA thesis, Carleton University, 1990.

Macintyre, D.E. *Canada at Vimy*. Toronto: P. Martin Associates, 1967.

MacKenzie, David, ed. *Canada and the First World War: Essays in Honour of Robert Craig Brown*. Toronto: University of Toronto Press, 2005.

Macksey, Kenneth. *The Penguin Encyclopedia of Weapons and Military Technology*. London: Penguin, 1995.

Macphail, Andrew. *Official History of the Canadian Forces in the Great War, 1914-19: Medical Services*. Ottawa: F.A. Acland, 1925. http://www.forces.gc.ca/dhh/collections/books/engraph/home_e.asp?=6.

MacPherson, J.S.B., ed. *Special Services, Heroic Deeds, etc.* Vol. 6, *Canada in the Great War: An Authentic Account of the Military History of Canada from the Earliest Days to the Close of the War of Nations 1918-1921*. Toronto: United Publishers of Canada, 1921.

Mann, Susan, ed. *The War Diary of Claire Glass, 1915-1918*. Montreal: McGill-Queen's University Press, 2000.

Mantle, Craig. *For Bully Beef and Biscuits: Charges of Mutiny in the 43rd Battalion, Canadian Expeditionary Force, November and December, 1917*. Kingston, ON: Canadian Defence Academy, Canadian Forces Leadership Institute, 2004.

–. *The "Moral Economy" as a Theoretical Model to Explain Acts of Protest in the Canadian Expeditionary Force, 1914-1918*. Kingston: Canadian Defence Academy, Canadian Forces Leadership Institute, 2004.

Marrin, Albert. *The Last Crusade: The Church of England in the First World War*. Durham, NC: Duke University Press, 1974.

Marteinson, John. *We Stand on Guard: An Illustrated History of the Canadian Army*. Montreal: Ovale, 1992.

Marwick, Arthur. *The Deluge: British Society and the First World War*. London: Macmillan, 1986.

Matthews, H.C.G., and Brian Harrison, eds. *Oxford Dictionary of National Biography*. Oxford: Oxford University Press, 2004.

Matthews, Mitford M. *A Dictionary of Americanisms*. Chicago: University of Chicago Press, 1956.

Meakin, Walter. *The Social and Economic Aspects of the Drink Problem*. London: V. Gollancz, 1931.

Middlebrook, Martin. *Your Country Needs You: Expansion of the British Army Infantry Divisions*. Barnsley, UK: Leo Cooper, 2000.

Miller, Ian Hugh MacLean. *Our Glory and Our Grief: Torontonians and the Great War*. Toronto: University of Toronto Press, 2002.

Millman, Brock. *Managing Domestic Dissent in First World War Britain*. London: Frank Cass, 2000.

Mills, Simon. *R.M.S. Olympic: The Old Reliable*. Launceston, UK: Waterfront Publications, 1995.

Mitchell, T.J., and G.M. Smith. *Casualties and Medical Statistics of the Great War*. 1931 reprint. Nashville: Imperial War Museum in association with Battery Press, 1997.

Mitchinson, K.W. *Pioneer Battalions in the Great War: Organized and Intelligent Labour*. London: Leo Cooper, 1997.

Morton, Desmond. "A Canadian Soldier in the Great War: The Experiences of Frank Maheux." *Canadian Military History* 1, 1-2 (1992):79-89.

–. *Fight or Pay: Soldiers' Families in the Great War*. Vancouver: UBC Press, 2004.

–. "'Kicking and Complaining': Demobilization Riots in the Canadian Expeditionary Force, 1918-19." *Canadian Historical Review* 61, 3 (1980):334-60.

–. "The Short Unhappy Life of the 41st Battalion CEF." *Queen's Quarterly* 81, 1 (1974):70-80.

–. *When Your Number's Up: The Canadian Soldier in the First World War*. Toronto: Random House, 1993.

Morton, Desmond, and J.L. Granatstein. *Marching to Armageddon: Canadians and the Great War 1914-1919*. Toronto: Lester and Orpen Dennys, 1989.

Murray, W.W. *History of the 2nd Canadian Battalion*. Ottawa: The Historical Committee, 2nd Battalion, Canadian Expeditionary Force, 1947.

Nasmith, George G. *Canada's Sons and Great Britain in the World War*. Toronto: Thomas Allen, 1919.

Neillands, Robin. *The Great War Generals on the Western Front 1914-1918*. London, Robinson Publishing, 1999.

Nicholson, G.W.L. *Canada's Nursing Sisters*. Toronto: A.M. Hakkert, 1975.

–. *Canadian Expeditionary Force, 1914-1919: Official History of the Canadian Army in the First World War*. Ottawa: Queen's Printer, 1962.

–. *The Fighting Newfoundlander: A History of the Royal Newfoundland Regiment*. St. John's: Government of Newfoundland, 1963.

Nicolson, Nigel. *Portrait of a Marriage*. London: Futura Publications, 1974.

The Official History of Australia in the War of 1914-1918. 12 vols. Sydney: Angus and Robertson, 1923-43.

Pope, Stephen, and Elizabeth-Anne Wheal. *The Macmillan Dictionary of the First World War*. London: Macmillan, 1997.

Prior, Robin, and Trevor Wilson. *Passchendaele: The Untold Story*. 2nd ed. New Haven, CT: Yale University Press, 2002.

Radecki, Henry. *A Member of a Distinguished Family: The Polish Group in Canada*. Toronto: McClelland and Stewart, 1976.

Radley, Kenneth. *We Lead, Others Follow: First Canadian Division, 1914-1918*. St. Catharines, ON: Vanwell Publishing, 2006.

Rawling, Bill. *Surviving Trench Warfare: Technology and the Canadian Corps*. Toronto: University of Toronto Press, 1992.

Reid, Gordon. *Poor Bloody Murder.* Oakville, ON: Mosaic Press, 1980.

Robb, George. *British Culture and the First World War.* Basingstoke, UK: Palgrave, 2002.

Robert McLaughlin Gallery. *The Ontario Regiment, R.C.A.C.: 125 years: 14 October-9 December, 1990.* Oshawa, ON: The Gallery, 1990.

Roberts, J.M. *Europe 1880-1945.* London: Longman, 1977.

Robertson, Peter. "Canadian Photojournalism during the First World War." *History of Photography* 2 (1978):37-52.

Roland, Charles G., ed. *Health, Disease and Medicine: Essays in Canadian History.* Toronto: Clarke Irwin for the Hannah Institute for the History of Medicine, 1984.

Rompkey, Bill, and Bert Riggs, eds. *Your Daughter, Fanny: The War Letters of Frances Cluett, VAD.* St. John's: Flanker Press, 2006.

Rutherdale, Robert. *Hometown Horizons: Local Responses to Canada's Great War.* Vancouver: UBC Press, 2004.

Ryan, Michael. "Supplying the Material Battle: Combined Logistics in the Canadian Corps, 1915-1918." MA thesis, Carleton University, 2005.

Schneider, Eric F. "What Britons Were Told about the War in the Trenches, 1914-1918." PhD diss., University of Oxford, 1997.

Schreiber, Shane B. *Shock Army of the British Empire: The Canadian Corps in the Last 100 Days of the Great War.* Westport, CT: Praeger, 1997.

Schwantes, Carlos A. *Coxey's Army: An American Odyssey.* Lincoln: University of Nebraska Press, 1985.

Searle, G.R. *Eugenics and Politics in Britain, 1900-1914.* Leyden: Noordhoff International Publishers, 1976.

Sheftall, Mark David. "The Glory and the Sadness: Shaping the Memory of the First World War in Great Britain, Canada and Australia, 1914-1939." PhD diss., Duke University, 2002.

Simpkins, Peter. *Kitchener's Army: The Raising of the New Armies, 1914-1916.* Manchester: Manchester University Press, 1988.

Singleton, John. "Britain's Military Use of Horses, 1914-1918." *Past and Present* 139 (1993):178-203.

Smith, Leonard V. *Between Mutiny and Obedience: The Case of the French Fifth Infantry Division during World War I.* Princeton, NJ: Princeton University Press, 1994.

Socknat, Thomas P. *Witness against War: Pacifism in Canada, 1900-1945.* Toronto: Toronto University Press, 1987.

Steele, H.E.R. *Canadians in France, 1915-1918.* London: T.F. Unwin, 1920.

Stevenson, David. *Cataclysm: The First World War as Political Tragedy.* New York: Basic Books, 2004.

–. *The First World War and International Politics.* Oxford: Clarendon Press, 1991.

Stevenson, John. *British History 1914-45.* London: Penguin, 1984.

Stone, Norman. *The Eastern Front, 1914-1917.* London: Hodder and Stoughton, 1975.

Sweetenham, John A., ed. *Valiant Men: Canada's Victoria Cross and George Cross Winners*. Toronto: A.M. Hakkert, 1973.

Tait, W. *1st Canadian Pioneers C.E.F.: Brief History of the Battalion France and Flanders, 1916-1918*. Calgary: 1st Pioneers Association, 1938.

The Times. London, UK.

Todman, Dan. *The Great War: Myth and Memory*. London: Hambledon Continuum, 2005.

Toronto Daily Star. Toronto, Ontario.

Toronto World. Toronto, Ontario.

Vance, Jonathan. *Death So Noble: Memory, Meaning, and the First World War*. Vancouver: UBC Press, 1997.

–. "Tangible Demonstrations of a Great Victory: War Trophies in Canada." *Material History* 42 (1995):47-56.

Van Creveld, Martin. *Technology and War: From 2000 B.C. to the Present*. New York: Free Press, 1989.

Wall, Richard, and J.M. Winter, eds. *The Upheaval of War: Family, Work and Welfare in Europe, 1914-1918*. Cambridge: Cambridge University Press, 1988.

Watson, Janet S.K. *Fighting Different Wars: Experience, Memory, and the First World War in Britain*. Cambridge: Cambridge University Press, 2004.

Whitehead, Ian R. *Doctors in the Great War*. Barnsley, UK: Leo Cooper, 1999.

Wilkinson, Allan. *The Church of England and the First World War*. London: SPCK Publishing, 1978.

Williams, John. *The Home Fronts: Britain, France and Germany 1914-1918*. London: Constable, 1972.

Wilson, Barbara. *Ontario and the First World War*. Toronto: Champlain Society, 1977.

Wilson, Trevor. *The Myriad Faces of War: Britain and the Great War 1914-1918*. Cambridge: Polity Press, 1986.

Winter, D. *Death's Men: Soldier's of the Great War*. London: Penguin, 1978.

Winter, J.M., and Antoine Prost, eds. *The Great War in History: Debates and Controversies, 1914 to the Present*. Cambridge: Cambridge University Press, 2005.

Winter, J.M., and Jean-Louis Robert. *Capital Cities at War: Paris, London, Berlin 1914-1919*. Cambridge, Cambridge University Press, 1997.

Woolf, Virginia. "Swift's 'Journal to Stella.'" In *The Common Reader*, edited by Andrew McNellie. Vol. 2. London: Hogarth Press, 1986, 67-77.

SELECTED WEB RESOURCES

Web resources have grown exponentially over the last decade. Library and Archives Canada and the Department of National Defence, Directorate of History and Heritage, have both made much historical material of military interest available to

Canadians online. The main address for the Library and Archives Canada website is http://www.collectionscanada.ca/. From here it is possible to follow links to the index provided by the Canadian Genealogy Centre of Library and Archives Canada, which can be found at http://www.collectionscanada.ca/genealogy/index-e.html. The index enables the reader to browse by topic. The military category provides the links to the enlistment papers of the members of the Canadian Expeditionary Force (CEF). These have now been digitized and serve as an index to the personnel files of members of the CEF. The War Dairies – the daily logs of wartime activities and operations – of the various battalions of the CEF are also now available digitally. The Canadian Genealogy Centre of Library and Archives Canada provides a link to the *Dictionary of Canadian Biography Online* and to an array of reputable websites, giving additional sources and links.

The Department of National Defence, Directorate of History and Heritage, has made several publications connected with the conduct of the First World War available for browsing and downloading at http://www.forces.gc.ca/hr/dhh/publications.

The Commonwealth War Graves Commission is the organization responsible for the care and maintenance of the records, graves, and memorials of the more than 1.7 million service personnel of the Commonwealth killed in the two world wars of the twentieth century. Its website can be found at http://www.cwgc.org and provides information on the history and activities of the commission, as well as a database of all the casualties, the Debt of Honour Register, which is searchable by name.

INDEX

Page numbers in italics indicate illustrations.

Printed and bound in Canada by Friesens

Set in Minion by Artegraphica Design Co. Ltd.

Copyedited by Judy Phillips

Proofread by Desne Ahlers

Indexed by Lillian Ashworth